The United States and Latin America

THE MAGILL BIBLIOGRAPHIES

The United States and Latin America

A Select Bibliography

John A. Britton

Magill Bibliographies

The Scarecrow Press, Inc.
Lanham, Md., & London
and
Salem Press
Pasadena, Calif., & Englewood Cliffs, N.J.
1997

F
1418
R4
B75
1997

SCARECROW PRESS, INC.

Published in the United States of America
by Scarecrow Press, Inc.
4720 Boston Way
Lanham, Maryland 20706

4 Pleydell Gardens, Folkestone
Kent CT20 2DN, England

British Cataloguing-in-Publication Information Available

Library of Congress Cataloging-in-Publication Data

Britton, John A.
    The United States and Latin America : a select bibliography / John
A. Britton.
        p.   cm. — (Magill bibliographies)
    Includes indexes.
    ISBN 0-8108-3248-8 (cloth : alk.paper)
    1. Latin America—Relations—United States—Bibliography.
    2. United States—Relations—Latin America—Bibliography.
    3. Central America—Relations—United States—Bibliography.
    4. United States—Relations—Central America—Bibliography.
    5. Caribbean Area—Relations—United States—Bibliography.
    6. United States—Relations—Caribbean Area—Bibliography.
    7. Andes Region—Relations—United States—Bibliography.
    8. United States—Relations—Andes Region—Bibliography.
    I. Title. II. Series.
    Z1609.R4B75   1997
    [F1418]
    016.30348 ' 27308—dc20   96-42962
                                                                    CIP

Contents

Chapter 1

INTRODUCTION

The purpose of this annotated bibliography is to provide the reader with a convenient description of the content of books and articles in the area of United States-Latin American relations. For the beginning researcher, some definitions are in order. A bibliography is simply a list of books and articles on a certain topic. An annotated bibliography includes some comments on the listed books and articles. The researcher can benefit from an annotated bibliography such as this one in at least two ways: First, it will identify books and articles on a particular topic; and second, it will offer a preliminary understanding of what these books and articles have to say about the topic. Students who do not have a specific topic in mind can find some possibilities by reading the table of contents. Students who have done some previous reading on topics such as the Monroe Doctrine, the Spanish-American War, economic development, or the international drug trade may want to go directly to the annotations in the relevant sections of Chapters 3, 4, or 5.

This bibliography covers a wide range of publications, and only a few libraries will have them all or even a high percentage of them. Large university and college libraries and the larger public library systems are most likely to have extensive holdings in the area of United States-Latin American relations. Students working through smaller colleges and high schools, however, can use this bibliography to determine the books and articles most relevant to their research topics and then locate these publications through the Library of Congress' *National Union Catalog* or through the *Online Computer Library Service*. Students can ask their library's reference staff for additional advice. Many local public and school libraries are connected to larger library systems that include access to computerized card catalogs. In such cases, students can survey the holdings of large numbers of libraries. After determining which publications are likely to be the most useful and the nearest location for these publications, the student can follow two possible courses: Make a research trip to a nearby large university, college, or public library; or apply through a local library to borrow the publications through interlibrary loan (articles can be photocopied and mailed to students for a fee). Remember that a thorough reading of the annotations in this bibliography *before* making a research trip or applying for an interlibrary loan can save the student much time and perhaps some money.

1

The subject of United States-Latin American relations generates much controversy among professional scholars and journalists. The reader should be aware that many of the books and articles listed in this bibliography take a certain point of view regarding some of these controversies. U.S. military interventions, the role of Communism, and the impact of revolutions tend to cause disagreements even among writers who try to be fair-minded. The reader, therefore, should not avoid books and articles that are involved in such debates. Instead, the reader should accept controversy as a normal and healthy aspect of the discussion of issues that inspire disagreement. The annotations usually draw attention to the author's point of view on key issues. In some cases, the annotations will include brief statements on the disagreements among authors within a particular section of the bibliography on a given topic. For example, the section titled "Democracy in Latin America" in Chapter 4 mentions the disagreements among authors whose publications are annotated in that section.

The annotations are intended to give the reader an understanding of the main themes or topics in each of the listed works. In addition, most annotations have comments on some of the specialized areas that are covered in depth. The chronological framework (the years under study) of each book is stated in the annotation if the title of the work does not include this information. When students begin to read one of these books or articles, they should keep in mind that scholars and journalists who write such publications often use words that may be unfamiliar to the general reader. Students should have access to a good dictionary and perhaps make a list of the definitions of unfamiliar words in the early stages of their study. Students who master the key terms early in the reading of the text will have a much better opportunity to grasp the full meaning of the material.

This bibliography offers only a sampling of the published works in this area. Many valuable studies are not included here. For example, this bibliography tends to favor books over articles because books usually give more depth in information and analysis than the shorter, generally more specialized articles. Students who want to learn more about a particular subject are advised to consult the bibliographies and footnotes in the books and articles annotated in this volume. Those studies with their own bibliographies and extensive footnotes offer the researcher an excellent opportunity to probe more deeply into the subject and to look into related topics.

There are many superb studies in this area in Spanish and Portuguese that have not been translated into English. For students who read these languages, the bibliographies and footnotes in many of the scholarly works annotated in this volume can provide important sources for additional research.

Two Approaches:
Diplomatic History and International History

The contrast between diplomatic history and international history is exemplified in the lives of two well-known figures of Cuban origins: Fidel Castro and Gloria Estefan. Castro's rise to power in 1959 caused diplomatic tensions between the United States and Cuba that resulted in an official break in relations between the two countries in early 1961. More crises soon followed. The U.S. Central Intelligence Agency (CIA) organized the unsuccessful Bay of Pigs invasion of April, 1961, in a vain effort to overthrow Castro. In October of 1962, the United States, Cuba, and the Soviet Union became entangled in the Cuban Missile Crisis, which very nearly plunged the world into nuclear war.

While Castro, U.S. presidents Dwight Eisenhower (1953-1961) and John F. Kennedy (1961-1963), and the leaders of the Soviet Union captured worldwide attention as they careened from one crisis to another, young Gloria Estefan and her family quietly adjusted to life as members of the Cuban immigrant community in Miami, Florida. Estefan's family left Cuba with thousands of other Cubans to find refuge from Castro's revolutionary government in southern Florida. In the early 1980's, Estefan blossomed into a major star in the highly competitive popular music business in the United States. A singer and songwriter, she used musical themes from her native Cuba to reach a mainstream audience in the United States, first as a vocalist for the group The Miami Sound Machine, then, by the late 1980's, as a solo performer.

Gloria Estefan and Fidel Castro had little in common except that they both were Cubans and both achieved a high level of public recognition in the United States. Indeed, Castro was the enemy of most members of the Cuban immigrant community in Miami. Estefan's father participated in and survived the ill-fated Bay of Pigs invasion.

In terms of the basic ideas used in this book, these two well-known Cubans exemplify the two approaches to the study of the relationships between nations. The conflict between the United States and Castro's Cuba is a story typical of traditional diplomatic history, which concentrates on the actions of political leaders, diplomats, and military officials. Castro's regime and his affiliation with Communism and the Soviet Union was a matter of great concern for several administrations in Washington. At the same time that Castro consolidated his power in Cuba, Gloria

Estefan was growing up in Miami. She and her fellow Cuban immigrants were typical of another kind of interaction between nations, often called international history. This approach is much broader than diplomatic history in that it includes topics such as immigration, popular culture, mass communications, and economic development.

Most of the readers of these pages know the names of Gloria Estefan and Fidel Castro, and most probably have seen a television news broadcast or a video documentary that deals with some aspect of the recent history of United States-Latin American relations. The international cocaine trade, the destruction of tropical rain forests, and the struggles of Latin American nations to achieve industrial development are typical of the images of Latin America that reach the public in the United States. Many people from the United States travel to one or more of the nations of the Caribbean and Latin America as tourists or as part of their university education. The fact that these channels of communication and travel have become open to so many people in the last decades of the twentieth century is connected to a basic concept in this book. The reader probably is aware that the relationship between the United States and the large, diverse region known as Latin America is influenced by coverage on television and in films, by popular images and stereotypes, and by immigration, trade, and missionary work as well as by the more traditional methods of international relations, which usually are dominated by political leaders, diplomats, and generals. The content of this book draws from both approaches to international relations. In short, the older view of diplomatic history as fundamentally the story of relations between governments fits into a much broader framework that recognizes the importance of cultural, social, and economic trends that reflect the lives of ordinary people who rarely are included in treaty negotiations and the formulation of foreign policy.

The increased interest in international history in recent decades is a reflection of widespread changes in technology. In the nineteenth century and earlier, international travelers were a small percentage of the total population. Diplomats and merchants were the most frequent travelers from nation to nation. Migration of ordinary citizens generally involved uncertainty and risk. Travel was too expensive and, in many cases, too dangerous to make tourism practical on a large scale. Improvements in transportation including steel-hulled, motor-driven ships; railroads; trucks; buses; automobiles; and airplanes made movement across international borders easier and safer. Information also began to cross borders with increasing volume and speed. Communications systems underwent revolutionary changes with the invention of mass printing, telegraphy, the telephone, transoceanic cable, radio, motion pictures, television, and means of bouncing electronic signals off satellites. In the latter half of the twentieth century, historians, political scientists, and other academics widened the focus of their studies to include not only politicians, diplomats, and generals but also immigrants, missionaries, musicians, and athletes who used these modern systems of transportation and communication. These changes in the technology of travel and the flow of information have increased the relevance of news coverage, the spread of popular stereotypes, and the influence of ideas.

The reader should keep in mind that these two categories—the new international history and traditional diplomatic history—are not always mutually exclusive. Many writers of traditional diplomatic history also included a wide array of factors in their studies. For example, Arthur Whitaker, who did most of his writing from the 1920's to the 1960's, frequently emphasized the activities of merchants, journalists, and intellectuals in his early studies. In his highly respected book *The Western Hemisphere Idea* (1954), he combined diplomatic themes with cultural and intellectual history to show how attitudes and ideas influence foreign policy. His studies of U.S.-Argentine relations in the late 1940's and 1950's—especially *The United States and Argentina* (1954)—emphasize the domestic politics of Juan Perón in the development of Argentina's foreign policy. Likewise, many international historians include basic trends in foreign policy as essential to their findings. For example, Emily Rosenberg, in her classic study titled *Spreading the American Dream* (1981), uses research on the Department of State and foreign policy to show how U.S. business practices, religious institutions, and popular culture spread into foreign lands. Therefore, these two categories can best be understood as convenient generalizations that give the student a way to understand two of the basic trends in the published writing in this field. The reader should also keep in mind that many of the works annotated in this bibliography contain elements of both traditional diplomatic history and the newer international history.

Introduction to the Annotations

This section is intended to give the reader some background information for the annotations in Chapters 2, 3, 4, and 5. Chapter 2 is titled "General Works" and contains commentary on books that deal with large themes in U.S.-Latin American relations or cover the histories of several countries in the region. Many of these books are college textbooks intended for the classroom, but they can be useful to the student researching a term paper because they contain summaries of major historical trends and biographical sketches of leading historical figures. The books annotated in this chapter are of three basic types: a survey (or overview) of U.S.-Latin American relations, a survey of U.S. foreign relations in which Latin America is discussed in some depth, or a survey of Latin American history that is intended to be an introduction to this subject.

Chapter 3, "The Nineteenth Century Background," encompasses three important topics in U.S.-Latin American relations. The first is the Monroe Doctrine. President James Monroe announced these policies (not treaties or international agreements) in 1823 to discourage the European powers from intervening in the Western Hemisphere. Most of the Latin American nations recently had achieved their independence from Spain (Brazil broke away from Portugal), and Monroe was concerned that other European nations would attempt to establish their own colonies in this region and thereby pose a threat to the United States. The second theme in this chapter ties together Manifest Destiny and the Mexican-American War. Manifest Destiny was an expression of the growing sense of national pride in the United States that included the idea that the country was destined to stretch from the Atlantic Ocean to the Pacific Ocean. Nearly half of Mexico's national territory lay in the path of this expansion. The victory of the United States over Mexico in the 1846-1848 war led to the annexation of western lands including California by the government in Washington. The section titled "The Spanish-American War" covers the last stage of U.S. expansion in the nineteenth century. Although the war itself lasted only four months, the U.S. victory over Spain brought it colonies in Puerto Rico (and Guam and the Philippines in the Pacific) and virtual control of Cuba's economy and political system. Taken together, the three sections of this chapter discuss books and articles that examine the growth of U.S. power in the Western Hemisphere from the 1820's to 1898.

Chapter 4 covers a wide-ranging set of topics under the title "The Twentieth Century: Main Themes in International History." This chapter concentrates on international history as defined on the previous pages of this introduction. The first section is concerned with the acquisition of the Panama Canal Zone by the United States in 1903, the construction of the canal (completed in 1914), and subsequent changes in U.S. policy in the Caribbean. U.S. military interventions in nations such as Haiti, the Dominican Republic, and Nicaragua were important not only because they were the results of the strategic objective of protecting the canal from intrusive European powers but also because they had profound political, economic, and cultural impacts on these Latin American nations. The Good Neighbor Policy brought an end to military interventions as the United States attempted to build harmony and unity in the Western

Hemisphere, especially in the late 1930's and early 1940's, when World War II was the main concern in U.S. foreign policy. Many of the books annotated in this section deal with the three-sided relationships involving the Latin American nations (especially Argentina and Brazil), the United States, and the Axis Powers not only in diplomacy but also in trade, propaganda, and espionage.

The next two sections of Chapter 4 are concerned with Communism and revolution. These two topics are closely connected. Indeed, one of the main problems for U.S. foreign policy and security experts was the challenge of determining if a radical insurgency that intended to overthrow an existing government was a part of the much-dreaded and often overrated international Communist network or, by contrast, was an outpouring of the outrage of local people directed against an abusive political/economic system. The section on Communism includes items by and about individuals who, in later years, admitted that they were active in Communist organizations. The section on revolutions concentrates on movements that tended to have their roots in particular local or national circumstances in Latin America.

The United States generally opposed both Communism and revolution. One of the most consistent U.S. policies in this area was to provide aid, advice, and training for the Latin American armed forces. The intention of the United States was to strengthen the professionalism and striking power of the military establishments in nations that seemed to be threatened by Communism and/or revolution. The results were not always what the United States intended. In some cases, a strengthened military became the power base for a military dictatorship that only added to the anti-United States resentments of many Latin Americans and worsened the U.S. position in the region.

The United States used other approaches to win friendships and to reduce the possibility of radical insurgencies. The section on economic development discusses items that examine the impact of U.S. economic influence in the region. Although most directors of U.S. corporations active in Latin America insisted that their goals were to bring economic growth and prosperity to their host nations, not all writers who have looked into this process agree that such beneficial results were typical. This section, therefore, mentions sources that are often in disagreement. Some authors accuse the United States of exploiting Latin America's resources and inexpensive labor, whereas other authors see U.S. business enterprises as providing a necessary stimulus and the proper economic model to establish the bases for the free enterprise system.

The next section examines publications on another debatable topic: the impact of the United States in the spread of democracy in Latin America.

There is little doubt that the U.S. government advocated democracy as the preferred political system (several of the annotated books cover this point), but some writers see more rhetoric, propaganda, and empty promises in this policy than meaningful support for the building of representative institutions and an open society. "Armed Forces in U.S.-Latin American Relations" discusses how military force was used to achieve various goals of the U.S. government, including spreading democracy.

Because of the dominant influence of the United States and its frequent use of aggressive policies, many Latin American writers have criticized the nation that they sometimes call "the colossus of the north." Several of their books are annotated in the section titled "Latin American Criticisms of the United States and U.S. Policy," which contains a sampling of the books on this topic translated into English. (Readers should keep in mind that some of the most important critical studies of the United States and its policies are not yet published in English translation.)

The next three sections of Chapter 4 encompass grassroots tendencies that usually originate with ordinary citizens throughout the Americas. The section on "Latin American Immigration" concerns movement to the United States, especially from Mexico, Cuba, Central America, Haiti, the Dominican Republic, and Puerto Rico, that played an increasingly important role in national and international affairs. The Hispanic population of the United States in general became a significant political and cultural influence during the middle and later decades of the twentieth century. "Mass Culture and the Mass Media," the next section, describes images and ideas that spread through mass society in the United States. The media and culture have contained sharp but often contradictory images of Latin America and its peoples. Stereotypes and prejudices have been prominent in news coverage, political debates, films, and fiction, but, at the same time, Latino musicians, athletes, actors and actresses, and artists have become widely accepted north of the Rio Grande. The third section on grassroots trends focuses on the spread of Protestantism. Although Catholicism for centuries was the main religious force in Latin America, U.S.-based Protestant missionaries began to acquire significant numbers of converts in the 1960's and 1970's, thereby establishing a rivalry with the Catholic church in Guatemala, Brazil, and other countries. By the 1990's, the rapid expansion of Protestantism was one of the largest challenges facing the Catholic church in the Western Hemisphere.

As global awareness of ecological problems emerged in the 1970's and 1980's, the quickening pace of economic change and its impact on the environment in Latin America became a subject of widespread concern throughout the hemisphere. U.S.-based corporations participated in the cutting of rain forests in Brazil and Panama at the same time that ecologists, anthropologists, journalists, and other specialists wrote books about the harmful effects of this process on the native peoples and on the world's ecological system.

Government officials and scholars largely ignored the international drug trade for many decades, until it suddenly surfaced in the 1970's and 1980's because of the dramatic increase in the consumption of illegal substances in the United States. At the same time, the primary suppliers of cocaine began to reap multibillion dollar profits from their operations in Colombia, Peru, and Bolivia. Soon these operations spread into Mexico, the Bahamas, and other nations in and around the Caribbean. Confronted by a huge, illegal, underground empire, journalists and academics wrote several items drawn from their difficult and sometimes risky investigations into this unusual if not unprecedented episode in international history.

Lawful trade also became an issue in these years. The North American Free Trade Agreement (NAFTA) brought Mexico, the United States, and Canada into a sweeping free trade arrangement that, in theory at least, was to benefit all three nations. This section discusses many of the books written while the three nations negotiated the treaty. Most authors agreed with political and business leaders that NAFTA would bring benefits to the economies of all three nations. Mexico's economic collapse of 1995 served as a reminder of the uncertainties of international economics and the difficulties in the journalistic and academic analysis of such large-scale undertakings.

Chapter 5 is titled "Nations and Diplomacy" and includes books that approach the subject matter from the perspective of the traditional patterns of relations between and among governments and their official representatives. Publications on the relations between the United States and the Latin American countries tend to be guided by proximity and controversy. The nations along the southern rim of the United States and the circum-Caribbean—especially Mexico, Cuba, and the Central American countries—have inspired the most attention from academics and journalists. The second prominent theme, controversy, is the result of the writers' interest in confrontation and conflict and their interest in situations in which diplomats argue, foreign business managers and native workers quarrel, revolutionaries mobilize their followers, and, in some cases, U.S. armed forces intervene. The Mexican Revolution in its most violent phase (1910-1920) offered several cases of tense diplomacy and two examples of U.S. armed interventions: the first in Veracruz in 1914 and the second in northern Mexico in 1916. As Mexico's leaders and the aroused peasant and worker masses carried the revolution through the next two decades of political ferment and social and economic experimentation, U.S. diplomats and political leaders struggled to find the policy best suited for these shifting situations.

Another obvious example in which proximity and controversy combined to produce a large number of books and articles is the troubled relationship between the United States and Cuba in the era of Fidel Castro. The Cuban guerrilla warrior turned Maximum Leader lost much of his revolutionary fire in the 1980's, but there is a broad consensus from many points of view that Castro was a painful, injurious thorn in the side of many presidential administrations, from the last two years of Dwight Eisenhower's tenure (1959-1961) through both terms of Ronald Reagan's presidency (1981-1989). The nationalization of U.S.-owned petroleum refineries in 1960, the CIA's failed Bay of Pigs invasion in 1961, and the Cuban Missile Crisis of 1962 set the tone for U.S. relations with Cuba for many years.

In Central America, the Caribbean nations of Haiti and the Dominican Republic, and Cuba (before and during the Castro years), the United States exerted much diplomatic pressure and engaged in frequent armed interventions that involved an array of people: professional diplomats, CIA agents, soldiers, sailors, Marines, pilots, and even mercenaries. When the government in Washington initiated these policies, the policymakers usually had some strategic goal or some political or economic purpose: the protection of the Panama Canal, the defeat of a revolutionary movement, or the protection of U.S. corporate interests. The results of these policies, as portrayed in many of the books annotated in the sections dealing with these countries, often brought unexpected and contradictory consequences. For example, in Nicaragua and the Dominican Republic, U.S. military interventions in the 1920's and 1930's left these two nations saddled with harsh dictators for several decades. These leaders eventually created problems for the United States.

Perched on the northwest corner of South America immediately south of Central America, Colombia had some of its most traumatic experiences as a result of its relationship with and proximity to the United States. In 1903, the Panamanian revolt for independence and the subsequent U.S.-Panamanian treaty stripped Colombia of one of its greatest resources—the route for an interoceanic canal. The Panama Canal was built and controlled by the United States. Eight decades later, the United States and Colombia again became entangled as a result of the rapid growth of the international cocaine trade. In the years between these two episodes, Washington and Bogotá experienced other periods of discord. The reader should note that the Panama Canal and the international drug trade are covered in separate sections in Chapter 4.

The three larger nations of southern South America (Argentina, Brazil, and Chile) were too distant from the United States to experience the threats and stresses of intervention that plagued the nations further to the north. Beginning in the early 1900's, however, the expansion of U.S. investment, trade, and communications systems began to have an impact in these nations at approximately the same time that U.S. military interventions became commonplace in Central America, Cuba, Haiti, the Dominican Republic, and Mexico. Argentine, Brazilian, and Chilean leaders pursued their own policies to fend off the aggressiveness of the United States, but by the World War II era of the 1930's and 1940's, U.S. pressures on all three of these nations intensified because of concerns about their apparent receptivity to the trade, propaganda, and ideas of the Axis Powers. Again in the 1960's and 1970's, U.S. security interests focused on these three countries because of expanding leftist movements—especially the election of Socialist Salvador Allende to the presidency of Chile in 1970.

Although U.S. concerns about other South American nations have remained dormant for extended periods of time, in general the growth of extremist movements on the far right and the far left have captured the attention of policymakers in Washington. For example, Bolivia's flirtation with Fascism in the 1930's and 1940's caused anxiety in Washington, as did that nation's rapid shift to the left in its revolution of 1952. Peru's troubles from the 1970's to the 1990's often revolved around challenges from the revolutionary organization known as Sendero Luminoso. United States relations with Venezuela, Ecuador, Paraguay, and Uruguay were not usually as troubled as relations with other Latin American nations, but in the last half of the twentieth century, these four countries felt the effects of expanding economic ties and the extension of international communications and mass media systems. The United States usually worked with these countries through routine diplomatic practices.

Chapter 2
GENERAL STUDIES

Aguilar, Alonso. *Pan-Americanism from Monroe to the Present: A View from the Other Side.* New York: Monthly Review Press, 1968.

The study of U.S.-Latin American relations often causes controversy, and this book is among the most controversial on the topic. Aguilar's text gives the reader the opportunity to ponder the judgments typical of the generation of Latin American leftists who saw Fidel Castro's revolution of 1959 as a turning point in the history of the hemisphere. Writing in the 1960's, when Castro's reputation was at its peak, Aguilar brought together a large number of quotations from noted leftist writers including Cuban revolutionary José Martí, Mexican Marxist Narciso Bassols, and U.S. radicals Scott Nearing and Joseph Freeman. Aguilar locates the economic power base in the U.S. industrial surge of the late 1800's that solidified U.S. control of Latin America's export economies by the 1920's. The author sees Franklin D. Roosevelt's Good Neighbor Policy as the brightest period in U.S.-Latin American relations because of its rejection of military intervention and its promotion of democracy against Fascism. The onset of the Cold War in the late 1940's, however, relegated Latin America to a place of peripheral importance until Castro reminded U.S. leaders of their vulnerability in their own neighborhood. Aguilar is especially critical of the U.S. military intervention in the Dominican Republic in 1965. A valuable source for leftist opinion, this book is to be used carefully and in conjunction with other studies.

Bemis, Samuel Flagg. *The Latin American Policy of the United States: An Historical Interpretation.* 1943. Reprint. New York: Norton, 1971.

This is a clearly written, well-organized historical survey of U.S. policy toward Latin America from the time of the American Revolution to the early phases of World War II. Bemis emphasizes the importance of national security in the formulation and enactment of U.S. policy from the Monroe Doctrine to the interventions in the early twentieth century. He uses the word "imperialism" to describe these interventions, but it was "protective imperialism" intended to secure the Panama Canal and other strategic interests from meddlesome European powers. This book remains a classic defense of U.S. policies in the Western Hemisphere, especially during the period from the 1890's through the 1920's. Many critics, however, point out that Bemis gave little attention to Latin

American perspectives on the interventions and included very little research from Latin American sources. Other authors place much heavier emphasis on the U.S. government's determination to protect U.S. corporate investments in the region. (See the works by Alonso Aguilar, Walter LaFeber, and Thomas Paterson, J. Garry Clifford, and Kenneth Hagan in this section.)

Burns, E. Bradford. *Latin America: A Concise Interpretative History.* 6th ed. Englewood Cliffs, NJ: Prentice Hall, 1994.
This single-volume college textbook devotes approximately 80% of its coverage to the period since independence and has much to offer the student seeking background information on the political, economic, and social conditions in Latin America. Burns has chapters that deal with the "Emergence of the Modern State" (which means the national or central government) and the rise of the middle class. He also discusses the role of the United States in the region. His chapter on the Mexican Revolution includes commentary on the U.S. responses to that revolution. The chapter titled "The Revolutionary Option" discusses more recent revolutions in Guatemala, Bolivia, Cuba, and Nicaragua, as well as U.S. policy toward these revolutions. In his analysis, Burns is often critical of U.S. policy. He finds a pattern of opposition to radical change that has frustrated local initiative and has contributed to the continuation of Latin America's enigma: large numbers of poor people living in lands of great potential wealth.

Connell-Smith, Gordon. *The United States and Latin America: An Historical Analysis of Inter-American Relations.* New York: John Wiley, 1974.
British historian Connell-Smith surveys a century and a half of inter-American relations from the Monroe Doctrine to the early 1970's. While expressing respect for Samuel Flagg Bemis' *The Latin American Policy of the United States*, Connell-Smith challenges some of its basic assumptions regarding the "flattering self image" of the United States as the dominant power of the Western Hemisphere that refused to follow the natural tendency toward European-style colonialism. Connell-Smith argues that the United States replaced colonialism with other methods of imperialism including military intervention, economic penetration, and diplomatic intimidation. He develops these arguments throughout chapters that focus on the following events and trends: the Monroe Doctrine, Manifest Destiny, the interventions of the early twentieth century, the Good Neighbor Policy, the early Cold War, and Castro's revolution in Cuba. Connell-Smith also emphasizes the

persistence of anti-United States attitudes in Latin America and the
efforts of Latin American diplomats and political leaders to deal with
the aggressive tendencies of the hemisphere's dominant power. Although this book examines many controversial issues, the author's
language is calm, and his ideas are presented in a thoughtful and
incisive style.

Crow, John A. *The Epic of Latin America*. 4th ed. Berkeley: University of
California Press, 1992.
This comprehensive college text devotes approximately half of its
contents to the independence movements of the early nineteenth century and the histories of the independent nations thereafter. The special
value of this textbook lies in its sensitivity to and clearly written
discussions of Latin American cultural life. Crow covers the nineteenth
century with brief country-by-country surveys, but his approach to the
twentieth century is broader. For example, he uses topical chapters such
as "Deep Womb, Dark Flower" on social and political change including
the Mexican Revolution to accompany standard political narratives. A
specialist in Latin American literature, Crow emphasizes the importance of cultural symbols such as the Argentine gaucho, military/po-
litical caudillos, and the lives of certain leaders such as Simón Bolívar
of Venezuela, Domingo Sarmiento of Argentina, and Emperor Dom
Pedro II of Brazil. The last 250 pages of the text integrate commentary
on the histories of individual nations with the expansion of internationalization in the Western Hemisphere in the areas of culture, politics,
and economics, including the multiple roles played by the United
States in this process.

Gil, Federico. *Latin American-United States Relations*. New York: Har-
court Brace Jovanovich, 1971.
Beginning students will find particular value in this brief survey text
because of its straightforward writing style and its smooth organization. Gil gives balanced discussions of topics that often spark disagreements, such as U.S. interventions in the first three decades of the
twentieth century in Cuba, Haiti, the Dominican Republic, and Mexico. In his own words, Gil shows "the blunders as well as the successes
of United States diplomacy." He continues this balanced approach to
analyze the Good Neighbor Policy, the rise of Fidel Castro, and the
Alliance for Progress. Researchers will benefit from a careful reading
of the annotated bibliographies at the end of each of the first eight
chapters. The annotations are brief but pointed and informative. They
include books that served as sources of information for the preceding

chapter. Some of these books may be difficult to find, but many of them are available in university, college, and larger public libraries.

Keen, Benjamin. *A History of Latin America*. 5th ed. Boston: Houghton Mifflin, 1996.
The impact of the United States in Latin America is a central theme in this college textbook. Chapter 20 gives a succinct general summary of U.S.-Latin American relations since 1810. Several of the chapters on individual countries explore the impact of the United States in these nations—especially Mexico, Cuba, and the Central American nations of Guatemala, Nicaragua, and El Salvador. A key concept in Keen's analysis is neocolonialism—the idea that after the Latin American nations broke away from the Spanish and Portuguese empires (the first form of colonialism), the United States came to have considerable power over these nations not as formal colonies but through the neocolonial system of trade, investments, control of valuable resources, diplomatic pressure, direct intervention, and the threat of such interventions. The earlier editions of this text were coauthored by Keen and Mark Wasserman. The fifth edition is available in a single volume and a two-volume edition in which Volume 2 covers U.S.-Latin American relations.

Kryzanek, Michael. *U.S.-Latin American Relations*. 2d ed. New York: Praeger, 1990.
Intended for the college undergraduate, this book is written in clear language free of technical jargon and follows a logical organization. The first third of the text is a chronological summary of U.S. policy from the Monroe Doctrine to the rise of Fidel Castro. The second and longest portion of the text is an informative explanation of how the U.S. government formulates its Latin American policies. This section discusses the activities of several parts of the government (including the office of the President, the State Department, the Defense Department, and the Central Intelligence Agency) as well as the growing roles of Congress and nongovernmental institutions such as businesses, human rights groups, and think tanks. This portion of the text is concerned primarily with U.S. policy in Central America in the 1980's and has commentary on the administration of President Ronald Reagan, the campaign of the contras against the Sandinista government of Nicaragua, and the violent struggle in El Salvador. The last section of the text includes a discussion of the "fragile hold of democracy" in Latin America and the author's contention that the ability of the United States to control events in the hemisphere is in decline. The footnotes

at the end of each chapter provide the reader with additional sources on these topics.

LaFeber, Walter. *The American Age: United States Policy at Home and Abroad Since 1750*. New York: Norton, 1989.

This textbook in United States diplomatic history devotes a large amount of attention to U.S.-Latin American relations. One of the main themes is the rise of the United States to "superpowerdom" or a position of authority in world affairs. LaFeber traces the roots of this position to the U.S. annexations of Texas and California and its subsequent activities in the Caribbean, Mexico, Central America, South America, and the Pacific. LaFeber emphasizes economic motives in U.S. foreign policy, but he also gives considerable attention to political and ideological factors. The last six chapters cover the Cold War era, with attention to Fidel Castro's Cuba and the Central American crises of the 1980's. The organization of this text is especially convenient. The table of contents lists not only each chapter title but also the chapter subheadings, making it easy to find specific topics. Each chapter is footnoted and includes an informative bibliographical essay.

Langley, Lester. *America and the Americans: The United States in the Western Hemisphere*. Athens: University of Georgia Press, 1989.

This innovative textbook applies the new emphasis on international history to U.S.-Latin American relations. Langley surveys basic economic, political, and social institutions from the colonial period to the late twentieth century in his analysis of the history of the Western Hemisphere. The book is not a lengthy accumulation of facts but rather a series of thoughtful generalizations supported by specific cases. For example, Langley finds that U.S. interventions from the 1890's to the 1920's established stability in some nations but left an unintended political consequence—a string of military dictators such as Anastasio Somoza, Fulgencio Batista, and Rafael Trujillo who later caused much difficulty for the United States. The last third of the book is an overview of the Cold War era. Langley criticizes both the United States and its adversaries, especially Fidel Castro. He also identifies goals that are widely shared among Western Hemisphere nations, including some form of representative government and respect for human rights. These goals constitute the symbolic importance in the title of the word "America," which is used not simply to refer to the United States but also to include the ideals (and sometimes the practices) of most Western Hemisphere nations.

Maingot, Anthony P. *The United States and the Caribbean: Challenges of an Asymmetrical Relationship.* Boulder, CO: Westview, 1994.
United States domination of the Caribbean area is the central theme of this brief, well-organized study. The word "asymmetrical" refers to the imbalance in power between the United States and the smaller island countries and colonial territories of the Caribbean as well as the nations of Central America. Maingot, a highly respected sociologist, includes a concise historical survey of the influence of the United States in this area from the Monroe Doctrine to World War II. He also provides a much-needed discussion of the German submarine campaign in the Caribbean in World War II and the U.S. response to this significant threat to hemisphere security. His discussion of the conflicts of the Cold War era that pitted the United States against radical movements in the region focuses on Costa Rica, British Guiana (now Guyana), Guatemala, and Cuba. The last portion of this text is especially innovative because it moves beyond the familiar themes of these Cold War conflicts to examine the new set of issues that arose in the 1970's and 1980's: drug trafficking, offshore banking, and migration. Maingot devotes particular attention to the continuing troubles of impoverished Haiti and the strained relationship between the United States and Puerto Rico. In his analysis of these and other major causes of tension in U.S.-Caribbean relations, the author maintains a calm, even-handed approach that, coupled with his clear prose style, gives the reader a solid background for understanding this complex but essential area.

Paterson, Thomas G., J. Garry Clifford, and Kenneth J. Hagan. *American Foreign Policy: A History.* 4th ed. Lexington, MA: D.C. Heath, 1994.
This general United States diplomatic history textbook gives considerable attention to Latin America. The chapter titled "Managing and Extending the American Empire, 1900-1914" offers especially strong coverage of the interventions in the Caribbean, Central America, and Mexico following the U.S. acquisition of the Panama Canal Zone. The chapter on the Good Neighbor Policy provides important insights into the origins and implementation of this approach to Latin America. In the discussion of the Cold War era, U.S.-Latin American relations are integrated with other foreign policy issues in a global setting. Throughout their discussions of Latin America, the authors use a broad factual base that includes much coverage of Latin American criticisms of U.S. interventions and the often unintended consequences of these interventions. This book is unusually well illustrated, including photographs and editorial cartoons from newspapers. Each chapter is thoroughly footnoted, giving the reader the opportunity to locate additional

sources. There is also a useful topical bibliography at the end of the
text.

Rosenberg, Emily. *Spreading the American Dream: American Economic
and Cultural Expansion, 1890-1945*. New York: Hill and Wang, 1981.
This classic study is an excellent introduction to often-underrated
aspects of U.S. expansion. Rosenberg concentrates on business enterprises and cultural activities rather than diplomacy and military interventions. Although she covers U.S. expansion in a worldwide context,
the author gives heavy emphasis to Latin America, where much of this
type of expansion had its first serious impact. Topics that receive
particular attention include the growth of private corporations that used
new technologies, including submarine cables, motion pictures, and
aviation. This text also deals with the work of missionaries and the
expansion of the YMCA. U.S. domination of the communications and
transportation industries in the Western Hemisphere solidified in the
1920's and 1930's, giving Washington a framework to mount an
extensive cultural and propaganda offensive against the Axis Powers
in the era of World War II. Rosenberg's use of the concept of liberal
developmentalism (the collaboration of the government with private-
sector businesses and voluntary organizations in the promotion of U.S.
expansionism) as the foundation of U.S. policy in this area gives this
book a coherence that both beginning students and more experienced
researchers will appreciate.

Skidmore, Thomas E., and Peter H. Smith. *Modern Latin America*. 3d ed.
New York: Oxford University Press, 1992.
International economics serves as the organizational basis for this
unique textbook. The authors include political, social, and cultural
factors, but their central theme is the interaction of the economies of
the Latin American nations with the world market—in particular, the
private sector businesses and government agencies of the United
States. Skidmore and Smith use strategies concerning Brazilian coffee,
Argentine beef, and Chilean copper from the late 1800's to the 1930's
as examples of export-oriented economics. The worldwide depression
of the 1930's pushed several Latin American nations to begin the
process of import substitution industrialization, in which local entrepreneurs (often with support from national governments) established
factories to manufacture products such as steel, automobiles, and
washing machines to replace similar products previously imported
from the United States or Europe. This text also has trenchant discussions of twentieth century governments that have wrestled with these

economic challenges. The authors include the radical experiments in Fidel Castro's Cuba and Salvador Allende's Chile, along with the revolutionary movements in Central America of the 1980's. There is also an interpretive chapter on U.S.-Latin American relations since the 1880's. In their conclusion, Skidmore and Smith argue that the Latin American nations have begun to play larger and more important roles in the Western Hemisphere and in world affairs.

Smith, Peter. *Talons of the Eagle: Dynamics of U.S.-Latin American Relations*. New York: Oxford University Press, 1996.
Respected historian Peter Smith has written a compact interpretive survey of U.S.-Latin American relations. He divides his book into three parts. The first part, "The Imperial Era," covers the expansion of U.S. power in the nineteenth century and the United States' displacement of Spanish, British, and other European rivals in the Western Hemisphere through the 1940's. The chapter titled "Latin American Responses to Imperialism" is an especially valuable analysis of an often neglected subject. Smith includes commentary on the Mexican Revolution and explores the ideas of José Martí and Augusto César Sandino. The second part of this book spans the Cold War (the late 1940's to the late 1980's), during which Latin America was an arena for conflicts involving United States interventions against international Communism and local revolutionary movements. Smith discusses U.S. interventions in Guatemala, Cuba, the Dominican Republic, Chile, and Central America. The final section, titled "The Age of Uncertainty," deals with shifting conditions in the post-Cold War era. Smith gives the reader thoughtful and thought-provoking assessments of issues such as international immigration and the drug trade as well as the challenges arising from burdensome foreign debts and the consequences of NAFTA.

Van Alstyne, Richard W. *The Rising American Empire*. Oxford, England: Blackwell, 1960.
This relatively brief account of the expansionist impulse of the United States from the Revolutionary War to the early twentieth century gives the student a stimulating overview. Van Alstyne emphasizes the importance of the aggressive policies that led to the Louisiana Purchase, Manifest Destiny, the war with Mexico, and the extension of U.S. power and influence into the Caribbean and the Pacific. He uses the terms "empire" and "imperialism" to explain this process in ways that many of his contemporaries such as Samuel Flagg Bemis, Dexter Perkins, and Frederick Merk did not accept. Van Alstyne argues that a

centralized nation-state and imperialistic expansion have been factors in United States history since the country's beginning, but that national leaders, political commentators, and even historians avoid use of these terms in favor of euphemistic phrases such as the Monroe Doctrine and Manifest Destiny. Chapters 5 and 7 deal specifically with U.S. policies in Latin America, but the entire text is a thoughtful examination of the rhetoric and reality of expansive nationalism.

Winn, Peter. *Americas: The Changing Face of Latin America and the Caribbean*. New York: Pantheon, 1992.

In this survey text with a heavy emphasis on the mid- and late twentieth century, Winn integrates the histories of the Latin American and Caribbean nations within the framework of international history. This approach includes the rise and fall of the ambitious economic nationalism of Juan Perón, some traditional diplomatic history, and a discussion of the United States' "hegemonic presumption" regarding its military and economic domination of the region. Winn also gives considerable attention to the international impact of Latin American literature and folk/popular music as well as the repercussions of the revolutionary movements led by Fidel Castro and the Sandinistas. The final chapter is a general study of Latin American immigration to the United States, including Mexicans to California, Cubans to Florida, and Puerto Ricans to New York. Winn's clear, unpretentious style effectively combines recent history with sociology and economics to give the reader a panoramic view of the internationalization of the Western Hemisphere. This book is the companion volume for the ten-part television documentary series titled *Americas*, produced by WGBH in 1990.

Chapter 3
THE NINETEENTH CENTURY BACKGROUND

The Monroe Doctrine

Bemis, Samuel Flagg. *John Quincy Adams and the Foundations of American Foreign Policy*. New York: Knopf, 1950.

This gracefully written study combines diplomatic history and biography to evaluate the career of one of the foremost international figures in the Western Hemisphere of the early nineteenth century. Even though Bemis is overly sympathetic to Adams, he gives sufficient attention to Adams' critics. For example, Bemis traces the clash between Adams' careful, reserved diplomacy and Henry Clay's ardent advocacy of recognition of the newly independent Spanish American republics in the 1810's. In a few years, Adams adjusted his views on Latin America to take a position close to Clay's call for recognition. Bemis argues that Adams was the main author of the Monroe Doctrine, especially the noncolonization principle, which was directed against the European powers. Furthermore, Bemis insists that the stand Adams and Monroe made in 1823 was courageous, because they did not know that there was very little chance of European intervention in the Americas. As president from 1825 to 1829, Adams selected his old rival Clay to be Secretary of State, but the two pursued initiatives that found little success, as exemplified in the unproductive inter-American conference in Panama in 1826. In the final chapter, Bemis explores the "fourteen fundamentals" in Adams' contributions to U.S. foreign policy, eight of which concerned U.S. policy toward Latin America—most obviously the Monroe Doctrine, Manifest Destiny, noncolonization, Pan-Americanism, and anti-imperialism.

Dozer, Donald M., ed. *The Monroe Doctrine: Its Modern Significance*. New York: Knopf, 1965.

Dozer selected twenty-six short essays and excerpts from books and articles to illustrate the controversies, twists, and turns in the history of the Monroe Doctrine. His thirty-six-page introductory essay gives the student a balanced overview of the evolution of the doctrine. The selected readings include official justifications of the doctrine by U.S. diplomats Elihu Root and Charles Evans Hughes, but the distinctive contributions of this collection are the often critical analyses by Latin

American and other foreign observers. Among the most critical are those by Mexican diplomats Carlos Pereyra and Isidro Fabela, Chilean lawyer Alejandro Alvarez, and Nobel Peace Prize winner Carlos Saavedra Lamas of Argentina. Peruvian historian-diplomat Felipe Barreda y Laos defends the early Monroe Doctrine as a barrier to European penetration but rejects its twentieth century version because, in his view, it became a rationalization for armed U.S. interventions to protect economic interests. Japanese scholar Katsuji Inahara praises the Monroe Doctrine but from an imperialistic point of view. His 1940 article uses the Monroe Doctrine as a parallel case in his defense of the Japanese Empire's Greater East Asia Co-Prosperity Sphere. Academics Basil Dmytryshyn and Jesse Gilmore present an analysis of the hostile attitudes toward the Monroe Doctrine that emerged in the Cold War decade of the 1950's.

Liss, Peggy K. *Atlantic Empires: The Network of Trade and Revolution, 1713-1826*. Baltimore: Johns Hopkins University Press, 1983.
This well-written, extensively researched study of the economics and politics of the British, Spanish, and Portuguese empires provides the essential background for understanding the Monroe Doctrine. Liss highlights patterns in the commerce of material goods and the ex-change of ideas that brought about a shared experience for the leaders of the new nations of the Americas in the last decades of the eighteenth century and the first decades of the nineteenth century. She identifies businesspeople, patriots, and intellectuals in the United States and in Venezuela, Argentina, and other Latin American nations who worked for free trade, national independence, and the promotion of modern culture. Venezuelan Francisco de Miranda was at the forefront of the struggle for independence in northern South America, and Argentine Mariano Moreno led a similar movement in Buenos Aires. Thomas Jefferson and John Quincy Adams observed the independence move-ments in Latin America with a mixture of skepticism and hope. They saw political instability and clerical influences as flaws in these emerg-ing nations, but they also saw opportunities for trade and for mutual resistance to the revival of Iberian imperialism and the arrival of any other type of European aggression in the Western Hemisphere. In this context, Adams and James Monroe produced the Monroe Doctrine.

May, Ernest. *The Making of the Monroe Doctrine*. Cambridge, MA: Belknap Press, 1975.
The author, a specialist in the analysis of the decision-making process at the higher levels of government, uses an incisive approach to

determine why the Monroe Doctrine emerged as a major foreign policy statement in 1823. May examines private correspondence, diaries, and speeches to explain what motivated James Monroe, John Quincy Adams, and other national leaders to formulate this policy. In addition, he includes the impact of foreign powers on this process, especially the British, the French, and the Russians. Although he gives substantial attention to ideological factors and the strategic interest of the United States, May concludes that the decisive influences on the formulation of the Monroe Doctrine were the policymakers jockeying for political advantage in the context of the highly competitive presidential election of 1824. For example, Adams saw the Monroe Doctrine as evidence that in his tenure as Secretary of State (1817-1825), the United States had followed an independent foreign policy free from British influence and outside the entanglements of European politics. Adams won a disputed election that was settled in the House of Representatives. May concludes that the Monroe Doctrine was the result of the give and take of democratic politics, not the result of the cold calculations of statecraft.

Merk, Frederick. *The Monroe Doctrine and American Expansionism, 1843-1849*. New York: Knopf, 1968.

The first major application of the Monroe Doctrine after 1823 came in the administration of President James K. Polk and concerned the decision to annex Texas to the United States. Merk examines the diplomatic pressures, political intrigues, ideological pronouncements, and propaganda devices that surrounded this crucial decision in North American history. He concludes that Polk went beyond the original defensive purposes of the Monroe Doctrine to include strategic and security factors to justify U.S. expansion. Polk was especially concerned about the British presence in Texas. One widely circulated, inflammatory tale alleged a plan by London abolitionists/entrepreneurs to form a loan fund to pay the costs of the emancipation of slaves in Texas to clear away this impediment to the addition of a new colony to the British Empire (at this time, the government in London had made abolition of slavery a priority throughout its empire). The Polk Administration's exaggeration of this threat spurred the annexation of Texas. Merk also explores U.S.-British rivalries and intrigues in California, Yucatán, and Cuba. His examination of political propaganda reveals the extent to which the proponents of expansion were willing to use rumor and innuendo to excite public opinion. This study links the Monroe Doctrine to the concept of Manifest Destiny and the Mexican-American War.

Perkins, Dexter. *A History of the Monroe Doctrine*. Boston: Little, Brown, 1955.

A single-volume condensation of Perkins' earlier studies and a revised version of *Hands Off: A History of the Monroe Doctrine* (published in 1941), this book has less detail in the narrative of events but presents the author's considered judgments on the origins and impact of key events such as the writing and announcement of the Monroe Doctrine and its revival by James K. Polk in the 1840's. In addition, Perkins incorporates more recent material on the interventions under the Roosevelt Corollary, the interaction of the Monroe Doctrine and the League of Nations in the wake of World War I, and the shared legacy of the Monroe Doctrine and the Good Neighbor Policy. The last two chapters, written during the era of World War II and the early Cold War, are heavily influenced by the perception that the American nations are obligated to safeguard the hemisphere from threats of external aggression—first Fascism and then Communism—that would undercut the ideals of the original doctrine.

_____. *The Monroe Doctrine, 1823-1826*. Cambridge, MA: Harvard University Press, 1927.

_____. *The Monroe Doctrine, 1826-1867*. Baltimore: Johns Hopkins University Press, 1933.

_____. *The Monroe Doctrine, 1867-1907*. Baltimore: Johns Hopkins University Press, 1937.

Traditionally considered the standard study of the Monroe Doctrine, these three volumes contain a detailed history of its first eighty-four years and are based on the author's research in the 1920's and 1930's. The first volume covers the diplomatic, ideological, and strategic sources for the Monroe Doctrine and its reception in Europe. The second moves through the period of neglect to concentrate on the doctrine's revival during the Mexican-American War and subsequent disputes with Great Britain concerning Central America and with the French and Spanish in Santo Domingo. The last part of the second volume covers the United States' response to the short-lived French imperial adventure in Mexico in the 1860's. The third volume emphasizes the assertive statement of Secretary of State Richard Olney to Great Britain regarding the Venezuelan boundary controversy in 1895 and the establishment of Theodore Roosevelt's Corollary to the Monroe Doctrine in 1904, but it gives little attention to the Spanish-American War and the Panama Canal episode. These volumes are useful sources of detailed information on nineteenth century diplomacy and include Perkins' positive evaluations of the doctrine originally expressed from his perspective in the 1920's and 1930's. On controversial issues, the researcher should consult some of the more recent works in this area such as the books by Donald M. Dozer, Ernest May, William Weeks, and Arthur Whitaker mentioned in this section of the bibliography.

Weeks, William Earl. *John Quincy Adams and American Global Empire.* Lexington: University Press of Kentucky, 1992.
   Although the center of attention in this thoroughly researched study is the negotiation of the Adams-Onís Treaty of 1819 (ratified in 1821), Weeks does an excellent job of placing this event in its broad historical setting. He gives a revealing biographical sketch of John Quincy Adams, whose struggle with the moral conflict between republican virtue and imperial expansion ended in victory for empire. Adams' use of maneuver and intimidation in the negotiations with Luis de Onís, the representative of Spain, included a defense of General Andrew Jackson's impulsive invasion of Spanish Florida in 1818. Under the Adams-Onís Treaty, the United States annexed Florida and established a highly favorable southern boundary between the Louisiana Purchase territory and New Spain, the vast viceroyalty of the Spanish Empire that was on the verge of acquiring its independence as the nation of Mexico. Weeks argues convincingly that the Adams-Onís Treaty was a vital component of the U.S. expansionist surge that soon brought forth the Monroe Doctrine.

Whitaker, Arthur P. *The United States and the Independence of Latin America, 1800-1830.* 1941. New York: Norton, 1964.
   This extensively researched study, originally published in 1941, provides important historical depth on this crucial period in U.S.-Latin American relations. The United States was the main beneficiary of Spanish Royal Order of 1797, which opened Spain's American colonial ports to neutral ships (those not involved in the European war). From this time, U.S. interest in Latin American trade and politics grew, although at an irregular pace because of wars and piracy. After the War of 1812, U.S. trade with the crumbling Spanish Empire increased substantially. Whitaker includes two excellent chapters on the image of Latin America that developed in the private letters and published writing of individual merchants, sailors, and government agents who wanted to promote trade with these emerging nations. He also provides examples of the propaganda work of Latin American revolutionaries

in the United States. Whitaker explains the well-known roles of John Quincy Adams and James Monroe, but he also includes Henry Clay's advocacy of expanding commercial and diplomatic relations in Latin America. There is a chapter on the extension of the U.S. Navy's presence in the Caribbean and along both coasts of South America; that presence was intended to combat piracy during the revolutionary period. In his assessment of the Monroe Doctrine, Whitaker differs from other historians in crediting primary authorship to Monroe and Thomas Jefferson, rather than John Quincy Adams.

_____. *The Western Hemisphere Idea: Its Rise and Decline.* Ithaca, NY: Cornell University Press, 1954.
This brief book is a tight summary of the author's thinking on the 150-year evolution of the concept that the United States and the Latin American nations have shared a unique and intimate relationship. A central theme is the Monroe Doctrine. James Monroe envisioned the doctrine as a barrier to European efforts to reestablish colonial bases in the Western Hemisphere. Manifest Destiny and the dismemberment of Mexico by the United States, however, pushed the notion of hemispheric unity into near oblivion. In the late 1800's, Domingo Sarmiento of Argentina and William Eleroy Curtis of the United States revived the Western Hemisphere Idea, but through different approaches. Sarmiento saw an expansion of U.S. cultural and educational influences as the keys to progress, but Curtis emphasized business and commerce. In the twentieth century, U.S. interventions in Latin America posed serious challenges to hemispheric harmony. Whitaker devotes a chapter to the efforts of Argentine diplomat Luis Drago to create a hemispheric mechanism to eliminate military intervention as a means of collecting foreign debts. Theodore Roosevelt and Elihu Root twisted the Drago Doctrine into the Roosevelt Corollary to the Monroe Doctrine, which provided a rationalization for one of the things that Drago wanted to prevent—U.S. interventions. The last chapter deals with the Good Neighbor Policy, in which hemispheric harmony was paramount, and the early phases of the Cold War, in which the United States lost interest in the Western Hemisphere Idea because of its commitment to global diplomacy.

Manifest Destiny and the Mexican-American War

Brack, Gene M. *Mexico Views Manifest Destiny, 1821-1846: An Essay on the Origins of the Mexican War*. Albuquerque: University of New Mexico Press, 1975.

This brief (194 pages) but important book traces the evolution of public opinion in Mexico (as expressed mainly in newspapers) regarding the United States, from vague and often favorable comments in the 1820's to expressions of distrust and anger in the 1840's. As Mexican writers began to examine the political and economic life of the United States, they saw a vigorous, assertive people. This image eventually conveyed a threat because the vigor and assertiveness formed the basis for westward expansion. As Anglo-American settlers from the United States moved into Texas, newspaper editors expressed fear that the loss of this province would be only the first step in the dismemberment of the Mexican nation. One of Brack's central contributions is to show that many Mexicans were not eager for war. While newspaper editors and other commentators called for armed resistance to the U.S. annexation of Texas, many Mexican political and military leaders saw the futility of such action. General Mariano Arista, who was in charge of the military zone along the border with Texas, reported to his superiors that his manpower and supplies were insufficient to engage U.S. forces. Foreign Minister Manuel de la Peña y Peña grasped the necessity of foreign support—especially from the British—and also realized that such support was not available.

Brown, Charles H. *Agents of Manifest Destiny: The Lives and Times of the Filibusters*. Chapel Hill: University of North Carolina Press, 1980.

The westward expansion of the United States in the 1840's had something of a counterpart in its irregular thrusts into the Caribbean region in the 1850's. In the aftermath of the war with Mexico, ambitious men from a variety of backgrounds led landing parties onto Caribbean shores in hopes of conquest or of carving out an independent nation, or, at least, a colonial settlement. Newspaper coverage of the Mexican-American War and the excited patriotic rhetoric celebrating the U.S. victory created an atmosphere in which former soldiers, scheming politicians, and greedy financial agents saw the tropical lands to the south as open areas for the realization of their grandiose plans. Brown uses clear prose, extensive reading in secondary sources, and a biographical approach to present the stated goals and actual accomplishments of these adventurous filibusters. Many of those who attempted military invasions paid with their lives. Two who met fatal outcomes

were Narciso López, a Venezuelan who tried in vain to liberate Cuba
from Spain, and William Walker, a Tennessean who led four expeditions to Central America. Others survived their risky undertakings only
to drift into obscurity. Texas-born Mexican José María Jesús Carvajal
attempted to found the Republic of Sierra Madre in northeastern
Mexico in the early 1850's, and Illinois farmer-merchant Henry L.
Kinney saw his plans for a colony on Nicaragua's Mosquito Coast go
awry. Brown also explains the efforts of government officials in the
United States to monitor the erratic actions of the filibusters and, in
some cases, to restrain them to avoid international crises.

Griswold del Castillo, Richard. *The Treaty of Guadalupe Hidalgo: A
Legacy of Conflict.* Norman: University of Oklahoma Press, 1990.
This short book covers an important, controversial, and complex topic.
The author devotes the first third of his text to the negotiation and
ratification of the Treaty of Guadalupe Hidalgo, which formally ended
the war between the United States and Mexico in 1848. The most
obvious result of this treaty was the transfer of the land between Texas
and the Pacific Ocean to the United States. Griswold del Castillo uses
the remaining two-thirds of this volume to explain another important
result of the treaty: its impact on land ownership in the southwestern
part of the United States. The treaty was supposed to protect the
property ownership of approximately 100,000 residents of the area
after the transfer of the region from Mexico to the United States, but,
for a variety of reasons, the U.S. courts have not consistently enforced
its provisions regarding the original land grants. Griswold del Castillo
explains the continued importance of the treaty in the actions and ideas
of Mexican Americans and native Americans in their efforts to reclaim
their landed heritage and to establish their cultural identities in the
twentieth century. He also covers the controversies concerning the
Mexican-U.S. border that have emerged since 1848. The appendices
include the complete text of the treaty.

Horsman, Reginald. *Race and Manifest Destiny: The Origins of American
Racial Anglo-Saxonism.* Cambridge, MA: Harvard University Press,
1981.
This important study explains the role of racist ideas in the development of Manifest Destiny. Although Horsman's study is mostly intellectual history, the text and its main ideas are within the grasp of the
beginning researcher. Chapters 2 and 3, which trace the history of racist
thought in science (pseudoscience by modern standards), are fairly
challenging, but the remainder of the book explores, in clear prose, the

spread of assumptions concerning Anglo-Saxon superiority in the United States from the early 1800's to 1850. The author discusses the ideas and actions not only of intellectuals but also of politicians, popular writers, the practitioners of phrenology (who searched for alleged physical bases of apparent racial differences), and romantic novelists. Horsman has chapters on how Anglo-Saxon racial suprema- cist assumptions denigrated Mexicans and native Americans and cre- ated a rationalization for U.S. expansion into lands west of the Louisi- ana Purchase territory, held by Mexico from its independence in 1821 until 1848. He argues that the U.S. sense of mission (the uplift of local peoples) was corrupted by the prejudices of Anglo-Saxon racial supe- riority.

Johannsen, Robert W. *To the Halls of the Montezumas: The Mexican War in the American Imagination.* New York: Oxford University Press, 1985.

This valuable study contends that the war with Mexico gave the United States its first intense experience with a nation-state made up of a people and cultures very different from those of its own heavily British background. Johannsen relies on popular books, newspapers, and magazines, which reveal that war hysteria swept the United States in the summer of 1846, when maps and books about Mexico suddenly were in great demand. The war with Mexico was the first major international event involving the United States to be covered by the penny press (inexpensive, mass circulation newspapers that empha- sized dramatic events in an often sensationalized style). Early press and public responses to U.S. victories stressed alleged racial inferiority of the Mexican soldiers. Many writers portrayed the war in a romanti- cized version of medieval chivalry combined with the rugged individu- alism of the frontier. Heroic images of generals Zachary Taylor and Winfield Scott dominated the pages of the penny press, and artillery major Samuel Ringgold became a martyred hero in the Battle of Palo Alto. Some writers went beyond frontier romanticism and racial preju- dice to present other dimensions of Mexico. Travel accounts of jour- nalists and soldiers included expression of awe in descriptions of preconquest native American pyramids as well as rugged mountains and deserts. Although most books and articles heaped praise on the U.S. military, Johanssen points out that a few writers condemned the war as unnecessary. Elder statesman Albert Gallatin warned that the invasion of Mexico City and the acquisition of California amounted to a conquest that threatened the principles that had guided the nation for half a century.

Merk, Frederick. *Manifest Destiny and Mission in American History: A Reinterpretation*. New York: Vintage Books, 1963.

This influential study concentrates on the importance of ideas and propaganda in the popular press and literary magazines that stimulated and supported the expansion of the United States in the 1840's. One of the central figures in this book is John L. O'Sullivan, a literary scholar, politician, and adventurer who was well known for his essays celebrating the virtues of the U.S. political system. O'Sullivan was the first to use the expression "Manifest Destiny," in the summer of 1845. Merk views Manifest Destiny as a political movement promoted and sustained by O'Sullivan, other writers, and politicians such as President James Polk to justify the expansion of the United States as a means of implanting the nation's political institutions in the annexed territory. Merk also discusses the strongly racist current in the United States of the 1840's that contributed to the defeat of the movement to acquire "All of Mexico." Although the word "mission" appears in the title of this book, Merk discusses it briefly only in the prologue and the last chapter. He defines this term as the effort to introduce the more democratic aspects of the U.S. political system to other peoples and sees it as a countervailing tendency to more aggressive forms of expansion, particularly the imperialism of the 1890's.

Pletcher, David M. *The Diplomacy of Annexation: Texas, Oregon, and the Mexican War*. Columbia: University of Missouri Press, 1973.

This clearly written, well-organized account of the causes and outcome of the war between the United States and Mexico strikes a healthy balance between traditional narrative and carefully reasoned analysis. Pletcher focuses on the role of President James Polk but also includes details on the three-sided diplomacy involving the United States, Mexico, and Great Britain. The author's archival research on these three nations makes this a uniquely valuable book. One of Pletcher's main theses is that this conflict was not only a war over territory but also the opening phase in a series of aggressive U.S. policies in the Western Hemisphere pitting that nation against Great Britain in an intermittent struggle for domination in Latin America. Pletcher includes biographical sketches of important personalities including Mexican general/president Antonio López de Santa Anna and statesman Valentín Gómez Farías, British diplomat Richard Packenham and policymaker Lord Palmerston, and several leaders in the United States including John C. Calhoun, Thomas Hart Benton, and James Buchanan. Although not a military history, this book includes assessments of the actions and ambitions of Zachary Taylor and Winfield Scott. The most comprehensive portrait is that of James K. Polk. Pletcher examines his controversial diplomacy and concludes that Polk's intentions were to take strong negotiating positions with the British and the Mexicans. According to Pletcher, Polk did not contrive the war with Mexico, but when the Mexicans continued to offer resistance to his aggressive policies, the United States pursued a diplomatic-military escalation that resulted in war.

Robinson, Cecil, trans. and ed. *The View from Chapultepec: Mexican Writers on the Mexican-American War*. Tucson: University of Arizona Press, 1989.
This collection of twelve essays written by Mexicans on the origins, course, and consequences of the war between Mexico and the United States offers several valuable insights from the point of view of the citizens of the nation that lost the war. Editor-translator Robinson's forty-four-page introduction is an informative overview of the 1820's, 1830's, and 1840's in Mexico. Robinson also has brief but helpful introductions for each selection, including biographical details on the Mexican authors. These selections range chronologically from Mariano Otero's essay originally published in 1847 to Josefina Vázquez's historical account written in 1972. The following comments on a sampling of these selections will give the reader some indication of their contents. Otero blamed the defeat of his nation on its divided society, corruption in government, and a general indifference toward the war. Also in 1847, the elderly Carlos María de Bustamante wrote with anger (and some inaccuracies) to explain the ongoing defeat of his homeland. Modern historians Leopoldo Zea, José Fuentes Mares, Carlos Bosch García, and Josefina Vázquez approach the subject with more restrained judgments and greater accuracy but also present perspectives on the war that many students in the United States will find enlightening.

Schroeder, John H. *Mr. Polk's War: American Opposition and Dissent, 1846-1848*. Madison: University of Wisconsin Press, 1973.
Schroeder's thought-provoking, well-researched study concentrates on domestic opponents of the United States' war against Mexico and its decision to annex the territory from Texas to California. The author explores the origins and ideas of the two major groups of dissenters: the political opponents who came largely from the Whig Party and religious and intellectual opponents who worked in the churches, academic institutions, and literary circles of the northeastern United States. The Whigs were the main political rivals of President James K.

Polk's Democratic Party. As General Winfield Scott's forces approached Mexico City, many Whigs argued that Polk had led the nation into a war of conquest for the purpose of expanding slave territory. Senator Thomas Corwin of Ohio, a Whig, denounced Polk's intention of taking California as comparable to horse stealing (a serious offense in the United States of the nineteenth century). Religious and intellectual dissent concentrated in New England, where reform ideals—especially opposition to slavery—were strong. James Russell Lowell satirized the prowar position in a series of poems known as the Biglow Papers. The Unitarian and Quaker churches used pacifist arguments against the war. Henry David Thoreau refused to pay his taxes as a symbolic gesture against the war and spent a night in jail as a result. In the 1849 novel *Mardi, and a Voyage Thither*, Herman Melville portrayed the war as the rash, ill-considered act of an immature nation. Schroeder shows that although these protests did not change Polk's policies, they did make it clear that aggressive territorial expansion could incite considerable opposition within the United States.

Smith, Justin H. *The War with Mexico*. 2 vols. 1919. Reprint. Gloucester, MA: Peter Smith, 1963.

In spite of its age and dated prejudices, this work retains value because of its account of the war itself. Smith wrote mostly military history but with some sharp commentary on politics and diplomacy. His text features detailed narratives of major battles such as those at Monterrey, Veracruz, and Mexico City, accompanied by relevant maps as well as information on many of the minor engagements. His one-sided condemnation of the Mexicans for starting the war offers a distinct contrast with the more recent findings of scholars such as David Pletcher and Gene Brack. Students can benefit by contrasting Smith's ethnic biases and historical misjudgments with these two works and other studies mentioned in this section.

Weber, David J. *The Mexican Frontier, 1821-1846: The American Southwest Under Mexico*. Albuquerque: University of New Mexico Press, 1982.

An important but little-understood chapter in inter-American relations took place in the northern provinces of Mexico in the quarter century after that nation acquired its independence. Texas, New Mexico, and California were home to active but scattered communities of Mexicans and native Americans but, at the same time, served as enticements for the land-hungry Anglo-Americans of the United States. Weber fills this historical gap with an excellent account of the Mexican government's efforts to administer these distant provinces. While Mexico's national political system suffered from factional wrangling, the provinces were left to sort out their own problems. Frontier traders from the United States exchanged firearms for furs and horses with Apaches, Comanches, and other tribes, which then raided the isolated Mexican settlements. In 1821, eager St. Louis merchants opened the Santa Fe Trail to New Mexico, beginning the first wave of an invasion of Missouri merchants into Mexican territory. In Texas, the Mexican government invited immigrants from the United States to settle rich farmlands, with disastrous results. Soon Anglo-Americans outnumbered Mexicans in Texas, which in 1835 established its independence in a bloody revolt. By the outbreak of the war between the United States and Mexico in 1846, the Mexican government's influence in its remaining northern provinces was weak and quickly collapsed. This volume has an informative thirty-page bibliographical essay that includes many recent publications in English.

The Spanish-American War

Beisner, Robert L. *From the Old Diplomacy to the New, 1865-1900*. New York: Crowell, 1986.
The United States' growing interest in Cuba and its decision to go to war against Spain were parts of a major transformation of the nation's foreign policy. Beisner's book is a short, highly perceptive survey of U.S. policy toward Latin America, Europe, and Asia, with a strong emphasis on the 1890's and the Spanish-American War. One of his main theses is that by this decade, U.S. presidents and diplomats had abandoned the older, case-by-case, crisis-by-crisis approach for more systematic methods in order to formulate a coherent foreign policy that would take into account the nation's interests across the globe. Beisner points out that this new system had its flaws and failures but that it was an important part of the emergence of the United States as a world power. As his account makes clear, relations with Spain and Cuba were important testing grounds in this process.

Cosmas, Graham. *An Army for Empire: The United States Army in the Spanish-American War*. Columbia: University of Missouri Press, 1971.
This study is military history in the full sense of the term. Cosmas devotes two chapters to the invasion of Cuba and actual combat, but most of the book is a perceptive, well-organized examination of the internal workings of the United States Army in transition from its

campaigns against native Americans in the West to the challenges of
fighting a war outside the boundaries of the country. Cosmas discusses
the problems involved in the rapid recruitment and training of officers
and enlisted men, the vacillating policies of President William McKinley, and the effects of politics in these areas. The chapter titled "Sick-
ness and Scandal" gives an incisive account of the impact of tropical
diseases, inadequate food supplies, and the struggle to provide medical
care for the troops. Given the complexity of these tasks and the War
Department's lack of experience in tropical areas, the Army managed
to cope with its problems and, according to Cosmas, was generally
successful in the creation of a structure of military command for duty
overseas, with the war in Cuba serving as the central event.

Foner, Philip S. *The Spanish-Cuban-American War and the Birth of
American Imperialism, 1895-1902.* 2 vols. New York: Monthly Review Press, 1972.
In this seminal and controversial study of the struggle involving Spain,
Cuba, and the United States, Foner challenges earlier historical works
that limited their research to diplomatic and military archives in the
United States, Spain, and Western Europe. Foner's research in Cuba
reinforces one of his central theses—that Cuba was a major factor in
the events from 1895 to 1902. Students will find extensive coverage
of the Cuban rebels inspired by José Martí (who fell in the insurgent
invasion of 1895) and led by Antonio Maceo and Máximo Gómez from
1895 to early 1898, before the United States entered the conflict. Foner
emphasizes the efforts of Cuban leaders to write their own constitution
and to establish a national government. He also points out the struggle
of working-class Cubans to start a labor movement. In both war and
peace, however, the United States imposed its powerful presence. The
U.S. Army arrived in the summer of 1898 to participate in the defeat
of the already beleaguered Spanish. U.S. military governors presided
over the formation of Cuban political institutions, and U.S. pressure
dictated that the new constitution include the Platt Amendment, which
provided for U.S. military interventions based on judgments made in
Washington. Foner's work has a strong Marxist slant. He stresses U.S.
economic expansion as a force behind the McKinley Administration's
decision to enter the war. Although several authorities disagree with
this emphasis on economic motives, there is more agreement with
Foner's assertion that, once the fighting ended, U.S. corporate interests
moved into railroads, sugar mills, and landed estates in a big way. The
United States was not only the most convenient market for Cuban sugar

but also became the locus for the capitalization and management of the island's economy.

Freidel, Frank. *The Splendid Little War*. Boston: Little Brown, 1958.
The text of this highly readable military-naval history of the Spanish-American War is reinforced by more than one hundred large and nicely reproduced photographs and sketches. Freidel's narrative stays close to the army camp, the naval squadron, and the battles on sea and land. Students will benefit from careful study of the illustrations and their captions as a way to acquire insights into particular events and (mostly U.S.) personalities. The text, however, should be supplemented by the works of Louis Pérez for discussions of the role of Cuban insurgents and John Offner's book for the causes of U.S. intervention. Both of these works are annotated in this section.

Gould, Lewis. *The Presidency of William McKinley*. Lawrence: Regents Press of Kansas, 1980.
This compact history of the McKinley presidency (1897-1901) has unusual depth for a brief book. Gould weaves his own archival research into the findings of other historians to give the reader insights into the president's perspective on the crises that he faced. The Cuban situation loomed quite large for McKinley, and Gould gives significant portions of four chapters to the Spanish-American War. His central thesis is that McKinley faced diplomatic and military crises directly and was an effective manager of the resources of the government in responding to the tense relations with Spain, the varied political pressures in the United States, the demands of the military, naval warfare, and postwar diplomacy. The leaders of the Cuban revolutionary movement had a different view of the McKinley Administration, as explained in the studies by Philip Foner, John Offner, Louis Pérez, and Gerald Poyo listed in this section.

Healy, David. *The United States in Cuba, 1898-1902*. Madison: University of Wisconsin Press, 1963.
The influence of the U.S. military in Cuba did not end with the defeat of the Spanish. Healy contends that the four-year U.S. military government of the island was a crucial experience not only for Cubans but also for policymakers in Washington. The process of establishing and maintaining a military presence for the purposes of achieving political order and economic stability became a pattern for U.S. actions in the Caribbean through the early decades of the twentieth century. Healy's detailed examination of the U.S. administration of Cuban affairs brings

to light bureaucratic and political infighting in the War Department, Congress, and the White House that eventually resulted in the rise of General Leonard Wood to the position of military governor. Healy also provides a valuable discussion of the origins of the Platt Amendment, which gave the United States the right to intervene in Cuba to maintain stability. According to Healy, competing factions in the U.S. Senate agreed to this imposition on the new Cuban constitution as a compromise between outright independence for Cuba and continued military occupation. Healy also points out the widespread opposition to the Platt Amendment in Cuba, underscoring the wide gap between policy-making in Washington and the political environment on the island.

May, Ernest R. *Imperial Democracy: The Emergence of the United States As a World Power.* New York: Harpers, 1961.
The Spanish-American War was a decisive event in the rise of the United States to a position of respect and authority in the competitive arena of world politics of the late nineteenth century. May views U.S. involvement in Cuba and the war with Spain in this larger context. He sees President William McKinley's policies as driven by the jingoism (extreme patriotism) of politicians and the New York press and by the excitability of the public mood throughout the nation. Although May gives considerable attention to Cuba and its image in U.S. public opinion and political rhetoric, his analysis of the fighting in the Caribbean and the Pacific and the subsequent U.S. annexation of the Philippines concentrates on the perspectives of European diplomats, who were increasingly concerned about the expanding presence of the United States in the Western Hemisphere and Asia. For more information on the place of Cuba in these events, the reader should consult the works of Philip Foner, Louis Pérez, and Gerald Poyo discussed in this section.

Milton, Joyce. *The Yellow Kids: Foreign Correspondents in the Heyday of Yellow Journalism.* New York: HarperCollins, 1989.
Cuba of the 1890's was the testing ground not only for the diplomatic and military prowess of the United States but also for the reporting skills and personal ambitions of the generation that made yellow journalism a prevalent orientation in the print media of North America. Milton disagrees with earlier studies that depict this generation of reporters as irresponsible alarmists who stirred the U.S. public into a frenzy for war. Instead, she finds some redeeming validity in the reporting of James Creelman, Richard Harding Davis, Stephen Crane, and especially Harry Scovel. As pugnacious and colorful as any of the

other yellow journalists, Scovel passed through the Spanish and Cuban lines in 1895 at considerable personal risk to report on the rebel side of the war. He eventually stumbled onto the army of Máximo Gómez and witnessed a clash between these Cuban rebels and Spanish forces. He also rode with the legendary Gómez and, after three months in rebel territory, returned to safer quarters with an understanding of guerrilla tactics and the inability of the Spanish to overcome them. Milton's study makes clear the extent to which Scovel and some of his colleagues moved beyond the simplistic, stereotypical coverage usually attributed to yellow journalists and also explores the interactions of Cubans, Spaniards, and U.S. journalists in a time of international crisis.

Offner, John L. *An Unwanted War: The Diplomacy of the United States and Spain over Cuba, 1895-1898.* Chapel Hill: University of North Carolina Press, 1992.

The main purpose of this study is to explain why the United States and Spain went to war in 1898. This question has drawn a variety of explanations. Many historians—especially William Appleman Williams—have emphasized U.S. economic interests, and Joyce Milton has stressed the role of the jingo press in New York. Offner sees several trends at work, but probably the central contribution of this stimulating study is the uncovering of a different set of causative factors in the vigorous political rivalry between Republicans and Democrats during the congressional election year of 1898. Republican President William McKinley did not want the Democrats to win more seats in the House of Representatives and the Senate; therefore, he took high-profile, firm stands in his dealings with Spain. Offner's research in U.S., Spanish, Cuban, and other European and Latin American archives reveals that McKinley, the Spanish, and the Cubans all wanted to avoid U.S. entry into the fight. McKinley's determination to display firm leadership, however, eventually brought the United States into the war that he had hoped to avoid.

Pérez, Louis A., Jr. *Cuba Between Empires, 1878-1902.* Pittsburgh: University of Pittsburgh Press, 1983.

This superb study of the Cuban people's struggle for independence from Spain also includes the subsequent disappointments in their relationship with the United States. The two empires in the title are the decaying remnants of the four-hundred-year-old Spanish Empire in the Caribbean and the rising new empire of the United States, which by 1902 managed to dominate Cuba without formal annexation. Unlike most students of the Spanish-American War, Pérez focuses on events and people in Cuba and presents the work of U.S. and Spanish diplomats, generals, and admirals in the context of the island's history. Pérez gives a challenging interpretation of the origins of the movement for independence in the eastern portion of the island. In his analysis of the social background of the insurgents led by rebel generals Máximo Gómez and Antonio Maceo, Pérez makes the point that the movement for independence was also a social revolution—the peasants' attempt to overthrow the economic system controlled by large estates and centralized sugar mills. This revolutionary uprising against the island's power structure conflicted with another segment of the independence movement in the United States, led by Tomás Estrada Palma. He and his followers wanted support for Cuban independence from U.S. corporate leaders, many of whom had invested in the very sugar business that Gómez and Maceo were fighting to control. Although the revolutionaries won major victories against Spanish forces, the intervention of the United States quickly turned the course of events away from social revolution. The Spanish Empire gave way to the economic domination of the United States. Estrada Palma became the new nation's first president under a constitution that included the Platt Amendment.

_____. "Insurrection, Intervention and the Transformation of Land Tenure Systems in Cuba, 1895-1902." *Hispanic American Historical Review* 65 (May, 1985): 229-254.
The Spanish-American War and the subsequent United States military government of the island brought a major transformation of the Cuban economy that is often overshadowed in histories that dwell on stories of combat on land and sea. Pérez's brief but profound explanation of the economic transformation of eastern Cuba gives much-needed depth to this often neglected area. Most of the fighting on the island before and during U.S. military involvement took place in eastern Cuba. Under the directions of the military government—particularly Civil Order Number 62—the rebuilding of the shattered economy of this area gave large corporate investors from the United States a clear advantage over traditional landholding village communities and small property owners. These changes enhanced the position of the foreign-owned sugar estates that became a dominant feature of the Cuban economy for many decades.

Poyo, Gerald E. *"With All, and for the Good of All": The Emergence of Popular Nationalism in the Cuban Communities of the United States, 1848-1898*. Durham, NC: Duke University Press, 1989.

Poyo examines a unique and important episode in the history of the special relationship between Cuba and the United States. In the half century covered in this book, Cuban nationalism became a potent force, but this process took place not on the home island but in the United States. Many émigrés who left Cuba in the waning years of the Spanish Empire took up residence in Florida, where they worked in the growing cigar industry of Key West and Tampa. Poyo gives ample attention to radical labor leaders among the cigar workers; these leaders' activism injected working-class issues and presence into Cuban nationalism. The author discusses the contributions of José Martí, who more than any other leader personified the Cuban independence movement. Poyo also examines the split that ultimately divided Martí and his ardent followers in Florida from the group headed by Tomás Estrada Palma in New York that favored U.S. intervention against the Spanish. The outcome of U.S. participation in the Cuban war for independence in 1898 favored the Estrada Palma group and frustrated the followers of Martí, who saw their nationalist goals sacrificed under the weight of continued U.S. interventions over the next several decades.

Trask, David F. *The War with Spain in 1898*. New York: MacMillan, 1981. This detailed, smoothly written narrative weaves together political and military history to give the reader impressive depth on the key events of 1898. Among the many themes in the nearly five hundred pages of Trask's text are the failure of U.S.-Spanish diplomacy; the lack of military preparedness in both nations; the establishment of the U.S. blockade of Cuba; the problems of logistics in Tampa; the sinking of the Spanish fleet in Santiago harbor; the military campaigns in Cuba, Puerto Rico, and the Philippines; and the signing of the Treaty of Paris. Trask revises the findings of earlier historians in his assessments of President William McKinley as a competent leader and of the U.S. Army's performance as generally capable. The author also supplies helpful biographical sketches of other important figures such as U.S. Secretary of War Russell Alger, Admiral William Sampson, General William Shafter, Spain's Admiral Pascual Cervera, and Cuba's General Calixto García. The extensive footnotes include many books, articles, and published government documents that are available in larger college and university libraries.

Williams, William Appleman. *The Roots of the Modern American Empire: A Study of the Growth and Shaping of Social Consciousness in a Marketplace Society*. New York: Random House, 1969.

This classic study of the causes of the involvement of the United States in the Spanish-American War continues to inspire both admiration and debate. Williams portrays the grain farmers of the Midwest as agricultural businesspeople who, from the 1860's to the 1890's, called for the opening of new markets in foreign countries as a solution to the periodic farm crises resulting from surpluses in wheat and corn production. Through newspaper editorials, magazine articles, and political speeches, Williams documents the growth of support for Republican Party presidential candidate William McKinley in the election of 1896. McKinley's victory owed much to the combined support of agricultural and business leaders who saw Cuba—and Latin America in general— as a potential market for U.S. agricultural and industrial surpluses and the Philippines as an embarkation point for the China trade.

Chapter 4
THE TWENTIETH CENTURY:
MAIN THEMES IN INTERNATIONAL HISTORY

The Panama Canal and Early United States Interventions

Arbena, Joseph L. "Colombian Reactions to the Independence of Panama, 1903-1904." *The Americas* 33 (July, 1976): 130-148.

This concise, well-written article covers an important subject that is often neglected in other studies of the Panama Canal. Arbena uses Colombian newspapers and archives to document the responses of the nation's leaders to the disturbing news that the province of Panama had declared its independence and, even more distressing, that the United States under President Theodore Roosevelt actively supported the new Panamanian regime. Arbena discusses the shock and dismay of the Colombians as they realized that a military response would have been too costly and that diplomatic pressure would not work because other Latin American and European nations were reluctant to challenge the United States on this issue. Arbena's article is especially revealing as it traces the reactions of acting President José Manuel Marroquín and other national leaders to their country's loss.

Callcott, Wilfrid H. *The Caribbean Policy of the United States, 1890-1920*. Baltimore: Johns Hopkins University Press, 1942.

This account of U.S. diplomacy in the Caribbean has the merits of clear, unpretentious prose and sensible organization. More recent studies have revised some of Callcott's generalizations, but his judicious use of quotations from leading personalities and key diplomatic agreements and his understated commentary give this book considerable value for the researcher. Callcott also studied many contemporary publications, and his footnotes give the reader numerous citations from books, magazines, journals of opinion, and scholarly articles published from the 1890's to the 1920's.

Challener, Richard D. *Admirals, Generals, and American Foreign Policy, 1898-1914*. Princeton, NJ: Princeton University Press, 1973.

During the Spanish-American War and the Panama Canal episode, military and naval officers began to play important roles in U.S. foreign policy. Challener's study of the relationship between the military services and the civilian foreign policy establishment traces the emergence of this new set of influences in the formulation and application of U.S. policy—especially in the Caribbean. Although generals such as Leonard Wood and admirals such as George Dewey acquired definite influence in the policy-making process, Challener indicates that their input did not become the essential determinant. Rather, they seemed to have an impact as individual advisers to leaders with military inclinations—Theodore Roosevelt, for example—but considerably less impact on the decisions of leaders who were less prone to adopt military solutions. Nevertheless, the uncertainties of political instability in Cuba, Central America, and Mexico; the need to protect the Panama Canal; and the importance of strategically located bases in responding to these problems brought the expertise, opinions, and institutional interests of military/naval officials into the formulation and implementation of U.S. policies. Approximately half the cases discussed in this text involve the Caribbean, Central America, and Mexico.

Collin, Richard. *Theodore Roosevelt's Caribbean: The Panama Canal, the Monroe Doctrine, and the Latin American Context.* Baton Rouge: Louisiana State University Press, 1991.

This broadly focused study assesses the historical circumstances and international repercussions of the 1903 taking of the Panama Canal Zone by the United States. Collin emphasizes the collision of strategic interests in the Caribbean. Although Venezuela, Colombia, the Dominican Republic, and Cuba were troubled by political instability, economic distress, and large foreign debts, they occupied a region of growing importance for the world's powers. Among those powers, the United States had the geographic advantage of proximity and, in 1903, established itself as the master of the Panama Canal. The British and French had small colonies in the Caribbean, important investments throughout Latin America, and a tendency to project their power into the area. Germany, although excluded from colonial holdings, nevertheless sought a larger commercial and diplomatic presence. This combination of expansive U.S. and European interests directed onto the Caribbean nations, with their political and economic problems, created a multidimensional struggle for power during the presidency of Theodore Roosevelt, one of the most ambitious heads of state in U.S. history. Collin gives particular attention to the domestic crises in Colombia that preceded the Panamanian revolt for independence and the rapid movement of the Roosevelt Administration to recognize the new nation and to negotiate the Panama Canal Treaty.

Conniff, Michael. *Black Labor on a White Canal: Panama, 1904-1981*. Pittsburgh: University of Pittsburgh Press, 1985.

Most studies of the Panama Canal deal with diplomacy, politics, and engineering, but Conniff provides deep insights into an area generally neglected by historians. In order to find workers for this massive undertaking, U.S. officials imported more than 100,000 West Indians, who carried the heavy burden of often risky construction work and were compensated with a very low level of pay. Recruited from British colonial islands in the West Indies, the migrants came to Panama in hopes of improving their living standards, but many encountered difficult working conditions, life-threatening diseases, and slum housing. They endured sharply defined barriers of ethnic discrimination both from U.S. managers and workers and from the Panamanians, who soon came to resent the West Indians as rivals for employment in the Canal Zone. Conniff's thorough research makes clear, however, that the West Indians struggled and survived in this hostile environment through their own closely knit communities. They also found a spokesman in journalist George Westerman, who used his newspaper to bring attention to their plight.

DuVal, Miles. *And the Mountains Will Move: The Story of the Building of the Panama Canal*. Stanford, CA: Stanford University Press, 1947.

The second volume of Duval's study of the Panama Canal (see below for the first volume) is concerned mainly with the construction of the waterway. Approximately one-third of the text deals with the French effort of the 1880's led by Ferdinand de Lesseps and includes an analysis of the reasons for its failure. Most of the text covers the operations of the U.S. Panama Canal Commission: its organization and early crises, the debate about and rejection of the sea-level canal, and the actual construction project. The main value of DuVal's work is the detailed coverage of the project's engineering and construction achievements. The author gives little attention to the plight of the workers (see Michael Conniff's book cited in this section). This study also includes twenty-five photographs and two maps.

_____. *Cadiz to Cathay: The Story of the Long Diplomatic Struggle for the Panama Canal*. Stanford, CA: Stanford University Press, 1940.

This detailed narrative of the plans, plots, and negotiations involving Panama and the United States combines depth and focus. Approximately 300 of the 450 pages of text cover events from 1896 to 1903, with the French engineer, entrepreneur, and diplomat Philippe Bunau-

Varilla as the central character. Later findings by other historians, particularly the article by John Major cited in this section, indicate that Bunau-Varilla was not as influential as DuVal's portrait indicates, but this book's narrative depth in other areas gives it much utility for students of the history of the Panama Canal. DuVal also appends more than sixty pages of documents, including the text of the Hay-Bunau-Varilla Treaty, by which the United States secured its access to the Panama Canal Zone.

Langley, Lester. *The Banana Wars: United States Interventions in the Caribbean, 1898-1934*. Chicago: Dorsey Press, 1988.
Soldiers, sailors, and Marines were the occupation force in these interventions; they were responsible for the day-to-day operations in defense of U.S. diplomats, citizens, government installations, and private companies located in these nations as well as for actual military/naval campaigns. Most studies of this era deal with diplomacy and politics, but Langley is concerned with military history and draws from his extensive research in government archives, official reports, and published memoirs. The deployment of these forces was an important phase in the history of the Western Hemisphere and also a significant but usually neglected chapter in the history of these three branches. Although presidents, cabinet officials, and high-level commanders set the broad policy, military and naval officers on the scene exercised their own judgment in the implementation of these directives, and the enlisted men on the streets of Havana, Cuba; Veracruz, Mexico; and Managua, Nicaragua—and in the fields and jungles of Central America and the Caribbean—actually carried out these orders, often with improvisations. Langley's balanced account includes the ethnic prejudices that U.S. officers and men brought with them in their exercise of imperial power. This book focuses on four themes: the Spanish-American War and its aftermath in Cuba; the Veracruz intervention of 1914 and similar, smaller-scale operations in Central America; the interventions in Haiti and the Dominican Republic; and the pursuit of Augusto César Sandino in Nicaragua.

McCullough, David. *The Path Between the Seas: The Creation of the Panama Canal, 1870-1914*. New York: Simon and Schuster, 1977.
The unique mixture of entrepreneurs, engineers, diplomats, and politicians who worked their way across a broad international panorama to build the Panama Canal is the subject of McCullough's smoothly written account. The author's special penchant for sharply edged biographical portraits is abundantly evident in his treatments of the

unsuccessful diplomat-promoter Ferdinand de Lesseps, the enigmatic Philippe Bunau-Varilla, and the irrepressible nationalist Theodore Roosevelt. McCullough also gives much-needed attention to two often neglected characters: Panamanian politician Manuel Amador Guerrero and U.S. engineer John Stevens. The text covers the failed French effort, the international intrigues leading to Panama's break with Colombia, and the challenges of swamps, mountains, and disease that dogged the U.S. construction project. McCullough's discussion of the various construction plans and engineering dilemmas is free of technical jargon and accessible to the general reader. The text is reinforced by eighty well-chosen photographs.

Major, John. "Who Wrote the Hay-Bunau-Varilla Convention?" *Diplomatic History* 8 (Spring, 1984): 115-123.
This short scholarly article contains an important revision of the role of Philippe Bunau-Varilla in the writing of the Panama Canal Treaty. In his 1913 memoir, Bunau-Varilla claimed that he was the sole author of the agreement later ratified by the U.S. Senate. His version of the treaty's origins had credibility among historians until Major discovered documents in the U.S. State Department archives and the papers of Elihu Root that identify Secretary of State John Hay as the primary author of the treaty. Bunau-Varilla made some important contributions to the text, but Major contends that Hay wrote most of the treaty's twenty-seven articles.

Munro, Dana G. *Intervention and Dollar Diplomacy in the Caribbean, 1900-1921*. Princeton, NJ: Princeton University Press, 1963.
This book provides a rare combination of firsthand experience and scholarly research in analyzing this crucial era in the history of the Western Hemisphere. As a young man, Munro studied and traveled in Central America from 1914 to 1916 and served in the State Department as a specialist on this region from 1919 to 1932. This book, therefore, is both a retrospective on political and diplomatic affairs that the author knew very well personally (in some cases as a participant) and a historical study in which Munro combed through State Department archives for documentary evidence to reconstruct a version of events several decades after they transpired. The result is a detailed discussion, often at a day-to-day pace, of why Presidents Theodore Roosevelt, William Howard Taft, and Woodrow Wilson made their decisions to intervene in Central America and the Caribbean. Munro covers various degrees of U.S. involvement in more than a dozen of these smaller nations, but his emphasis is on the Dominican Republic

debt crisis of 1904, which was the immediate cause for the announcement of Theodore Roosevelt's Corollary to the Monroe Doctrine. Munro also provides narrative depth on U.S. military interventions in Nicaragua in 1912 and U.S. actions in Cuba and Haiti. Some of Munro's critics charge that he was an apologist for U.S. interventions, but a close reading of his conclusion to this volume reveals an effort to include failed policies in his evaluation of the era.

_____. *The United States and the Caribbean Republics, 1921-1933.* Princeton, NJ: Princeton University Press, 1974.
This continuation of Munro's 1963 study of the U.S. role in the region covers the transition period between the aggressive diplomacy and frequent interventions of the early decades of the twentieth century and the arrival of the Good Neighbor Policy of the 1930's, with its emphasis on nonintervention and harmony. Munro gives much attention to Nicaragua in the 1920's, when U.S. Marines embarked on an unsuccessful effort to defeat Augusto César Sandino, but his thesis is that, in general, policymakers in Washington turned away from such military involvement in this decade. The intervention in Nicaragua was an exception that actually reinforced the growing disillusionment with the results of armed interventions. Munro's personal experiences are evident in the chapter on the U.S. withdrawal of its financial supervision and military presence in Haiti in the early 1930's. He served as U.S. minister to that island nation during an important part of the negotiations.

Perkins, Whitney T. *Constraint of Empire: The United States and Caribbean Interventions.* Westport, CT: Greenwood Press, 1981.
Many U.S. interventions in the Caribbean and Central America took place under comparable circumstances. In this book, Perkins presents a comparative analysis of the origins, implementation, disengagement, and long-term consequences of U.S. interventions in Cuba, Nicaragua, the Dominican Republic, and Haiti. As one volume in a series of comparative studies of colonial systems, this book operates on the assumption that the United States enjoyed an imperialistic domination over these countries. Because he emphasizes the political aspects of the interventions, however, Perkins reaches conclusions considerably different from the findings of Marxists and other economic determinists. The United States sought stable, responsible governments in the region. When stability broke down and responsibility gave way to corruption and civil strife, the United States intervened, in part to establish good government and in part to protect its strategic interests.

The interventions brought forth a variety of results, most of them far removed from the original intentions of the United States. Internal political problems in these four nations entangled the United States in unwanted complications. U.S. diplomatic and military officials often turned to local military or law enforcement institutions to establish stability and, in the process, laid the foundations for troublesome dictators such as Nicaragua's Anastasio Somoza and Cuba's Fulgencio Batista. Overall, Perkins' analysis of these controversial issues is restrained and perceptive.

The Good Neighbor Policy and World War II

Beals, Carleton. *The Coming Struggle for Latin America*. Philadelphia: Lippincott, 1938.
A journalist who specialized in Latin America, Beals was one of the foremost alarmists on the issue of Axis penetration of the Western Hemisphere. Beals discusses Nazi Germany's economic, political, and cultural activities in the region and also points out evidence of growing Japanese immigration and trade. His picture of the expansion of fascist tendencies through the sense of identity with Benito Mussolini in the large Italian immigrant groups in Argentina and Brazil touched on a sensitive issue in the late 1930's, much like his account of the apparent strength of Spain's Francisco Franco among powerful segments of the region's predominantly Spanish population. By combining these ethnic groups and ideological tendencies, Beals provides a concentrated if somewhat exaggerated view of Axis influence. This book is a forceful statement of the alarmist position and should be read in conjunction with more recent historical studies that point out the limits of Axis influence, especially the works of Alton Frye, R. A. Humphreys, and Leslie Rout and John Bratzel mentioned in this section.

DeConde, Alexander. *Herbert Hoover's Latin American Policy*. Palo Alto, CA: Stanford University Press, 1951.
In this brief, well-organized study, DeConde makes a case for placing the origins of the Good Neighbor Policy in the administration of Herbert Hoover (1929-1933). DeConde covers Hoover's promotion of trade and investment in Latin America while he was Secretary of Commerce from 1921 to 1929. He also discusses Hoover's ten-week goodwill tour of the region soon after his November, 1929, election to the presidency. DeConde explains Hoover's implementation of the withdrawal of U.S. military interventions from Haiti and Nicaragua

and his upgrading of the standards for U.S. diplomats serving in Latin America. Although Hoover had long championed lower tariffs and free trade, the economic collapse of the early 1930's led him to sign into effect the Smoot-Hawley Act, which raised U.S. tariffs on imports. This action caused loud protests from U.S. trading partners in Latin America and was one of the main impediments to Hoover's efforts to improve relations in the Western Hemisphere. In spite of this depression-inspired tariff, DeConde concludes that Hoover's Latin American policy improved the image of and broadened the influence of the United States before Franklin D. Roosevelt assumed the presidency.

Dozer, Donald M. *Are We Good Neighbors? Three Decades of Inter-American Relations, 1930-1960.* Gainesville: University of Florida Press, 1961.
Dozer's evaluation of the Good Neighbor Policy goes beyond the boundaries of diplomacy to consider economic, political, and cultural factors in U.S.-Latin American relations. In addition to being one of the first historians to use U.S. State Department records from the Good Neighbor era, Dozer also incorporates into this book a broad survey of Latin American newspaper editorials, essays in journals of opinion, and books written by leading political and intellectual figures. The reader not only acquires insights into what diplomats from Washington, D.C., Bogotá, Colombia, Rio de Janiero, Brazil, and Buenos Aires, Argentina, were trying to accomplish but also finds pithy quotations from important newspapers such as *El Tiempo* of Bogotá, *Jornal do Brasil* of Rio de Janiero, and *La Nacion* of Buenos Aires. The first six chapters cover the period from 1930 to the mid-1940's, and the last four chapters discuss the decline of the Good Neighbor Policy in the late 1940's and the 1950's. Dozer emphasizes economic issues such as trade, investment, and the role of government in the promotion of development.

Frye, Alton M. *Nazi Germany and the American Hemisphere, 1933-1941.* New Haven, CT: Yale University Press, 1967.
Germany's use of propaganda and subversion in the Western Hemisphere was the subject of speculation, rumor, and even panic in the period leading up to U.S. involvement in World War II. Frye's research in German records reveals that Nazi leaders, especially propaganda chief Joseph Goebbels, attempted to acquire support among ethnic German communities in Latin America and also to disrupt the political systems of several nations. After the outbreak of fighting in Europe in September of 1939, Germany focused its propaganda efforts on Argen-

tina, where the political environment seemed most conducive to building support for the Third Reich. Frye finds that Nazi ideas and institutions made few inroads in Latin America, but he also provides evidence that Hitler's grandiose vision of Germany replacing Spain and Portugal as the cultural mentor for the Latin American nations, coupled with the actions of his agents in the Americas, reinforced fears in Washington that somehow the Nazis would use stealth and deception to gain a strategically important foothold in the southern part of the Western Hemisphere. Approximately half of this book concerns Nazi operations in the United States.

Gellman, Irwin F. *Good Neighbor Diplomacy: United States Policies in Latin America, 1933-1945*. Baltimore: Johns Hopkins University Press, 1979.

Foreign policy usually has political and personal dimensions. Gellman's study of the internal dynamics of the U.S. State Department in its development and implementation of the Good Neighbor Policy places at the center of this process the political astuteness of President Franklin D. Roosevelt and the assertive maneuvering and intellectual acuteness of Under Secretary of State Sumner Welles. These two often moved around Secretary of State Cordell Hull, who served as the administration's public spokesman on Latin American policy. Gellman emphasizes the importance of economic factors in the diplomacy of both peace and war, the growing perception of Nazi penetration of the Western Hemisphere in the late 1930's and the early war years, Roosevelt's use of the apparent Nazi threat to build public support for the Good Neighbor Policy, and the problems of inter-American diplomacy during the war—especially in U.S.-Argentine relations. The informative footnotes indicate that this book is based on extensive research in State Department files and the records of the Federal Bureau of Investigation.

Green, David. *The Containment of Latin America: A History of the Myths and Realities of the Good Neighbor Policy*. Chicago: Quadrangle Books, 1971.

This book rejects the view that the Good Neighbor Policy was a sincere effort by the administration of President Franklin D. Roosevelt to improve relations with the Latin American nations. Green argues that the United States replaced direct military intervention with more subtle means of domination. He insists that the Good Neighbor Policy placed Latin America under the economic hegemony of the United States in order to make the Western Hemisphere a bastion of U.S. strength, whether the threat was Fascism or Communism. U.S. officials pressured Latin American governments to open their markets to U.S. private corporations and to accept loans from the Export-Import Bank and other U.S. lending institutions. Green concludes that the Good Neighbor Policy ultimately failed because Latin American nationalism emerged after World War II to assert local demands for broadly based economic expansion, often through government-run enterprises. Even more radical outbursts took place in Bolivia's revolution of 1952 and in Cuba with the rise of Fidel Castro in 1959. This book remains a controversial but important study that reflects the leftist historical writing of the 1960's and 1970's.

Haglund, David. *Latin America and the Transformation of U.S. Strategic Thought, 1936-1940.* Albuquerque: University of New Mexico Press, 1984.

Most students of the 1930's have little awareness of the importance of Latin America in the strategic planning and diplomatic policies of the United States as the Roosevelt Administration adjusted to events leading to the outbreak of World War II. Haglund develops the thesis that the grave concerns (at times intense fears) about the German threat in Brazil, Argentina, Chile, and even Mexico led the Roosevelt Administration to take a more aggressive position in support of Great Britain—especially in 1940 after the Nazi defeat of France. Haglund uses the statements of Roosevelt and Secretary of State Cordell Hull, the reports of State Department and military intelligence officials, the U.S. military's contingency plans for the defense of South America, and the writings of journalists and other concerned citizens to explore the atmosphere that prevailed in the high echelons of the government. Although there were many different theories, one of the most widespread involved Nazi exploitation of political unrest in Argentina, Brazil, or Chile through the ethnic German communities in those nations to seize political power and thereby establish a base for the extension of a significant Axis military presence in the Western Hemisphere. Some historians have criticized Haglund for exaggerating the impact of this threat on general U.S. foreign policy, but his basic point—that the security of Latin America was a vital concern of the United States government—is an important contribution to understanding the history of the Western Hemisphere and the place of inter-American relations in the World War II era.

Humphreys, R. A. *Latin America and the Second World War.* War II2 vols. London: Athlone Press, 1981 and 1982.

There is a common assumption that World War II had little impact in Latin America. Humphreys disproves this assumption in these two volumes, which connect the military and naval battles in Europe, in the Atlantic (including the sinking of the German battleship *Graf Spee* off the coast of Uruguay), and in the Pacific theater with the diplomatic, political, and economic histories of individual countries. Emphasis is on Argentina, Brazil, Mexico, and the nations with coastlines on the Caribbean. The first volume reveals that after the outbreak of hostilities in Europe in September of 1939, the United States assumed the initiative in bolstering hemispheric defense and boosting trade in essential minerals and other raw materials. With the defeat of France in June, 1940, the U.S. and Latin American governments considered the Axis military threat quite real and also shared concerns about political subversion. The Japanese attack on Pearl Harbor in December, 1941, did much to stimulate both Washington's push for access to military bases in the region and Latin American cooperation in hemispheric defense. The main exception to this hemispheric harmony was Argentina, which maintained a conspicuous neutrality that tilted toward the Axis. The second volume gives a country-by-country survey of the political, economic, and military effects of the last four years of the war and brings to the reader's attention a general pattern of closer relations between the United States and most nations of the hemisphere. Humphreys also mentions the combat experiences of twenty-five thousand Brazilian soldiers in Italy and of the Mexican fighter squadron that flew missions in the Philippines. The unfriendly and sometimes hostile relations between Argentina and the United States are covered in three chapters that feature the political intrigues of Argentine military officers, their Fascist sympathies, U.S. Secretary of State Cordell Hull's conviction that by 1943 Argentina had converted to Fascism, and the rise of Juan Perón within this time of turmoil and tension.

Rout, Leslie B., and John F. Bratzel. *The Shadow War: German Espionage and United States Counterespionage in Latin America During World War II*. Frederick, MD: University Publications of America, 1986.
Rout and Bratzel use extensive research in U.S. and German archives to explore the murky environment of World War II espionage. The substance of their research reveals that the head of Germany's Abwehr (military intelligence), William Canaris, was a determined spymaster who had to devote much of his energy to a defense of his bureaucratic "turf" from his ambitious rivals, particularly Heinrich Himmler. According to Rout and Bratzel, espionage in Latin America was of

marginal interest to Germany until the Luftwaffe's failure in the Battle of Britain in the late summer of 1940 convinced Canaris and other high officials in the Reich that the war would last for several years. With the Roosevelt Administration furnishing valuable support for the British, German espionage concentrated on Latin America as the "soft underbelly" of the United States. One of the most successful spies was Chilean Emilio Schonherr, who took advanced pilot training in the United States and supplied information on U.S. aircraft. Abwehr operations in Latin America, however, seldom reached their full potential because of communications problems, inadequate resources, and bureaucratic rivalries. U.S. counterespionage work often was ineffective, and agents often were disappointed by reluctant and sometimes nonexistent cooperation of officials in Argentina, Chile, and Mexico, where the local German population, anti-U.S. sentiment, and highly placed Nazi sympathizers frustrated efforts to deal with the Abwehr.

Steward, Dick. *Trade and Hemisphere: The Good Neighbor Policy and Reciprocal Trade.* Columbia: University of Missouri Press, 1975.
The diplomatic and political successes attributed to the Good Neighbor Policy often overshadow its economic aspects. Steward's examination of Secretary of State Cordell Hull's campaign for reciprocal trade agreements with the Latin American nations in the 1930's throws well-placed light on this area. The goal of reciprocal trade agreements is for the two nations involved to reduce their tariffs (taxes on imported goods) to their lowest levels, generally called the tariff rate of the most favored nation. Hull, an admirer of President Woodrow Wilson's ideal of free trade, pursued this goal with great determination in spite of only lukewarm support from other members of the Roosevelt Administration. By 1940, Hull had signed reciprocal trade agreements with eleven Latin American nations. Steward emphasizes that these agreements brought opportunities for U.S. corporations to open new markets for the sale of their manufactured goods. Hull's policies favored U.S. businesses at a time when most of the rhetoric of the Good Neighbor Policy and the New Deal took a more skeptical view of private enterprise. Hull's plan to continue his campaign for reciprocal trade came to an end around 1940 with growing competition from Germany, Japan, and Great Britain, which used government policies such as quotas, currency exchange deals, and barter to take advantage of trading opportunities.

Wood, Bryce. *The Making of the Good Neighbor Policy.* New York: Norton, 1961.

This standard study of the emergence of the Good Neighbor Policy identifies the administration of President Franklin D. Roosevelt as the chief catalyst for this transformation of U.S.-Latin American relations. Wood analyzes the troubling consequences of U.S. intervention in Nicaragua in the 1920's and interference in Cuba in the early 1930's as the proximate experiences that led Roosevelt, Secretary of State Cordell Hull, Under Secretary of State Sumner Welles, and Ambassador to Mexico Josephus Daniels to chart this course in foreign policy. The U.S. government discontinued its use of military intervention and pulled back from a position of close support for U.S. corporations operating in Latin America. Disputes concerning U.S.-owned properties were settled by negotiations rather than interventions and intimidation, as exemplified by the Mexican oil expropriation of 1938. As the threat of world war loomed in the late 1930's, the United States and most of the Latin American nations worked together in preparation for the defense of the Western Hemisphere. Wood's meticulous research in Department of State archives is reflected in the footnotes, which also contain useful commentary for the reader who wants to probe further into the origins of the Good Neighbor Policy.

Communism in Latin America

Alexander, Robert J. *Communism in Latin America.* New Brunswick, NJ: Rutgers University Press, 1957.

This pioneering study of Communist influence in Latin America appeared originally at a time when few students of the region attributed any importance to the subject. Fidel Castro's unexpected revolutionary triumph in Cuba in 1959 and his subsequent alliance with Cuban Communists (who had not been with him in the Sierra Maestra campaign) made Alexander's work essential reading for those who wanted to assess the possibilities for similar movements elsewhere. Alexander's book was reprinted in 1960 and 1963, each time with new introductions to update the reader on recent trends. The first six chapters of the text constitute an introduction to the core of the book and include some trenchant observations on the social and economic conditions that contributed to the growth of Communist parties. Alexander also has chapters on the Communist presence in labor unions and the potential "military danger" of Latin American Communism to the United States. The main part of the text is an encyclopedic, country-by-country survey of Communist political activities, with extensive treatments of Brazil, Chile, Peru, Mexico, Guatemala, and Cuba. The last chapter contains Alexander's prescriptions for U.S. policy responses to Communism. Alexander's sources of information include party publications and interviews with Communist leaders.

_____. *Trotskyism in Latin America*. Stanford, CA: Hoover Institution Press, 1973.

Leon Trotsky was one of the primary leaders of the Russian Revolution of 1917 but lost out in the ensuing power struggles in Moscow and went into exile in 1929. He settled in 1937 in Mexico, where he was assassinated by a Soviet agent in 1940. Alexander explores Trotsky's lasting influence in Latin America as the symbolic leader of a small but determined group within international Communism. Trotskyism rejected Joseph Stalin as a corrupting usurper of the Marxist-Leninist movement. Beyond this rejection of Stalin and bureaucratic authoritarianism, Trotsky's followers seem to lack political unity and ideological coherence. Alexander traces Trotsky's uneven influence through several countries, with special emphasis on Mexico and Bolivia and the work of J. Posadas, who organized the Fourth International. Alexander's analysis reveals the bitter internal quarrels that have dominated Trotskyism and greatly limited its influence.

Blasier, Cole. *The Giant's Rival: The USSR and Latin America*. Pittsburgh: University of Pittsburgh Press, 1983.

"The Giant" in the title is the United States, and its rival is the Soviet Union. Blasier, an expert in Soviet foreign policy, presents a careful, balanced analysis of Moscow's expansive role in Latin America in the 1970's. He does not include dire warnings of a rising tide of Communism in the Americas. Instead, he sees Moscow finding a much-needed sense of legitimacy through its achievement of normal diplomatic relations with many of the Latin American nations. He also reviews the growth of Soviet trade and cultural influence as part of the larger effort to secure both material benefits and respected status among the nations in the backyard of the United States. Policymakers in Washington tended to see the Communists' hands in political agitation and revolutionary schemes when, in reality, direct Soviet involvement was rather limited. The Soviets' greatest success in the Western Hemisphere, the Castro revolution, was a definite political achievement but, in Blasier's estimate, a serious economic burden because it required extensive support from Moscow.

Caballero, Manuel. *Latin America and the Comintern, 1919-1943*. Cambridge, England: Cambridge University Press, 1986.

Soon after the Communists took control of Russia in 1917, they established the Comintern, or Communist International, to promote revolution in other countries. The Comintern was to be a tool for exporting revolution based on the theory and practice of the Russian Revolution of 1917. Caballero's study shows that the Comintern gave few resources to its operations in Latin America before 1928 and only marginal attention thereafter. Major themes in this book are the tensions, bickering, and profound disagreements among Comintern leaders and agents on how to proceed in Latin America. Caballero argues that Marxism had a great impact on intellectuals throughout the hemisphere but that Leninism, which was concerned mainly with the problems of how to carry out a revolution, often caused divisive disputes. Caballero identifies several important Communists who participated in these discussions, including Victorio Codovilla, an Argentine of Italian origin who became arguably the foremost Comintern leader in Latin America. In contrast, Jules Humbert-Droz, a Swiss-born student of Latin American society, advocated a prominent role for the peasantry in Communist revolutionary movements, an approach that met a sharp defeat at the hands of Comintern strategists. Luis Carlos Prestes, a Brazilian military officer who converted to Communism, led a large but unsuccessful revolutionary movement in his homeland in the 1930's. Caballero concludes that even though the Comintern did not achieve a single revolutionary triumph, it did leave a legacy of radical thought and activism that had continued relevance into the era of Castro and the Sandinistas.

Debray, Regis. *Revolution in the Revolution? Armed Struggle and Political Struggle in Latin America*. New York: Grove Press, 1967.

Debray was a young philosopher and student of revolutions whose analysis of the reasons for Castro's victory in Cuba brought a different perspective to the strategy of and tactics for revolutionary change in Latin America, as well as in Africa and Asia. Debray argued that reliance on traditional Communist parties, with their ties to industrial labor and cities, was misplaced. He advocated that small bands of guerrillas establish a base of operations in rural areas. These "focos," or focal points, were to be primarily military in nature and were to function as the principal organizational units for the rise of a people's (or popular) army that would overthrow the established government and take power. Debray relied heavily on the experience of Castro and Che Guevara in eastern Cuba in the formulation of his theories.

Guevara's death in a futile effort to instigate a revolution in Bolivia in 1967 called into question some of this book's conclusions, but both Soviet Communists and the U.S. Central Intelligence Agency regarded this formula for revolution as a threat to their particular interests.

Guevara, Ernesto "Che." *"Che" Guevara on Revolution: A Documentary Overview*. Coral Gables, FL: University of Miami Press, 1969.
Guevara's brief but spectacular career as a practitioner and strategist of guerrilla warfare is the subject of much disagreement. His contributions to Fidel Castro's victories in eastern Cuba in 1957 and 1958 were impressive, but in 1967 Guevara died in a futile effort to prod Bolivian peasants to revolution. Editor Jay Mallin's twenty-seven-page introduction to this volume is a sharply worded, critical summary of Guevara's life, with special attention to his contributions to the theory and practice of guerrilla warfare in the context of the ideas of China's Mao Tse-tung and Vietnam's Vo Nguyen Giap. The fourteen selections in this volume include Guevara's own account of the campaign in eastern Cuba, several of his speeches and articles—particularly "Guerrilla Warfare: A Method"—and five documents from his ill-fated efforts in Bolivia.

Liss, Sheldon. *Marxist Thought in Latin America*. Berkeley: University of California Press, 1984.
The presence of Communism in Latin America extended beyond efforts to organize political parties and to foment revolutions. Liss gives the reader a broad survey of Marxism as an intellectual movement in the region. Not all the Marxist thinkers in this book were members of the Communist Party, and most Communist Party members did not publish books and essays on Marxism. In spite of these limitations on the relationship between Marxist thought and Communism, this book makes it clear that Marxism had a deep and lasting influence on many important intellectual and political leaders in Latin America. Liss adroitly combines biographical sketches with commentary on Marxist theory to present his subjects' views on the nature of revolution, ideal forms of community, and the main political and economic issues in their countries and in the region. Most Marxist thinkers were highly critical of capitalism and saw the United States as a powerful force in opposition to their goals. Among the individuals examined in this volume are Chile's Salvador Allende, Brazil's Luis Carlos Prestes, Colombia's Camilo Torres, and Cuba's Fidel Castro and Che Guevara.

Parkinson, F. *Latin America, the Cold War and the World Powers, 1945-1973*. Beverly Hills, CA: Sage Publications, 1974.

Parkinson's study is one of the first important efforts to discuss the broader aspects of the rivalry between the United States and the Soviet Union in Latin America during the early and middle phases of the Cold War. Drawing from academic monographs and journalistic reports, Parkinson constructs a well-organized narrative of events including the overthrow of the leftist government of Guatemala in 1954, the rise of Fidel Castro to power in Cuba in the late 1950's, Castro's victory at the Bay of Pigs in 1961, and the U.S.-Soviet confrontation in the Cuban Missile Crisis in 1962. Parkinson also examines less publicized events such as Castro's attempt to promote revolution in Venezuela in the early 1960's and the U.S. intervention in the Dominican Republic in 1965. The United States and the Soviet Union are the "world powers" in this book, but Parkinson also gives attention to the diplomacy of Mexico, Brazil, and Argentina, which had considerable importance in this period. Published in 1974, this book has information that is out of date in a few places (especially the commentary on the Cuban Missile Crisis and guerrilla movements) and should be used in conjunction with more recent studies in these areas (see the section on Cuba in Chapter 5 for the Cuban Missile Crisis and the section in this chapter on revolution for guerrilla movements).

Poppino, Rollie. *International Communism in Latin America: A History of the Movement, 1917-1963*. Glencoe, NY: Free Press, 1964.

Writing soon after Fidel Castro's early triumphs in Cuba, Poppino emphasizes the confidence and competence of the Communist leaders in Latin America. He points out that although the Communists had insufficient numbers to take power by revolution or the ballot box, they did have a significant potential to acquire influence through collaboration with other leftist organizations—especially in countries beset by social and economic problems. Communist inroads in Latin America parallel the political situations in Third World countries that emerged after the collapse of the old European empires in the 1950's and 1960's. Poppino sees additional parallels in the growth of anti-imperialist movements in Latin America that are generally opposed to the United States and sympathetic to Communism. Chapter 5 is especially valuable because it describes Communist appeals to certain social and economic groups such as labor, peasants, the middle class, university students, and intellectuals. The last third of this book deals with Soviet propaganda, diplomacy, and economic efforts in the region. Poppino also takes into account the internal squabbles and frequent failures of

Communists before Castro but stresses their expansive optimism of the early and middle 1960's.

Rabe, Stephen G. *Eisenhower and Latin America: The Foreign Policy of Anticommunism.* Chapel Hill: University of North Carolina Press, 1988.
In the United States and throughout the Western Hemisphere, contemporary critics of Dwight Eisenhower's administration (1953-1961) argued that the policymakers in Washington deliberately chose to neglect Latin America in order to concentrate on Asia and Europe as the main areas of confrontation with Communism. Rabe challenges that school of thought in his clearly written, well-organized discussion of Eisenhower's persistent and consistent involvement in the region, including the CIA-directed overthrow of Jacobo Arbenz Guzmán's leftist government in Guatemala in 1954 and the support of right-wing dictatorships and free enterprise economics as antidotes to Communism. Rabe's text contains supportive evidence for his thesis that the central thrust in Eisenhower's eight years was a sharply focused anticommunism. After January, 1959, Fidel Castro and his revolutionary example preoccupied Washington in both Latin American and wider global concerns. Rabe concludes that, in spite of these considerable exertions, the Eisenhower Administration did not achieve its goal of maintaining a Latin America committed to stability and security and free of Communist influence.

Ravines, Eudocio. *The Yenan Way.* New York: Scribners, 1951.
Ravines was born in Cajamarca, Peru, in 1897 and became involved in the political-intellectual circle around Peruvian radical Víctor Raúl Haya de la Torre in the early 1920's. After his conversion to Communism in the mid-1920's, Ravines traveled to Paris and then to Moscow, where he became an important figure in the Communist International's Latin American section. He returned to South America in the 1930's as a Comintern agent in Peru, Chile, and Argentina, and was an activist in the hectic odyssey of the Communists' "flying brigade" that scrambled from "one place to another at a moment's notice." His meeting with Mao Tse-tung introduced him to the "Yenan Way," which, according to Ravines, was Mao's plan for using any method available (including the exploitation of fear, greed, and vengeance) to secure the support of the middle class as well as peasants and workers. Ravines also discusses the Popular Front era of the late 1930's, when he worked with Communists in Chile to form alliances with other political parties. By the time he wrote this book, Ravines had broken his ties with the

Communist Party and was often critical of its operations in his commentary.

Shipman, Charles. *It Had to Be Revolution: Memoirs of an American Radical.* Ithaca, NY: Cornell University Press, 1993.
Shipman was a member of the Communist Party in Mexico from 1918 to 1922 and a participant in the Latin American section of the Comintern until the mid-1920's. Born with the name Charles Phillips in 1895, he studied at Columbia University's journalism school, where he became involved in radical activities. Once a member of the Communist Party in Mexico, he used several aliases, including Frank Seamen and Jesús Ramírez, and worked with several Communist agents including Bertram Wolfe and Michael Borodin. Shipman was a member of the first generation of Communists who traveled from Mexico to Europe, the United States, and various Latin American countries to establish the Comintern. His memoirs reveal the sporadic, unstable internal operations of the Comintern in Latin America in these years. Pages 50 to 169 cover this phase of Shipman's life. He left the party in the 1930's.

Smith, Gaddis. *The Last Years of the Monroe Doctrine, 1945-1993.* New York: Hill and Wang, 1994.
Smith's study of the Monroe Doctrine in the Cold War era is a model for pointed, provocative commentary on an important series of episodes in U.S.-Latin American relations. He defines the Monroe Doctrine as a set of U.S. policies intended to defend the Western Hemisphere from a large external threat. The sources of these threats varied from the time of President James Monroe's formal statement in 1823 through World War II (see the section in Chapter 3 on the Monroe Doctrine), but for the period under study in this book, Smith convincingly argues that Communism had by far the greatest impact on the minds of the U.S. policymakers and public alike. He emphasizes Soviet expert George Kennan's 1950 report on Latin America, in which the architect of the containment policy (prudent but firm opposition to the expansion of Communism around the globe) saw immense potential for the spread of Communism among the poor and politically alienated in Latin America. According to Smith, these assumptions (held by Kennan and many others) led to the undermining of the original Monroe Doctrine because they pushed the United States toward alliances with brutal anti-Communist dictators who violated the original doctrine's ideals of democracy and human rights. The rise of Fidel Castro in Cuba in 1959 and the Sandinistas in Nicaragua in 1979

provided apparent strongholds for Communism and therefore embod-
ied threats to the security of the Western Hemisphere. Presidents John
F. Kennedy, Lyndon Johnson, and Ronald Reagan resorted to deception, intrigue, hypocrisy, and armed intervention in their efforts to
defeat these challenges to U.S. hegemony in the region. The author is
especially critical of the Reagan Administration's policies in Central
America. Smith sees the end of the Monroe Doctrine with the collapse
of the Soviet Union in 1989 and its aftermath; these events seemed to
terminate the threat of the spread of the discredited doctrine of Communism.

Revolution

Blasier, Cole. *The Hovering Giant: U.S. Responses to Revolutionary
Change in Latin America.* 2d ed. Pittsburgh: University of Pittsburgh
Press, 1986.
One of the most important studies of United States responses to
revolution, this book analyzes the origins and outcomes of four major
case studies: Mexico from 1911 to 1940, Bolivia from 1943 to 1964,
Guatemala from 1945 to 1954, and Cuba from 1959 to 1961. Blasier
uses a comparative approach that begins with the early stages of the
revolutionary movements and then considers the rise of reformist (or
moderate) governments in Mexico, Bolivia, and Guatemala (but not
Cuba); the seizure of property owned by U.S. citizens in all four cases;
and the two contrasting types of outcomes—negotiation and reconciliation with Mexico and Bolivia, and hostility and paramilitary expeditions against Guatemala and Cuba. The chapter titled "Explaining U.S.
Responses" is a model for thoughtful comparisons and contrasts of the
various policies discussed earlier in the book. Like many students of
this subject, Blasier considers both Communist and non-Communist
revolutions in his analysis. In an epilogue, the author adds helpful
generalizations about U.S. responses to revolutions after 1961. The text
has several useful charts, and the footnotes, often containing Blaiser's
comments, mention valuable books and articles.

Cockcroft, James D. *Neighbors in Turmoil: Latin America.* New York:
Harper and Row, 1989.
Cockcroft, a university teacher and leading research professor in the
field of Latin American history for more than a quarter of a century,
has written a textbook intended for college students and the general
public alike. Written during the peak of the hostilities involving the

United States, Nicaragua, and El Salvador, this book contains a general view of the causes of social and political unrest in Latin American history. Explanations are contained in country-by-country survey chapters (including a chapter on Puerto Rico). Cockcroft has been a consistent critic of U.S. policies toward revolutionary movements, and this book is both a continuation and a refinement of this point of view. He gives intensive coverage to Central America and Mexico, with more than 170 pages on these nations. One of his main themes is that the movements of the 1980's constituted "a second revolution for independence" by attempting to go beyond political independence (accomplished in most nations in the early part of the nineteenth century) toward autonomy in the area of economic development in order to remedy problems of poverty and social inequality. Cockcroft's judgments on these issues may conflict with the opinions of many readers, but his perspective represents an important school of thought among students of Latin American affairs in the United States. The text is supported by bibliographies at the end of each chapter that include films and video documentaries as well as printed material. The author provides brief annotations on some of these items.

Gott, Richard. *Guerrilla Movements in Latin America*. Garden City, NY: Doubleday, 1971.

Gott took on the difficult task of assessing the importance of guerrillas in Latin America in 1971 when, in spite of the death of Che Guevara in a failed uprising in Bolivia four years earlier, such movements had taken hold in several countries. Gott focuses on Guatemala, Venezuela, Colombia, and Peru in addition to offering commentary on crucial events in Cuba and Bolivia. In his analysis of this wide variety of movements, Gott includes several theoreticians and field leaders, from Fidel Castro and Guevara to French philosopher Regis Debray, Guatemalan rebel leader Marco Antonio Yon Sosa, and radical Colombian priest Camilo Torres. Gott's conclusions point out the many problems that confronted the guerrillas, including the lack of support from other leftist groups and the absence of widespread acceptance among peasants and urban workers. Another factor that mitigates against the guerrillas is the growing presence of the United States Special Forces units charged specifically with countering the operations of revolutionaries. Gott concludes that weaker movements will fail but that the stronger, better-prepared guerrillas have a chance to establish an authentic revolutionary tradition. The 496-page text is followed by a sampling of revolutionary documents and a 23-page month-by-month chronology of guerrilla activities in the six countries under study in the text.

Guillen, Abraham. *Philosophy of the Urban Guerrilla*. New York: William Morrow, 1973.

Although Fidel Castro and Che Guevara made bearded, khaki-clad rural guerrillas the most prominent figures of the radical left after 1959, revolutionary movements also appeared in large cities such as Buenos Aires, Argentina, and Montevideo, Uruguay. Guillen was an urban guerrilla leader who attempted to devise the means to overthrow the existing regimes in Argentina and Uruguay in the 1960's and 1970's. Born in Spain in 1913, he was a veteran of the Spanish Civil War (1936-1939) who migrated to South America to continue his revolutionary efforts. Guillen accepted Marxism as a powerful set of ideas, but he did not advocate reliance on the Soviet Union as a source of material support or ideological inspiration. Guillen's theories reflected the strategies of the Montoneros of Argentina and Tupamaros of Uruguay, two of the most active urban guerrilla movements of the 1960's and 1970's. A major strength of this book is the fifty-five-page introduction by Donald Hodges, which gives essential biographical and analytical background to Guillen's writings.

Hodges, Donald. *Intellectual Foundations of the Nicaraguan Revolution*. Austin: University of Texas Press, 1986.

The resilience of the Sandinista regime that came to power by revolution in 1979 surprised many observers, including its ardent opponents in the administration of President Ronald Reagan. Even after the stormy 1980's, with the constant opposition of the U.S.-backed contra rebels and the defeat of their candidate (also the incumbent president), Daniel Ortega, in the 1990 election, the Sandinistas maintained a strong base of support among peasants, workers, and intellectuals. Philosopher Donald Hodges explains the foundations of this hard-core support in his exceptional study of the ideas, personality, and mythical status of Augusto César Sandino, the rebel who stood up against U.S. intervention in the 1920's. The Sandino legacy played an essential role in the rise of the Sandinistas in the 1960's and 1970's, first as a fringe group, then as successful revolutionaries in 1979, and eventually as an organized political party in the 1980's. Hodges explores how the Sandinistas developed their own uniquely Nicaraguan ideology and organization, which were very much at variance with Communist tactics but, nevertheless, provided an example to disaffected groups of peasants, workers, and intellectuals in other nations. Hodges' book contains many valuable insights for students interested in U.S. policy toward revolutions because of its penetrating examination of this indigenous revolution.

Kolko, Gabriel. *Confronting the Third World: United States Foreign Policy, 1945-1980.* New York: Pantheon, 1988.
In spite of more than a century of unique and often intimate relationships between the Latin American nations and the United States, foreign policy experts in Washington after 1945 placed the American nations south of the Rio Grande in the same category as the countries of Africa, the Middle East, and Asia—the Third World. As Kolko explains in his well-written text, "Third World" is a Cold War expression used to describe nations that were neither Communist with links to the Soviet Union nor free enterprise representative democracies tied to the United States. Kolko devotes about one-fourth of his book to Latin America, with emphasis on the revolutions in Guatemala (1944-1954), Bolivia (1952), and Cuba (1959). He gives special attention to the administration of President John F. Kennedy (1961-1963) as a turning point for liberal foreign policy in the United States. Kennedy and his liberal foreign policy specialists turned against revolutionary movements after Fidel Castro's defeat of the U.S.-sponsored Bay of Pigs invasion in 1961. Kolko tends to be critical of U.S. policy in general and provides an especially sharp critique of President Ronald Reagan's campaign against the Sandinista government in Nicaragua in the 1980's.

Mander, John. *The Unrevolutionary Society: The Power of Latin American Conservatism in a Changing World.* New York: Harper and Row, 1969.
Fidel Castro's revolutionary triumph in 1959 conveyed the message to many observers that Latin American society was an overheated cauldron, ready to boil over at any moment with radical movements that could transform the economic structure and international politics of the region. British journalist Mander takes the contrary point of view— Latin American society is, in his judgment, very conservative in that it rejects most forms of change, especially revolutionary change. Mander uses quotations and paraphrasings from leading Latin American intellectuals. The beginning student may be a bit intimidated by some of these sophisticated statements, but the central themes developed in the text are quite clear and are not difficult to grasp. Mander insists that the bases of Latin American conservatism lie in several areas: the influence of the military in national affairs, the tendency of the caudillo

(the man on horseback) to dominate politics, the Spanish heritage of the colonial period (especially the Catholic church), and the example of the transformation of the Mexican Revolution into a conservative to moderate probusiness presidential system in the 1940's and 1950's. Mander offers some balance to those writers who develop a narrow concentration on the revolutionary potential in the region.

Silvert, Kalmon H. *The Conflict Society: Reaction and Revolution in Latin America.* 1961. 2d ed. New York: Harper and Row, 1968.
Silvert was one of the first U.S. political scientists to make an in-depth study of the phenomenon of revolution in Latin America during the Cold War. His research on Guatemala in the late 1940's and early 1950's formed the basis for much of this book in its first edition and the considerably revised edition seven years later. By 1968, Silvert and most students of contemporary Latin America were engaged in an effort to explain the underlying causes of domestic instability in the region. His brief, straightforward definition of revolution (pages 19-22) is presented in a chapter titled "National Political Change" and is free of the alarmism of much of the writing on this subject in the 1960's. Silvert takes a broad view of conditions in Latin America, in which the quest for modernization (the development of modern institutions such as representative democracy, public universities, and stable governments) establishes the setting for the implementation of U.S. policies as much as the challenge posed by Castro's revolution. His commentary on the role of the military in Argentine politics presents a critique not only of the troubles of that nation but also of the potential problems associated with military governments as barriers to change in other nations.

Vanden, Harry E. *National Marxism in Latin America: José Carlos Mariátegui's Thought and Politics.* Boulder, CO: Lynne Rienner, 1986.
Mariátegui was one of Latin America's most original political thinkers, but he remains one of the least recognized in the United States. Born in 1895 in Peru, Mariátegui not only examined his nation's centuries-old Inca traditions and the economic and political injustices of his contemporary environment but also read deeply in the writings of Karl Marx, Georges Sorel, and other leftist European intellectuals. Vanden's well-structured text explains the nature of Mariátegui's synthesis of these various historical, political, economic, and ideological currents to produce an innovative, "nationalist" form of Marxism adapted to fit into Peruvian society and culture. Mariátegui reached his peak as a revolutionary thinker in the 1920's. In many ways, Vanden's study of

Mariátegui parallels Hodges' analysis of the Sandinistas. The Sandinistas achieved power and Mariátegui and his followers did not; the main point, however, is that in both cases revolutionary thinkers used Marxism, but only as one of several components in movements that found support from local and national populations much more than from international Communism or other outside influences.

Wickham-Crowley, Timothy. *Exploring Revolution: Essays on Latin American Insurgency and Revolutionary Theory.* London: M. E. Sharpe, 1991.

More than most political movements, revolutions have close connections to theory. Karl Marx, V. I. Lenin, Che Guevara, and Regis Debray, among others, have contributed to the debates surrounding the optimal theoretical approach to planning and accomplishing the overthrow of existing political and economic systems. Wickham-Crowley examines the positions of revolutionaries, revolutionary sympathizers, and academic analysts to determine how revolutions work. His conclusions reflect his own determination to avoid any romantic or sympathetic reaction to the revolutionary process. In general, Wickham-Crowley contends that revolutionary movements have failed to mobilize enough support to gain power. The two exceptions are Castro's movement in Cuba and the Sandinistas' in Nicaragua. Among the crucial variables in these two exceptional movements, Wickham-Crowley cites the location of guerrilla activities in areas on the fringe of the national government's police and military control and the guerrillas' success in creating organized networks that reach beyond peasants and workers. The author also presents his summaries of and commentaries on the work of other students of revolution, including Barrington Moore, Charles Tilly, Theda Skocpol, James Scott, and Eric Wolfe.

_____. *Guerrillas and Revolution in Latin America: A Comparative Study of Insurgents and Regimes Since 1956.* Princeton, NJ: Princeton University Press, 1992.

Wickham-Crowley's second book on this vital topic is a comparative study of the revolutions that succeeded (in Cuba and Nicaragua) and the larger number that failed (in Venezuela, Colombia, Bolivia, Peru, and Guatemala). The author's carefully organized, sophisticated comparative analysis will provide stimulation for students who want to probe the motives of individuals and groups who chose to risk their lives in this dangerous enterprise. The author's conclusions are of particular relevance to U.S.-Latin American relations. Wickham-Crowley argues that although U.S. military and economic aid to governments facing a serious threat from revolutionaries may have been decisive in some cases (Guatemala, for example), other factors are more important in determining the outcome of a revolutionary struggle. He singles out the inability of "mafiacracies" to deal with revolutionary crises. These "mafiacracies" are defined as corrupt dictatorships that serve to benefit dictators and their families at the expense of wealthy landowners and business entrepreneurs. More than ideology and revolutionary theory, the internal weaknesses of these "mafiacracies" are crucial to understanding the successes and failures of revolutionaries in acquiring and maintaining power.

Wolfe, Eric. *Peasant Wars of the Twentieth Century*. New York: Harper and Row, 1969.
In this highly respected comparative analysis of peasant revolutions, Wolfe develops a set of structured generalizations drawn from six case studies: Mexico, Cuba, Russia, China, North Vietnam, and Algeria. An anthropologist by training, Wolfe examines closely the roots of revolutionary movements within peasant communities. Many U.S. leaders in the Cold War era insisted that revolutions were the work of Communist conspiracies that placed professional agitators in rural areas. Wolfe rejects this assumption. His findings assert that it is the arrival of the market economy—and not Communists—that disrupts peasant life and creates circumstances in which frustrated individuals and groups come together to try to restore their traditional social and economic arrangements. Rebels such as Emiliano Zapata and Pancho Villa of Mexico and the peasants of the Sierra Maestra of Cuba rose as a result of their own frustrations and not in response to the appeals of Communist persuasion. Wolfe devotes single chapters to Mexico and Cuba and provides a nicely written summary of his findings in his conclusion.

Wright, Thomas C. *Latin America in the Era of the Cuban Revolution*. New York: Praeger, 1991.
In the three decades after Fidel Castro seized power in Cuba, the threat of revolution seemed to be quite real throughout Latin America. Wright's incisive examination of the success of Castro and Che Guevara in eastern Cuba, which inspired similar movements elsewhere, not only reveals the appeals of guerrilla war as a revolutionary tool but also uncovers the weaknesses and failures of such undertakings. In particular, Wright's account of Guevara's failure and death in Bolivia is impressive. This book contains much of relevance to the study of the U.S. responses to Communism. Wright, however, is careful

to keep Communism within its parameters and explains several revolutionary movements, such as the Sendero Luminoso of Peru and the Sandinistas of Nicaragua, in their particular national environments, where an outside influence such as Communism was only one of many factors. Wright also discusses U.S. efforts to block several of these revolutionary movements and the pressures that the United States, brought to bear against established leftist governments in Cuba under Castro, Chile under Salvador Allende, and Nicaragua under the Sandinistas. Each chapter has informative footnotes, and there is a useful bibliography at the end of the book.

Economic Development in Latin America

Bulmer-Thomas, Victor. *The Economic History of Latin America Since Independence*. Cambridge, England: Cambridge University Press, 1994.

Economic history is an imposing subject of broad significance, and Bulmer-Thomas rises to meet the challenge of presenting it quite well in a textbook that is both comprehensive and comprehensible. Where difficult terminology appears, the author explains it in language suitable for the general reader. The first half of the text covers the first century after independence (1820's-1920's) and concentrates on the theme of export-led growth, or reliance on the sale in foreign markets of primary products such as grains, meat, coffee, and minerals. The last half of the book deals with the repercussions of the Great Depression of the 1930's, World War II, and the emergence of a new international economic order thereafter. In the 1940's and 1950's, Latin American nations entered a phase that Bulmer-Thomas calls inwardly looking development, with an emphasis on local industries and nationalism. The small size of local markets placed limits on economic growth in this phase. From the 1960's to the 1980's, debt-led development policies based on borrowing from foreign (largely U.S.) banks were widespread, with an unfortunate climax in the debt crisis of 1982. The author makes some interesting commentary on the Latin American nations' problems in dealing with the intense competitiveness of the increasingly integrated world economy of the 1990's. Throughout his analyses, Bulmer-Thomas places reminders of the chronic inequalities in wealth and income in most nations of the region and the social as well as the economic implications of this issue.

Clayton, Lawrence A. *Grace: W. R. Grace & Co., the Formative Years, 1850-1930*. Ottawa, IL: Jameson, 1985.

The history of one of the Western Hemisphere's first genuinely multinational companies was dominated by the Grace family. W. R. Grace, the founder of the company, migrated from his birthplace in Ireland to Peru in the 1850's to become active in the business of trading guano (fertilizer made from heaps of bird droppings) to the United States. From these origins, Grace and his family built a large, diversified international company that included sugar mills in Peru and nitrate mines in Chile. This company also ran a famous shipping operation— the Grace Line—that boasted high-masted clipper ships as well as steamships that linked the Pacific coast of South America with the United States. In the midst of these business undertakings, W. R. Grace, who had established his home in New York City, jumped into big-city politics and served as mayor of that metropolis from 1880 to 1886. Clayton's thoroughly researched, clearly written text adroitly combines family history with economics, technology, and business practices. His thesis—that the Grace Company made vital contributions to the modernization of Peru, Chile, and Bolivia—is reinforced by several case studies in the introduction of modern transportation, mining, and agricultural practices in the company's operations in these countries. This book contains excellent illustrations and maps.

Drake, Paul W. *The Money Doctor in the Andes: The Kemmerer Missions, 1923-1933*. Durham, NC: Duke University Press, 1989.

Many Western Hemisphere nations took substantial steps toward the establishment of modern business practices in the 1920's, and much of this tendency flowed from the expert advice offered by U.S. economist Edwin W. Kemmerer. Drake examines Kemmerer's work in Colombia, Chile, Ecuador, Bolivia, and Peru, where governments generally followed his advice on monetary and banking policies patterned on the U.S. model. Kemmerer's international reputation reached its peak in the late 1920's as these five Andean nations developed uniform national currencies, centralized banking institutions, and regulated commercial banking. U.S. private investments moved into these nations to a large extent because of confidence in Kemmerer's work. Within the Andean nations, import merchants, private bankers, local industrialists, and even labor unions saw advantages in a stable national currency and increased foreign investments. Kemmerer's influence declined, however, with the worldwide depression of the 1930's, when close ties with the United States came to mean a burdensome debt that the Andean nations could not pay. Drake explains these economic issues in a clear, unpretentious style with relevant comparisons and contrasts between the boom-bust cycles of the 1920's and 1930's and those of the 1970's and 1980's.

Edwards, Sebastian, and Alejandra Cox Edwards. *Monetarism and Liberalization: The Chilean Experiment.* Cambridge, MA: Ballinger, 1987.

In the decade after the overthrow of President Salvador Allende's socialist government, Chile's military regime engaged in a vast economic experiment—a shift from state-controlled (or socialized) enterprises and a tightly managed economy to private enterprise with few regulations or restraints. The military government that formulated these policies relied heavily on the so-called "Chicago boys," the group of free enterprise economists trained at the University of Chicago under the influence of Milton Friedman, an internationally recognized advocate of private entrepreneurship. The results resembled a roller-coaster ride. The Chilean economy surged in the middle and late 1970's only to experience a severe downturn in the early 1980's. Economists Edwards and Edwards examine both stages of this process in their carefully organized study, which generally avoids technical jargon to provide a balanced evaluation of what went wrong in the Chilean experiment in addition to what these policies accomplished. The expression "monetarism" in the title refers to policies that tend to reduce the money supply in the economy and to reduce government spending as means to rein in inflation. "Liberalization" refers to privatization, or the sale of government-owned corporations to individuals or businesses and the removal of regulations from several areas of economic activity.

Frank, Andre Gunder. *Capitalism and Underdevelopment in Latin America: Historical Studies of Chile and Brazil.* 2d ed. New York: Monthly Review Press, 1969.

In this controversial study, Frank discusses the United States' displacement of Great Britain as the dominant imperial power in the economic struggles of Chile and Brazil in the early to middle decades of the twentieth century. Although international economic relations are central to this study, Frank also portrays a more complex relationship in which capitalist domination from abroad links up with internal exploitation of impoverished areas (the Brazilian Northeast, for example) by domestic enclaves of modern industry and commerce (São Paulo) that have closer ties to New York and London than to their own rural backwaters. This book had a large impact on serious students of Latin

American affairs when it appeared in 1967 and two years later, when the revised edition came out. This neo-Marxist polemic has value as an expression of opinion in many ways typical of the Left in the 1960's and 1970's. For balance, students should consult other studies of international economics mentioned in this section.

Furtado, Celso. *Economic Development of Latin America: A Survey from Colonial Times to the Cuban Revolution.* 2d ed. Cambridge, England: Cambridge University Press, 1976.

This historical overview includes brief chapters on the geography of the region and the colonial period (1492 to the 1820's), but most of its contents cover the century after the 1850's. One of the main unifying themes is the impact of international trade and investment on the Latin American nations. Furtado provides critical assessments of import substitution industrialization typical of the 1930's and 1940's, in which imports of manufactured goods such as processed food, clothing, and building materials were replaced by the same or similar items manufactured in local factories. He also discusses other issues, including inflation, stagnation, and the transfer of technology. He examines what he considers to be the "immutable" long-term trends in the relationships between the Latin American nations and their sources of investment and trade—Great Britain in the nineteenth century and the United States in the twentieth century. In Furtado's view, even the more industrialized economies in the region, such as Argentina, Brazil, and Mexico, continue to rely on the export of primary products such as wheat, meat, coffee, and petroleum for their economic well-being. Events of the 1980's and 1990's have introduced many new issues, but Furtado's work retains considerable value in its coverage of the crucial century that ended in the 1960's.

Hirschman, Albert O. *Getting Ahead Collectively: Grassroots Experiences in Latin America.* New York: Pergamon Press, 1984.

Hirschman is one of the foremost academic specialists in the field of economic development in Latin America. He has written numerous articles and books (including *Journeys Toward Progress* in 1973) that explore the complexities of how and why economic activity originates and what makes it continue or fail. In *Getting Ahead Collectively*, Hirschman combines his years of study on the larger issues of economic growth with personal observations that he made on a six-nation trip through Latin America in 1983. The result is a brief, clearly written text that most readers will find informative and stimulating. The author uses little technical jargon and enhances his presentation through several photographs of the people and communities that he describes. He is concerned primarily with the work of the Inter-American Foundation and other international nongovernmental organizations that support small-scale economic activities in local communities. His wide range of examples includes a dairy cooperative in Durazno, Uruguay; a loan fund for *tricicleros* (operators of three-wheeled produce carriers) in Santo Domingo, Dominican Republic; and land-hungry peasants along the Caribbean coast of Colombia who turned to fishing when agricultural land was not available to them. Hirschman explains these and other grassroots phenomena to give the reader case studies in the process of economic change, then connects these case studies to some of the fundamental trends in the field.

Karnes, Thomas L.*Tropical Enterprise: The Standard Fruit and Steamship Company in Latin America*. Baton Rouge: Louisiana State University Press, 1978.
Karnes gives a unique inside examination of the workings of one of the premier banana businesses of the Western Hemisphere. Based in New Orleans, Louisiana, Standard established a system of procurement, transportation, and marketing that stretched from the north coast of Honduras into the major cities of the United States. Founded by Joseph Vaccaro, his two brothers, and Salvador D'Antoni, the company was under family management from 1899 until the 1960's. It faced a multitude of challenges, including political instability and strife around its Honduran base of operations (and also near its enterprises in Nicaragua and Mexico), the dangers to humans from tropical diseases, the devastation of banana crops by sigatoka and other natural afflictions, and shipwrecks during the hurricane season. In addition, Standard had to confront competition from its rivals, the United Fruit Company and Cuyamel, and the uncertainties of the business cycle. Karnes makes excellent use of Standard's internal records as well as interviews, government records, and relevant published studies in Central American, Mexican, and United States history to tell his story in its full historical context.

Krenn, Michael L. *U.S. Policy Toward Economic Nationalism in Latin America, 1917-1929*. Wilmington, DE: Scholarly Resources, 1990.
This tightly organized analysis of U.S. responses to economic nationalism focuses on the attitudes and policies of government officials such as Secretaries of State Robert Lansing, Charles Evans Hughes, and Frank Kellogg, and State Department Counselor Frank Polk. Krenn views their rejection of economic nationalism as an outgrowth of

negative attitudes in the United States toward Latin America in general, the exaggerated fears of the spread of Communism in the region, and the more realistic concerns regarding the precedent set by Article 27 of the Mexican Constitution of 1917, which established a legal basis for government nationalization of foreign-owned private property. In addition to Mexico, Krenn provides case studies of U.S. policies toward Colombia, Venezuela, and Brazil. Students may benefit by a comparison of Krenn's findings with Drake's book on the Kemmerer missions to promote U.S. banking and monetary policies in the Andean nations in the same period.

Kuczynski, Pedro-Pablo. *Latin American Debt.* Baltimore: Johns Hopkins University Press, 1988.

In 1982, Mexico and Brazil sent shock waves through the international banking system when these nations were unable to make the scheduled payments on their debts owed to U.S. and other foreign-owned banks. Soon afterward, Argentina, Peru, and other Latin American nations made front-page news throughout the world as the debt crises of the early 1980's became a major international issue. Kuczynski's text presents the causes and consequences of the crisis in a calm, common-sense fashion. A cabinet officer in Peru during the crisis period, Kuczynski moved to the World Bank and then took a position as an investment banker with the First Boston Corporation in the United States. With this experience in both government and the private sector, he gives important insights into the internal dynamics of the negotiation of the original loans as well as the arrangement of the settlements that helped to end the immediate crisis. The author is quick to point out, however, that the basic problems were not solved—they were merely contained. The establishment of a new package of loans from U.S. and international lending institutions such as the World Bank and the International Monetary Fund, accompanied by austerity programs (increased taxation and reduction of government social programs) in Mexico and other Latin American nations, did not solve the larger problems, which include unstable world prices for exports such as petroleum, cotton, and food crops; rising interest rates; and changes in government policies. As this book and the study by Carlos Marichal described in this section make clear, the problems of international debt have a long history and the potential for an enduring presence in the Western Hemisphere.

Lewis, Paul H. *The Crisis of Argentine Capitalism.* Chapel Hill: University of North Carolina Press, 1990.

Like many commentators on recent Argentine history, Lewis views his subject as an enigma—a nation with immense potential that has never realized its greatness. With rich farmland, petroleum reserves, and a well-educated population, Argentina emerged in the world economy in the early twentieth century as a major exporter of grains and meat. It seemed poised on the brink of a breakthrough into the ranks of the world's upper echelon of prosperous nations. The next half century, however, saw this promise denied as Argentina floundered from one crisis to another. In his study of this environment of frustration and disappointment, Lewis concentrates on business entrepreneurs. The early twentieth century spurt of expansive free enterprise built on an infusion of foreign investment and then continued into the 1920's based on healthy rates of domestic capital savings. Lewis identifies a vibrant entrepreneurial spirit in a series of biographical sketches of business leaders from this period. This spontaneous upswing in the private sector soon languished and nearly perished in the depression of the 1930's. More important, according to Lewis, were the mistaken policies and mismanagement of the government of Juan Perón from 1946 to 1955. Perón's heavy dose of populist economics, in which the landowners who produced wheat and meat were taxed heavily in order to support industrial development, weakened both agriculture and industry (where investments were channeled into inefficient enterprises). The inflation, capital shortages, and debt crises of the decades after Perón have their beginnings in these troubled years. Although the United States played a limited role in this story, Lewis' account of the rise and fall of Argentine capitalism provides a revealing analytical case study of the type of free enterprise initiatives that U.S. policymakers generally have favored.

Marichal, Carlos. *A Century of Debt Crises in Latin America: From Independence to the Great Depression, 1820-1930.* Princeton, NJ: Princeton University Press, 1989.

Marichal's study is a much-needed historical perspective on international debt problems in Latin America. The basic organization is chronological, beginning with the negotiation of the first group of loans to the newly established Latin American governments in the 1820's, soon followed by the financial crises of 1825-1826. In the 1850's, British bankers "rediscovered" Latin America and its economic potential, but the loan arrangements extended to governments for the construction of railroads and port facilities soon collapsed in another series of financial crises in the 1870's. This pattern of private loans to Latin American governments followed by periods of crisis often resulting in defaults (cancellation of debt payments) reappeared in the last two decades of the nineteenth century and again in the 1920's and 1930's. Although the specific circumstances of each of these episodes tend to vary from cycle to cycle, Marichal maintains a firm grasp on the macroeconomics (larger economic environment and trends) of the loans, the finances of the governments that received the loans, and the circumstances that triggered the debt crises. His "Epilogue" presents thoughtful comparisons and contrasts of these financial problems with the debt crisis of the 1980's, which Marichal, like Pedro-Pablo Kuczynski (cited in this section), considers to be part of a long-term process.

Newton, Wesley Phillips. *The Perilous Sky: U.S. Aviation Diplomacy in Latin America, 1919-1931.* Coral Gables, FL: University of Miami Press, 1978.

The arrival of air transportation in Latin America in the 1920's was a mixture of risky exploratory flights, conflicting government policies, international rivalries, and aggressive business entrepreneurship. Although Newton's study is based in diplomatic archives, it also includes considerable information on the competition between the Colombian-German Air Transportation Company (SCADTA) and the U.S. corporation Pan American Airways (PAA). Newton's detailed research clarifies the connection between the national security interests of the United States in the Western Hemisphere—especially the Panama Canal—and the emergence of PAA as a rival to the German-backed SCADTA. The text includes impressive portraits of Juan Terry Trippe, the sharp-witted head of PAA; Peter Paul von Bauer, the cultured, competitive representative of SCADTA; and Francis White, the U.S. State Department official whose support of PAA was crucial to its success. In addition to archival sources, the bibliography lists several contemporary books and magazine articles on aviation history in Latin America.

Park, James William. *Latin American Underdevelopment: A History of Perspectives in the United States, 1870-1965.* Baton Rouge: Louisiana State University Press, 1995.

Serious observers have spent much time and effort trying to explain why Latin America's level of economic and political development has lagged behind that of the United States. As Park makes clear in this innovative study, their efforts have ranged from sympathetic, seeing signs of improvement in spite of past frustrations, to pessimistic, seeing little potential for economic and cultural advancement. The author finds that from the 1870's to the 1920's, three heavily pessimistic types of explanations emerged: the fundamentally racist doctrine that ascribed biological inferiority to the Latin American peoples, the environmental determinism interpretation that claimed that a tropical climate made progress impossible, and the cultural argument that emphasized that peculiar forms of Hispanic values molded by Catholicism created barriers to material and social advancement. Park notes that in the 1930's and succeeding decades, the quality of U.S. observers' analyses improved as journalists, academics, and government officials moved away from convenient and simplistic assumptions. Chapter 6 is a penetrating discussion of the "discovery of underdevelopment" among U.S. writers and the impact of this insight on their perception of Latin America. Park carefully discusses modernization theory, a complex social science approach that set up the economic and political systems of the United States and Western Europe as proper models for the measurement of progress. This approach found approval among both academics and the general public in the 1950's and 1960's. Park also supplies a succinct examination of dependency theory, which was based on the argument that the United States and Western Europe drained Latin America of its most valuable resources, inhibiting the region's development and leaving it dependent on the more prosperous dominant economies. Throughout his discussions of these controversial themes, Park maintains a steady, fair-minded grasp of the subject matter.

Prebisch, Raul. *Change and Development—Latin America's Great Task: A Report Submitted to the Inter-American Development Bank.* New York: Praeger, 1971.

Prebisch emerged as perhaps the foremost Latin American economist from the 1940's to the 1960's, and he was one of the first members of this profession from a Third World nation to challenge the international consequences of free enterprise economics as advocated in the United States in those years. For much of this period, Prebisch worked with the United Nations Economic Commission for Latin America. A native of Argentina who followed closely the harmful effects of the depression of the 1930's and the distortions of populist economics as practiced by Juan Perón from 1946 to 1955 (in brief, the redistribution of income from corporations and landed estates to workers), Prebisch advocates a form of free enterprise especially designed to respond to the needs of the developing nations of Latin America. This book is a report to the Inter-American Development Bank, one of the main international financial institutions operating in the Western Hemisphere. Prebisch surveys several of the paramount questions surrounding economic development in the middle decades of the twentieth

century: population growth, occupational structure, technology transfer, and the imbalances of trade and investment between wealthier
modernized nations and nations in the early stages of industrialization.
One of Prebisch's main points is his emphasis on the risks of reliance
on foreign investment (largely from the United States) and the need to
stimulate higher rates of private savings and investment in industry
within individual Latin American countries. This book has several
helpful charts and tables and few complicated mathematical formulas.
Most readers will find the literate prose style appealing.

Tulchin, Joseph. *The Aftermath of War: World War I and U.S. Policy
Toward Latin America*. New York: New York University Press, 1971.
During the decade following the outbreak of World War I in 1914, the
United States surpassed Great Britain as the chief source of loans and
investment to Latin America. Tulchin uses information from U.S.
government archives to explain the aggressive actions of the State
Department, Commerce Department, and other official agencies in the
promotion of U.S. financial and commercial interests from Mexico to
Argentina. He also points out the political stresses and bureaucratic
rivalries that complicated the implementation of U.S. policies. In his
overview, Tulchin finds more continuities than variations in the change
of administrations from Democratic President Woodrow Wilson
(1913-1921) to his Republican successors, Warren G. Harding (1921-
1923) and Calvin Coolidge (1923-1929). The author provides case
studies in three areas of strategic importance: petroleum, banking, and
cables (telegraph lines). He identifies Secretary of State Charles Evans
Hughes (1921-1925) as probably the most perceptive government
official directly involved in the formulation of policy in this period of
transition, when the United States achieved a position of economic
dominance in the Western Hemisphere at the same time that it moved
away from controversial military/naval interventions to more subtle
forms of exerting influence and pressure through diplomacy.

Democracy in Latin America

Castañeda, Jorge. *Utopia Unarmed: The Latin American Left After the
Cold War*. New York: Knopf, 1993.
Many U.S. policymakers watched with a sense of triumph as the appeal
of Communism weakened and calls for democracy grew stronger
throughout the Western Hemisphere in the 1980's and early 1990's.
The decline of Fidel Castro and the Sandinistas' loss of the Nicaraguan

presidential election of 1990 marked low points, if not the demise, of Communism in Latin America. Castañeda's discussion of the rise, the meandering course, and the fall of Communism from Argentina and Chile to Mexico and Central America forms an important part of his interpretive study of politics in Latin America. He makes only a few references to U.S. responses to Latin American politics, but his first five chapters make clear that, except in Cuba, Communism in the region had at best a narrow base of political support, which implies that Washington's perceptions of the Communist menace were often exaggerated. Castañeda also examines the diversity of the region's political parties and the sociocultural environments in which Communism gave way to other tendencies, including left-wing nationalism, grassroots movements such as liberation theology, growing demands for democratization, and the possibility of a revival of populism. Castañeda sees little, if any, U.S. influence in these movements. His thoughtful verdict on the Latin American Left is that, even without Communism, it retains considerable potential for expansion because of the many opportunities to recruit political support for innovative programs in government-directed economic development, labor unionization, and humane responses to urban poverty.

Collier, Ruth Berins, and David Collier. *The Shaping of the Political Arena: Critical Junctures, the Labor Movement, and Regime Dynamics in Latin America.* Princeton, NJ: Princeton University Press, 1991. Democratic tendencies are more often the results of domestic or internal factors than of external influences coming from the United States. This section of the bibliography is concerned primarily with the role of the United States in the furtherance of democracy in Latin America, but for those students who want to look into the origins of democratic tendencies within specific countries, Collier and Collier have written a study that provides an excellent starting point. They concentrate on how labor movements become important participants in the political life of certain nations (Brazil, Chile, Mexico, Venezuela, Uruguay, Colombia, Peru, and Argentina) and use scholarly studies of these eight countries for their basic information and analysis. The authors arrange their material in a sensibly conceptualized framework that focuses on "critical junctures" or periods in which labor movements entered into the highly competitive and combative arena of national politics. This concentration on specific time periods (for example, in Mexico the two decades of political and structural change after 1920 that followed a decade of revolutionary civil strife) allows the authors to examine each case in some detail regarding the actions of individual labor and political leaders and the important events that constituted the turning points for the labor movements. Students should not be intimidated by the length of this book (nearly 800 pages) because the authors have organized their material in a convenient way, making it possible to trace one or two case studies through the text. The book has a useful glossary and a fifty-seven-page bibliography that lists many published works on democratic tendencies in Latin America.

Frieden, Jeffry. *Debt, Development, and Democracy: Modern Political Economy and Latin America, 1965-1985.* Princeton, NJ: Princeton University Press, 1991.

The debt crisis of the early 1980's had a heavy impact on politics and government in most Latin American countries. Frieden examines this process with special attention to the connection between the burdens of these debts owed to foreign banks—many of them based in the United States—and the functioning of democratic institutions. He uses five case studies (Argentina, Brazil, Chile, Mexico, and Venezuela) to see how Latin American governments, under pressure from external debts, formulated their nations' economic policies. Frieden concentrates on the varied capacities of the five governments to respond to the crisis. He provides an incisive account of each case so that readers interested in the record of one or more of these countries over this two-decade period can find much material of value presented in a succinct format. Frieden's conclusions tend to support the notion that the more open systems with some of the characteristics of democracy (Mexico and Venezuela) tended to formulate better responses to the economic crisis than did the authoritarian regimes (Argentina and Brazil). The exception to this generalization was Chile, where the military government, in Frieden's estimate, adapted well to the economic situation. In general, this study stresses the challenges faced by both democratic and nondemocratic governments that rely on large external debts to finance their development goals.

Johnson, John J. *Political Change in Latin America: The Emergence of the Middle Sectors.* Stanford, CA: Stanford University Press, 1958.

Many informed observers of United States history have seen the presence of a prosperous middle class as one of the essential building blocks for a democratic political system. Historian Johnson detects the rise of what he terms the "middle sectors" to positions of political and social leadership in several Latin American nations in the period from the 1910's to the 1950's. Johnson identifies several characteristics of the group: location in large cities, employment in industry or government, commitment to public education, and a sense of nationalism in economic policies. After three introductory chapters that cover the historical background of the Latin American middle sectors from the independence movements of the 1810's and 1820's into the early twentieth century, Johnson delves into five case studies: Uruguay, Chile, Argentina, Mexico, and Brazil. His analysis indicates little direct U.S. influence on the expansion of these middle sectors. Readers should be aware that Johnson, writing in the relatively prosperous 1950's, tends to overestimate the importance and influence of the middle sectors, but his use of this term (and not the U.S. expression "middle class") implies an appropriate element of skepticism. He chose the term "middle sectors" mainly because, in his judgment, these groups in Latin America lacked the cohesiveness typical of the U.S. middle class. The turmoil that has occurred in many Latin American countries since this book appeared supports the notion that these groups indeed lacked unity and singleness of purpose in the political arena. The sixty-seven-page annotated bibliography will be of much help for research on publications on this subject up to the mid-1950's.

Levinson, Jerome, and Juan de Onís. *The Alliance That Lost Its Way: A Critical Report on the Alliance for Progress.* Chicago: Quadrangle Books, 1970.

The uproar following Fidel Castro's commitment to Communism in the early 1960's included President John F. Kennedy's heavily publi- cized program to promote democratic institutions as safeguards against the spread of similar radical movements elsewhere in the Western Hemisphere. At the end of the decade, foreign service officer Levinson and journalist de Onís wrote this evaluation of the Alliance for Pro- gress, which found Kennedy's idealistic goals abandoned or frustrated in almost every sphere of activity. U.S. private investments for eco- nomic development did not reach anticipated levels, and U.S. govern- ment aid flowed mainly to elites or to military-dominated governments that showed little interest in democratic practices. Instead of free enterprise and representative governments opening channels of oppor- tunity for the masses, the authors saw the same old patterns of privi- leged family control of business and political institutions. Unlike many academic writers, Levinson and de Onís express their judgments in sharp, unequivocal language.

Lowenthal, Abraham F., ed. *Exporting Democracy: The United States and Latin America, Case Studies.* Baltimore: Johns Hopkins University Press, 1991.

_____. *Exporting Democracy: The United States and Latin America, Themes and Issues.* Baltimore: Johns Hopkins University Press, 1991.

The flurry of interest in the 1980's in the possibility that the United States could promote democracy in Latin America prompted Lowenthal to bring together fourteen thought-provoking essays by fifteen respected scholars from several Western Hemisphere nations in these two paperback volumes (also available in a single-volume hardback edition from the same publisher). The "Themes and Issues" volume includes essays on each of the four periods in which the United States actively pursued prodemocracy policies: the era of the Woodrow Wilson presidency through the 1920's, the spurt of interest in democracy during the last stages of World War II and the early Cold War, the Alliance for Progress, and the presidency of Ronald Reagan. The "Case Studies" include examinations of United States policies toward Argentina, Chile, the Dominican Republic, Mexico, and Nicaragua during the Cold War period. In addition, both paperback volumes contain the same general essays, which give the reader broad perspectives on several key issues. Two insightful contributions explore the connections between the operations of U.S. private corporations and labor unions and the emergence of democratic tendencies in the region. Three overview essays assess the general effectiveness of U.S. efforts to promote democracy. Editor Lowenthal's conclusions are representative of the entire work. He sees little historical evidence to support the idea that previous attempts to export democracy have worked. Much of his pessimism is shared by the other writers in these volumes and is based on the widely held conclusions that democratic institutions are difficult to export and are most likely to be viable when they arise as spontaneous local and national movements and are not artificial implants from abroad.

Muravchik, Joshua. *Exporting Democracy: Fulfilling America's Destiny.* Washington, DC: American Enterprise Institute Press, 1991.

The collapse of the Soviet Union in 1989 inspired a wave of confidence in the spread of democratic institutions around the world. Muravchik's book contains a heavy portion of that optimism. He identifies several policies that he believes should contribute to the achievement of that goal, including prodemocracy propaganda, cultural exchanges, foreign economic aid, and "the force of example" supplied largely by the historical record of the United States. Muravchik also advocates the use of more aggressive methods such as military occupation, covert action, and assertive crisis diplomacy. In this last category, he includes four examples of U.S. involvement in Latin America during the Cold War years: Haiti, the Dominican Republic, Nicaragua, and Panama. The reader should be aware that this book is not limited to Latin America but rather addresses the general methods by which the United States could stimulate the spread of democratic institutions throughout the world. Muravchik makes it clear that he considers these methods to be applicable to Latin America. The author's optimistic assumptions should be studied along with the more pessimistic views expressed by John Sheahan, Robert Packenham, Ruth Berins Collier and David Collier, and the essayists in the volumes edited by Abraham F. Lowenthal, all of which are cited in this section.

Packenham, Robert. *Liberal America and the Third World.* Princeton, NJ: Princeton University Press, 1973.

Researched and written in the middle years of the Cold War, this book offers a penetrating critique of the ideas that dominated U.S. policies toward the Third World, including Latin America. One of Packenham's main topics is the promotion of political development, which, in these years, meant the transfer of the U.S. model of democracy (or something close to it) to Third World nations. Packenham examines how U.S. diplomats, foreign aid officials, politicians, and social scientists built their case for the exportation of the values and institutions associated with democratic politics and free enterprise economics in an environment that lacked diversity of opinion and exemplified the more narrow-minded aspects of ethnocentrism. Packenham insists that the optimism about programs such as the Alliance for Progress (see the book by Jerome Levinson and Juan de Onís mentioned in this section) was based on erroneous assumptions formulated in this ethnocentric setting. He sees the officials and academics who put together the agenda for liberal development as the required formula for nation-building (the creation of the basic political, economic, and social institutions needed by modern countries) in the Third World as the formulators of a type of ideological dogmatism that in many ways was as rigid and unimaginative as the Marxist doctrines of the Soviet Union and Castro's Cuba. Packenham's sharp criticism of the idea that certain democratic practices can be transplanted from one nation to another may disturb some readers, but most ultimately will agree that the strength and clarity of his argument deserves a fair hearing.

Peeler, John A. *Latin American Democracies: Colombia, Costa Rica, and Venezuela.* Chapel Hill: University of North Carolina Press, 1985.

The discussion of democratic government has entered the political life of every Latin American nation through speeches, pamphlets, and even constitutional reform, but the actual existence of democratic practices over an extended period of time is unusual. Peeler selects three countries that, from the 1950's to the early 1980's, established and maintained what he calls liberal democracy. The practice of this type of democracy includes a prominent place for traditionally wealthy and powerful groups that accept some aspects of representative government, including popular election of the nation's chief executive and legislature. In these three nations, liberal democratic governments have enacted limited reforms with little threat to the property and power base of the elites. Peeler does a good job of explaining the relevant background in political theory necessary for understanding the developments in these three countries in a comparative perspective that includes other Latin American nations and the United States. Unlike Muravchik, Peeler finds only a marginal potential for the United States to promote democratic tendencies in Latin America.

Sheahan, John. *Patterns of Development in Latin America: Poverty, Repression, and Economic Strategy.* Princeton, NJ: Princeton University Press, 1987.

This provocative, pessimistic appraisal of the possibilities of representative government and economic growth taking hold in Latin America provides a useful summary of the evolution of the debates surrounding these and other issues over the four decades of the Cold War, from the 1940's to the 1980's. Sheahan views political democracy and economic development as closely connected parts of a large, complex process that also encompasses issues such as inflation, currency devaluation, external (or foreign) debt, land reform, multinational corporations, and public (or government) enterprises. His range of case studies includes Argentina, Brazil, Cuba, and Peru. He also has a chapter on Chile that emphasizes its difficulties in the rough transitions from the reformism of the 1960's to Salvador Allende's socialism (1970-1973) to the military government's imposition of strict monetary policies after Allende's overthrow. Many readers will find much of value in Sheahan's chapter that examines the impact of U.S. policies on the potential for democracy. Sheahan surveys the Alliance for Progress, the International Monetary Fund, and Washington's Cold War concerns about the security of the region in the face of Communism and other radical movements.

Armed Forces in U.S.-Latin American Relations

Barber, William F., and C. Neal Ronning. *Internal Security and Military Power: Counterinsurgency and Civic Action in Latin America.* Columbus: Ohio State University Press, 1966.

The primary value of this book is that it expresses both the "climate of urgency" and the sense of optimism that were evident in U.S. military policy toward Latin America during the early 1960's. The urgency arose from concern about the outbreak of revolutions (or insurgencies) following the example of Fidel Castro's movement. The optimism came from the confidence of the U.S. military that it could devise programs to deal with insurgency. Barber and Ronning examine in detail the origins and early implementation of civic action programs in which the U.S. military provided advisers and funding for the armed forces of most Latin American nations. These advisers performed a variety of noncombat duties, including road building, school construction, and reforestation. The purposes of these projects were to respond to the problems of poverty and neglect as potential causes of revolutions and to introduce the military to local peoples in friendly and supportive roles. The long-term outcomes of these projects were not as positive as many of these early signs indicated (see discussions by Edwin Lieuwen and Michael McClintock in their books annotated in this section), but this study captures the optimism of the early years of civic action.

Danner, Mark. *The Massacre at El Mozote: A Parable of the Cold War.* New York: Vintage Books, 1993.

Guerrilla warfare and the responses to it, particularly counterinsurgency, involve great risks to the noncombatant civilian population. Danner's account of such a bloody incident gives the reader a close-up view of one of the most disturbing events in Central America's recent history. In late 1981, the mountain village of El Mozote in northeastern El Salvador was the scene of a massacre of at least one hundred civilians by that nation's Atlacatl Battalion. That unit, like many in the Salvadoran army, had received training and material support from U.S. officials. Much of Danner's text concerns the forensic investigation of El Mozote by anthropologists, archaeologists, and medical doctors in the early 1990's to confirm earlier reports of the massacre by U.S. journalists. Danner also examines the efforts of U.S. government agencies to block the journalists' reportage on the incident. This book reprints more than one hundred pages of documents concerning the deaths in El Mozote.

Desch, Michael C. *When the Third World Matters: Latin America and United States Grand Strategy.* Baltimore: Johns Hopkins University Press, 1991.

The United States has not fought a major conventional war in the Western Hemisphere in the twentieth century, but, as Desch explains, Latin America consistently appears in U.S. strategic considerations mainly because of its proximity—particularly Mexico, Cuba, and the other nations that border on the Caribbean. One of the strengths of Desch's research is his examination of the U.S. military's contingency plans for invasions of and military engagements in Western Hemisphere nations. For example, during the time that the violent phase of the Mexican Revolution overlapped with World War I (1914-1918), U.S. military planners estimated that a force of nearly one million men would be required to subdue the Mexican army and various insurgent movements, which would have been a serious drain on resources needed for the fighting in Europe. Desch also explains the combination of Axis influence in South America, the German submarine offensive in the Caribbean, and the perceived threat to Brazil from Axis-controlled North Africa that caused Franklin D. Roosevelt's administration serious concerns early in World War II. Desch also presents a thorough discussion of Defense Department plans for a conventional, combined forces (sea, air, and land) invasion of Cuba during the period of the Cuban Missile Crisis. The author includes discussions of the nature of strategic thought and a concluding chapter on the place of peripheral areas in the post-Cold War world.

Dickey, Christopher. *With the Contras: A Reporter in the Wilds of Nicaragua.* New York: Simon and Schuster, 1987.

The contras were the subject of much controversy in the United States. The official position of the administration of President Ronald Reagan (1981-1989) was that they were "freedom fighters" who were engaged in a praiseworthy attempt to overthrow the leftist government of the Sandinistas in their homeland, Nicaragua. Dickey, a journalist stationed in Central America in the early 1980's, took an entirely different point of view. Drawing from his own observations and interviews, he traces the organization of the contras, who included not only Nicaragua-born soldiers but also Argentine anti-insurgency specialists and several CIA and U.S. Army experts in guerrilla warfare. Dickey concentrates on the infamous contra known as Suicida, whose atrocities created problems for the entire movement. Apparently, his fellow contras executed him after one of his violent rampages. Dickey's story of events in Central America complements Bob Woodward's book on

CIA decision making and the political maneuvering in Washington discussed in this section.

Dillon, Sam. *Commandos: The CIA and Nicaragua's Contra Rebels*. New York: Henry Holt, 1991.

The central character in this book is Luis Fley, a Nicaraguan farmer who first joined the Sandinista rebels and later switched sides to become a field commander for the U.S.-sponsored contras. Journalist Dillon first interviewed Fley in 1988. Utilizing these interviews and other sources, Dillon assembles a detailed narrative of the fighting in northern Nicaragua throughout the 1980's. He also provides commentary on the involvements of the CIA, the State Department, and other U.S. government agencies with the contras' training camps in Honduras and their campaigns in Nicaragua. Fley emerges in Dillon's text as an idealist disillusioned as a result of the death and destruction of the war and the pressures brought to bear on the contras by the United States. Another vivid portrait is that of Enrique Bermúdez, the contra commander and former colonel in the Somoza regime's National Guard. Through the lives of Bermúdez and Fley, Dillon gives an inside view of the operations of the contras that carries up to 1990 some of the issues of the early 1980's raised in Christopher Dickey's book (annotated in this section).

Farcau, Bruce W. *The Coup: Tactics in the Seizure of Power*. Westport, CT: Praeger, 1994.

Farcau defines a coup d'état as a sudden military or quasi-military action with the purpose of overthrowing an existing government. The perpetrators of the coup almost always are citizens of the country involved and generally are members of its armed forces. Farcau, a former U.S. State Department officer, makes clear the interest of diplomats, intelligence experts, and military leaders in trying to anticipate these dramatic changes in government, which have been fairly common in Third World countries over the last half of the twentieth century. Latin American coups have been a special concern of policymakers in Washington, and Farcau's study concentrates on this region. Drawing on his own experience in Bolivia, books and articles by academics and journalists, and government reports, Farcau provides an analytical breakdown of how coups are planned and carried out, and why some fail and some succeed. Most of the text is concerned with the work of the armed forces in the process. His findings underscore the point that there is little the United States (or any other power) can do to control or even to predict the outcome of coup attempts. To a large extent, this volatility is the result of the internal workings of the coup, in which the decision of whether or not to join the plot is very much a personal choice for many military officers, who may be concerned with a wide array of factors from promotion to patriotism to the charisma (or lack thereof) of the coup leader.

Freedman, Lawrence, and Virginia Gamba-Stonehouse. *Signals of War: The Falklands Conflict of 1982.* Princeton, NJ: Princeton University Press, 1991.

The United States was caught by surprise when the Argentine military occupied the British-held Falkland (Malvinas in Argentina) Islands. The British dispatched an invasion fleet to remove the Argentines by force. President Ronald Reagan (1981-1989) and his Secretary of State, Alexander Haig, were in a difficult situation between two allies on a collision course for war. U.S.-British ties were rooted in tradition and formalized in the North Atlantic Treaty Organization. The Argentine military was working with the United States in Central America in training the contras to fight against the Sandinista government of Nicaragua (see books by Christopher Dickey, Sam Dillon, and Bob Woodward mentioned in this section). Although Freedman and Gamba-Stonehouse are concerned primarily with Argentina and Great Britain, they also examine the role of the United States in this conflict. Argentine President Leopoldo Galtieri, also an army general well known in Washington, believed that the United States would remain neutral and work for a negotiated settlement. Instead, the United States supplied satellite intelligence to the British and in other ways supported their invasion effort. Problems of long-distance logistics and the performance of the Argentine fighter and bomber aircraft made the British margin of victory narrow and gave the U.S. tilt in favor of London an even greater significance. The research value of this book is enhanced by extensive footnotes and a bibliography.

Lieuwen, Edwin. *Arms and Politics in Latin America.* 2d ed. New York: Praeger, 1961.

The persistence of military dictatorships in Latin America from the early years of independence to the second half of the twentieth century prompted historian Lieuwen to write this lucid study that connects history with contemporary events. The author defines nineteenth century caudillismo as political rule by the strong man on horseback, then traces the arrival of professionalism in the Latin American armed forces in the late 1800's and the early decades of the twentieth century. The old caudillo often acquired power by a combination of charisma and brute force, but the requirements of professional military service tend to restrict these forces. In Lieuwen's view, however, the professional military with its modern weapons and greater mobility remained a threat to civilian government, especially in the Cold War period in which national security concerns often expanded to include internal political movements of the Left. The last 123 pages of his text constitute a thoughtful examination of U.S. policy toward Latin American armed forces from 1898 to 1961, including the author's prescription for the future. Lieuwen is especially critical of U.S. support during the Cold War era for military forces and military dictatorships that used their training and equipment to suppress leftist movements and to intimidate a broad spectrum of reform advocates. The first edition of this book appeared in 1960, and the second edition (1961) added a chapter on the U.S.-directed Bay of Pigs invasion of Cuba and the general security problems posed by Castro. In spite of its age, this book remains a valuable contribution. The annotated bibliography is especially helpful for material published in the 1940's and 1950's.

McClintock, Michael. *Instruments of Statecraft: U.S. Guerrilla Warfare, Counter-insurgency, and Counter-terrorism, 1940-1990.* New York: Pantheon, 1992.

The military conflicts of the Cold War did not take the form of massive, heavily equipped armies facing each other on a European battlefield. In most cases, they consisted of smaller units carrying hand-held weapons engaged in the hit-and-run tactics typical of guerrilla warfare. The United States grasped the nature of this type of engagement in World War II through the work of the Office of Strategic Services in Southern Europe and Southeast Asia and incorporated these experiences into the operations of the Central Intelligence Agency in the late 1940's and into elements of the U.S. Army that came to be known as Special Forces in the 1960's. According to McClintock, President John F. Kennedy (1961-1963) and his chief adviser in this area, General Edward Lansdale, were the main architects of these types of strategies and tactics in the United States. McClintock includes examples of counterinsurgency and counterterrorism from Vietnam, the Middle East, and Africa as well as a large amount of material on Latin America, from the CIA intervention in Guatemala in 1954 to U.S. operations in Central America in the 1980's. McClintock also deals with U.S. military and CIA collaboration with the armed forces of Guatemala (after 1954), El Salvador, and Colombia, as well as the role of U.S. forces in efforts to overthrow the governments of Cuba and Nicaragua. McClintock's overall evaluation of counterinsurgency as "an un-

American way of war" may disturb some readers, but the depth of his research and analysis in this book makes it essential reading on this subject. The footnotes offer a wide range of references to other published studies, some of which tend to disagree with McClintock's conclusions.

Millett, Richard. *Guardians of the Dynasty: A History of the U.S. Created Guardia Nacional de Nicaragua and the Somoza Family.* Maryknoll, NY: Orbis Books, 1977.

The impact of the United States in twentieth century Nicaragua is closely connected to the dominance of the military in that Central American nation's history. After a survey of historical background, Millett begins his fast-paced discussion in 1925, when retired U.S. Army Major Calvin Carter, who had been a training officer for the Philippine constabulary in the early 1900's, took charge of the newly formed Nicaraguan National Guard. His efforts to establish a professional military collapsed in the civil unrest of 1926. Augusto César Sandino's armed resistance to the U.S. military presence in Nicaragua soon spurred the formation of another version of the National Guard under the direct command of U.S. Marine officers. By 1928, Nicaragua had 173 officers and more than 1,600 enlisted men in this new force, most of whom were involved in the fight against Sandino. The U.S. military determined that the training of a Nicaraguan officer corps was essential and, in 1930, opened the Nicaraguan military academy to meet that responsibility. U.S. troops withdrew in 1933, leaving behind the best-trained, best-equipped, and most modern army that Nicaragua had ever known. U.S. and Nicaraguan officials placed Anastasio Somoza in command of this new force. In the following year, the National Guard under Somoza assassinated the popular rebel leader Sandino. Somoza quickly consolidated not only military but also political power in his own hands to create the family dynasty that ruled Nicaragua until 1979. Millett's research and analysis give a detailed picture of how the National Guard and Somoza, supported by U.S. military and economic aid, implanted a harsh military dictatorship. Although the burst of interest in Central America in the 1980's produced many solid studies in this area after Millett's volume appeared, his thorough research and efficient writing style give this study enduring value.

Nunn, Frederick M. *The Time of the Generals: Latin American Professional Militarism in World Perspective.* Lincoln: University of Nebraska Press, 1992.

The United States government frequently worked with Latin American armed forces during the Cold War years, to a large extent, to strengthen hemispheric opposition to the spread of Communism. Nunn's study gives fascinating insights into the ideas and ideals of Latin American officers in comparison with military leaders in other countries. His main sources of information are professional military journals published in the 1970's and 1980's. One of his central theses is that the Latin American officers, like many of their counterparts in the United States, strongly oppose Communism and other left-wing movements. Nunn also finds a contrast between the Latin American military mind and the values of U.S. officers. Latin American military leaders have a widespread belief that they are obligated to lead not only troops but also the civilian population—in other words, the entire nation—in times of crisis. This belief helps to explain military interventions in politics and coups d'état discussed in the books by Bruce Farcau, Edwin Lieuwen, and Richard Millett annotated in this section.

Rodríguez, Felix I., and John Weisman. *Shadow Warrior: The CIA Hero of a Hundred Unknown Battles.* New York: Simon and Schuster, 1989. The Cold War spawned several small but important military conflicts. Rodríguez worked on both sides of revolutionary insurgency: as a clandestine infiltrator of Castro's Cuba in 1961 to help prepare the way for the Bay of Pigs invasion and as a military adviser in El Salvador in the mid-1980's to help to foil the leftist guerrillas in that nation. A native of the Cuban city of Sancti Spiritus who went to the United States for his education in 1954, the eighteen-year-old Rodríguez joined an ill-fated expedition to overthrow Castro in 1959 and, thereafter, committed himself to the fight against Communism, often working for the Central Intelligence Agency. Probably his greatest personal triumph was his contribution as a CIA intelligence analyst in 1967 in Bolivia, where, according to Rodríguez, his interrogations and insights contributed to the Bolivian army's capture of Che Guevara. Pages 127 to 173 present Rodríguez's first-person account of his meeting with Guevara and his recollections of the Bolivian army's decision to execute the legendary guerrilla on the spot. The last portion of the book presents Rodríguez's often frustrating efforts in Central America in the 1980's. His judgments are clear-cut. His expression of admiration for the ability and attitude of General Juan Rafael Bustillo of the Salvadoran Air Force contrasts with his disdain for the covert operations claims of Colonel Oliver North, who, in Rodríguez's estimation, was "wet behind the ears." Much of the material in this book tends to be controversial and is sometimes at variance with other sources. This book is a valuable primary source to be used with other accounts of the events under study.

White, Richard Alan. *The Morass: United States Intervention in Central America*. New York: Harper and Row, 1984.

White's discussion of the buildup of the U.S. military presence in Central America in the early 1980's combines sensible organization, clear writing style, and a sharply critical perspective on the policies of Ronald Reagan's administration. White discusses the U.S. military's theory and practice of counterinsurgency as well as the activities of the Central Intelligence Agency. One of the strengths of this book is the inclusion of separate chapters on each of the three countries where the U.S. military and CIA worked intensively with the national armed forces: Guatemala, El Salvador, and Honduras. White questions the Reagan Administration's categorization of the majority of its foreign aid as nonmilitary in a chapter titled "It Depends on the Way You Count." Like many critics of U.S. intervention, White sees the conflicts in Central America as outgrowths of the Cold War competition between the United States and the Soviet Union, which, in his view, had little connection with the basic political and economic issues in the region.

Woodward, Bob. *Veil: The Secret Wars of the CIA*. New York: Pocket Books, 1987.

The Central American crises of the 1980's became significant political issues in the United States. Woodward, a well-known investigative journalist, wrote this best-selling exposé of the secret operations of the Central Intelligence Agency to support the contras by concentrating his interviews on several dozen informants inside that agency, the State and Defense departments, other parts of the Reagan Administration, and the House of Representatives and the Senate. This book gives very little information on the actual operations of the contras in Nicaragua. Instead, Woodward concentrates on personalities and events in Washington to explain how the CIA, aided by powerful allies in the administration, organized, trained, and supplied these opponents of the left-wing Sandinista government in Nicaragua as part of a campaign to defeat what Reagan and his followers feared was the expanding menace of Communism in the Western Hemisphere. He also examines the mining of Nicaraguan harbors and traces the long and complex trail of money that flowed from arms sales to the Iranian government through Europe and across the Atlantic to support the contras in their fight to overthrow the Sandinistas. Many important figures play out their shadowy roles in this book, including Oliver North and John

Poindexter, but the central personality is CIA Director William Casey, whose anti-Communist zeal matched that of President Reagan.

Yerxa, Donald. *Admirals and Empire: The United States Navy and the Caribbean, 1898-1945.* Columbia: University of South Carolina Press, 1991.

Historians typically discuss gunboat diplomacy as a part of diplomatic history, but Yerxa's excellent study makes it clear that the U.S. Navy played a major role in this era of Caribbean history. Based on extensive research in the archives of the U.S. Navy, this book covers strategic planning, the establishment of naval bases, training exercises and war games, and the actual deployment of naval vessels in times of political and diplomatic crisis (the action often identified as gunboat diplomacy). Yerxa's broad perspective on the U.S. Navy's operations in the Caribbean emphasizes that this region was an essential component in U.S. strategic thinking because of its location on the southern flank of the eastern half of the United States and because of the integral role of the Panama Canal in the deployment of U.S. warships. The author integrates these larger strategic concerns with the often difficult and frustrating tasks of intervention in nations such as Haiti, the Dominican Republic, Cuba, Nicaragua, and Honduras for the purposes of maintaining political stability and economic order, thereby removing the justification for intervention by a European power. Many readers may be surprised to learn of the extent of the German threat posed in the Caribbean from the joint British-German intervention in Venezuela in 1902-1903 to strategic concerns about the Kaiser's desire for a naval base in the region prior to World War I to the successful German submarine campaign against allied shipping in the early part of World War II. The footnotes and bibliography contain many useful citations for publications in English.

Latin American Criticisms of the United States and U.S. Policy

Arévalo, Juan José. *The Shark and the Sardines.* New York: Lyle Stuart, 1961.

This book is an expression of indignation, as the author admits in the introduction. Arévalo, a former president of Guatemala (1945-1950), does not attempt to disguise his disgust with the United States, which in 1954 overthrew the administration of his elected successor, Jacobo Arbenz Guzmán, because of the latter's alleged connections with Communists. Arévalo begins his book with a short fable that embodies his main thesis—that the Latin American nations (the sardines in the title) face humiliation and domination by the voracious and powerful United States (the shark). He reinforces his historical argument by citing the U.S. domination of Nicaragua in the early decades of the twentieth century. Translators June Cobb and Raúl Oseguedo capture the biting cynicism in Arévalo's judgments on the harmful effects of the power of the United States in inter-American relations, from the Pan-American conferences where "traitorous" Latino diplomats vote to satisfy the wishes of the government in Washington to the profit-hungry actions of U.S. corporations such as Standard Oil, Du Pont, and Anaconda Copper. Arévalo condemns the close alliance of these and other corporations with the State Department and, in particular, renders a harsh indictment of John Foster Dulles, who was Secretary of State in 1954. Although this book lacks the support of archival research, it does convey with force and clarity the anger of a political leader who saw the violation of the sovereignty of his nation.

Beals, Carleton, Herschell Brickell, Samuel Guy Inman, and Bryce Oliver. *What the South Americans Think of Us*. New York: McBride, 1945.
World War II and the threat of Axis penetration into the Western Hemisphere stimulated concern about the image of the United States in the nations of South America. Beals and his coauthors attempt to assess both public opinion and the judgments of political and cultural leaders in the nine largest countries of that continent. Although these essays do not have the support of public opinion polls (not available in Latin America at the time) and extensive survey data, they do contain informed impressions about the status of the United States as a neighbor after more than a decade of the Good Neighbor Policy. Beals covers Peru, Ecuador, and Bolivia, where he found much cynicism about the results of the Good Neighbor Policy and much interest in U.S. films, fashions, and popular culture. Journalist and radio commentator Bryce Oliver reports on Brazil's ambiguous flirtation with fascism, and historian Samuel Guy Inman sees much more than flirtations in Argentina's inclinations toward Germany and Italy. The fourth contributor, Herschel Brickell, combines his experience as a journalist and as a diplomat to describe the efforts of the U.S. Coordinator of Inter-American Affairs to build goodwill in Colombia and Venezuela. Chile (covered by Inman) and Uruguay (covered by Oliver) are also included in this volume.

Bosch, Juan. *Pentagonism: A Substitute for Imperialism.* New York: Grove Press, 1968.

This book is an angry attack on the role of the United States Defense Department in international affairs. The author, the former president of the Dominican Republic who was removed from office by a military coup in 1963 and blocked from his return to the presidency by the U.S. military intervention in his home country in 1965, expresses an intense mistrust of the influence of armed forces in the foreign policy arena. Bosch argues that "pentagonism" differs from imperialism in that the purpose of the intervention is no longer conquest of material resources but rather the justification of high-level military budgets in the United States. In his preface, Bosch connects his idea of pentagonism with U.S. Senator J. William Fulbright's criticisms of the military-industrial complex and its commitment of U.S. soldiers and weapons in the Vietnam War, which was a source of great controversy in the United States at the time that this book appeared. Bosch sees pentagonism as an evil that poses a threat to less-developed nations in Latin America, Asia, the Middle East, and Africa. He argues that it is a form of corruption in which military officials, government bureaucrats, and the executives of large corporations combine their selfish interests to promote warfare in developing nations.

Cosío Villegas, Daniel. *American Extremes.* Austin: University of Texas Press, 1964.

Cosío Villegas earned the respect of scholars, journalists, and policy-makers throughout the Western Hemisphere with his versatility as a diplomat, banker, historian, and university administrator. The main value of this collection of his essays comes from his work as a sharp-eyed critic of contemporary events. The essays were published in Latin America and Europe between 1940 and 1962. Translated by Americo Paredes and accompanied by John P. Harrison's biographical sketch, Cosío Villegas' essays concentrate on the issues of the early Cold War era and the problems of economic development in the Western Hemisphere. Five of these ten essays contain extensive commentary on the United States. The author has an understandable preoccupation with U.S. Latin American policy, but he probes more deeply into the political life of the United States than do most of his fellow Hispanic commentators. He examines the Korean War, U.S. policy toward the Soviet Union, and the psychology of public opinion in the United States as well the often neglected inter-American conference at Chapultepec in 1945 and the seldom neglected Cuban Revolution of 1959.

Fanon, Frantz. *The Wretched of the Earth.* New York: Grove Press, 1963.
   Fanon, born on the French colonial island of Martinique in the Caribbean in 1925, brought forth in his short life an intellectual condensation
   of the meanings of imperial domination, racism, revolution, and violence. Fanon's perspective bears the marks of a childhood and adoles-
   cence in the deeply divided society in which the African population,
   descendants of slaves imported to the West Indies generations earlier,
   endured the anguish of colonial discrimination. Fanon earned a medical degree in psychiatry in France after World War II and then turned
   his attention to the psychological and sociological implications of
   imperialism. Constance Farrington's translation expresses Fanon's
   provocative mix of psychiatric analysis, historical awareness, and
   passionate advocacy. Although most of the cases cited in the book are
   from his experiences in the Algerian anticolonial revolution against
   France, Fanon's broader conclusions have much to say about West
   Indian and Latin American societies, the tensions created by white
   domination of Third World nations, and the potential for violent
   revolution against such domination. Fanon does not discuss the United
   States in depth, but his book found a wide readership in the United
   States in the 1960's and 1970's, when the governments in Washington
   pursued policies of anti-Communism and counterinsurgency that
   seemed to fit into his analysis. The preface by French philosopher
   Jean-Paul Sartre places Fanon's work in the international context of
   the period.

Galeano, Eduardo. *Open Veins of Latin America: Five Centuries of the
   Pillage of a Continent.* New York: Monthly Review Press, 1973.
   This harsh indictment of the imperial exploitation of Latin America
   conveys the emotional intensity manifested by many leftist observers
   in the 1960's and 1970's. Galeano, a Uruguayan scholar, links the
   region's poverty and economic underdevelopment to the absorption of
   its natural resources such as gold, silver, and sugar by the Spanish and
   Portuguese empires. After independence, British merchants and U.S.
   bankers and industrialists removed oil, copper, coffee, and meat, often
   in league with Latin America's elitist diplomats and generals. The last
   chapter, titled "The Contemporary Structure of Plunder," is a fifty-
   eight-page attack on the policies of the U.S. government and U.S.
   corporations in Latin America. The reader can find a clear, unequivocal
   condemnation of the United States in Galeano's work, which can be
   read in conjunction with other less-strident studies of the same issues
   to obtain a broader perspective.

Haring, Clarence. *South America Looks at the United States*. 1928. Reprint. New York: Arno Press, 1970.

Haring, a history professor at Harvard University, traveled in South America for about a year in 1925 and 1926 in order to gauge the continent's attitudes toward the United States. For nearly three decades, the United States had been active in military interventions, economic investments, and the construction and operation of the Panama Canal. Haring's text includes translated quotations from several leading critics of the United States, including José Ingenieros and Manuel Ugarte of Argentina, Alejandro Alvarez of Chile, and José Enrique Rodó of Uruguay. Haring also summarizes opinions found in newspapers and magazines and the policy statements of several governments. The issues emphasized in this book include U.S. racial prejudice, U.S. economic penetration, the Monroe Doctrine, and the movement toward Latin American unity and the revival of Spanish influence as counterbalances to the expansive United States.

Liss, Sheldon. *Fidel! Castro's Political and Social Thought*. Boulder, CO: Westview Press, 1994.

The hostility between Castro's Cuba and the United States has been evident for more than a third of a century. Castro's criticisms of the United States have been frequent over these years, but, unfortunately for the interested English-language reader, these comments are scattered through a large variety of publications, many of which have not been translated. Liss, a specialist in the history of the Latin American left, examines Castro's voluminous publications, interviews, and speeches to construct a clearly organized explication of the Cuban leader's ideas on several topics, including capitalism, internationalism, imperialism, democracy, and human rights, all of which relate to his opinions of the United States. In particular, Chapter 6, titled "The Americas," deals with Castro's views of the United States and U.S. policy in the Western Hemisphere. Liss includes many valuable books and articles in his footnotes, which give the reader considerable guidance for consulting Castro's published writing and speeches available in English as well as Spanish.

Martí, José. *Martí on the U.S.A.* Carbondale: Southern Illinois University Press, 1966.

Martí, a Cuban intellectual and instigator of the island's revolution for independence against Spain in 1895, was one of Latin America's foremost commentators on the political conditions and social customs of the United States. For approximately a decade and a half before the outbreak of the revolution (in which he lost his life), Martí made his home base in New York City while he traveled throughout the United States as a journalist writing for Spanish-language newspapers and magazines. Editor and translator Luis A. Baralt provides an interesting selection of Martí's essays, including biographical sketches (originally obituaries) of poet Walt Whitman, President James Garfield, philosopher Ralph Waldo Emerson, and outlaw Jesse James. Martí also wrote about the Charleston, South Carolina, earthquake of 1886 and the dedication of the Statue of Liberty. The last fifty pages include Martí's responses to the emergence of a national popular culture in the United States, from Buffalo Bill Cody's Wild West Show and the bustling shores of New York's Coney Island to the horror of mob violence in the streets of New Orleans, Louisiana, to the excitement of political campaigning in the 1880's. Editor Baralt has added useful explanatory footnotes for some of the more obscure references in Martí's text.

Quintanilla, Luis. *A Latin American Speaks*. New York: Macmillan, 1943.
The Axis threat in World War II created a widespread, if only temporary, harmony in the Western Hemisphere. Mexican diplomat Quintanilla incorporates this sense of unity into his book, which emphasizes the themes of cultural and political democracy as the bases for international cooperation among the American nations. In general, Quintanilla's judgments are quite favorable on the Roosevelt Administration, its Good Neighbor Policy, and the historical champions of democracy from Thomas Jefferson to Abraham Lincoln. He is much more critical of U.S. interventions in the Caribbean in the early decades of the twentieth century and the superficiality of what he terms the "blah blah" Pan-Americanism of the United States from the 1880's to the 1920's. Quintanilla also provides interesting commentary on the social and economic life of the United States, including an extended critique of the hardships of small farmers and migrant workers in the South and the West as well as the escapism of Hollywood's motion pictures. Quintanilla's overriding theme, however, is hemispheric unity through democratic idealism, a perspective that is in contrast to the often strident criticism of the United States offered by most of the commentators mentioned in this section.

Reid, John T. *Spanish American Images in the United States, 1790-1960*. Gainesville: University of Florida Press, 1977.
Reid's selection of several leading intellectual and political figures who visited the United States and then published their impressions provides the basis for this well-organized and clearly written study.

These individuals include Benjamín Vicuña Mackenna, a Chilean statesman and writer who traveled in the United States in the 1850's, and his contemporary, Argentine educator Domingo Sarmiento. Twentieth century observers include Mexican philosopher and educator José Vasconcelos, poets Rubén Darío of Nicaragua and Gabriela Mistral of Chile, and politician-social critic Luis Alberto Sánchez of Peru. Reid's discussion of the views of these individuals gives the reader a sampling from important works that, in many cases, have not been translated into English. In addition, Reid incorporates his explication of the writing of several of the authors annotated in this section, including José Martí and José Enrique Rodó. Some of the themes in U.S. history and culture addressed in Reid's study are economic imperialism, education, materialism, racism, and hemispheric solidarity. Reid's assessment of this wide range of commentary is thoughtful and balanced, taking into account several different ideological tendencies.

Rodó, José Enrique. *Ariel*. Austin: University of Texas Press, 1988.
Rodó's extended essay, originally published in 1900, was a landmark in Latin America's struggle to come to an understanding of the nature and purpose of the projection of the United States' power throughout the Western Hemisphere. A native of the small South American nation of Uruguay, Rodó was less concerned with the U.S. victory in the Spanish-American War than were other writers of his generation and was more inclined to view the issues of his time in cultural and philosophical terms. Margaret Peden's translation of this essay conveys the literary dimensions in Rodó's use of characters from William Shakespeare's play *The Tempest* in order to contrast and compare the fundamental values of the United States with those of Latin America. Although literary critics and political commentators disagree on Rodó's intent in this essay, it seems fairly clear that he was trying to alert the first generation of twentieth century Latin American university students that the commercial values of the United States (represented by Shakespeare's character Caliban) posed a sharp contrast and something of a threat to the abstract idealism typical of many of the region's literary intellectuals (represented by the character Ariel). Rodó deals with few specific events or individuals, but his broad cultural commentary is a valid expression of enduring themes in the history of the Western Hemisphere.

Sáenz, Vicente. *Latin America Against the Colonial System*. Mexico City: Central American Union, 1949.

Sáenz was one of the Western Hemisphere's most outspoken opponents of imperialism. A native of Costa Rica who headed the Central American Union (with headquarters in Mexico City, Mexico), Sáenz published a long series of diatribes against many forms of imperialism, from the territorial empire of the Spanish in the colonial period to the British outposts in the Caribbean and the Malvinas (Falkland) Islands. In this volume, one of his main targets is the rapidly growing U.S. economic domination of the Latin American nations, which was becoming increasingly evident as Sáenz wrote in the late 1940's. Throughout this book, Sáenz praises the high ideals of the Monroe Doctrine—democracy and anticolonialism—and identifies several U.S. political leaders (including Presidents Woodrow Wilson and Franklin D. Roosevelt) and writers (including William Krehm, former *Time* correspondent) who advocated these positions. Sáenz also criticizes the United States for its failure to incorporate these ideals into its policies in the 1940's. He strongly advocates that the United States side with the Latin American nations against the decision by Great Britain to tighten its grasp on Western Hemisphere colonies. His last chapter is an appeal to President Harry Truman to take action to restrict, if not to end, both U.S. and British imperialism (territorial and economic) in the Americas.

Ugarte, Manuel. *The Destiny of a Continent*. 1925. Reprint. New York: AMS Press, 1970.

This book expresses the provocative opinions of an Argentine critic of United States imperialism in Latin America. Ugarte was born and educated in Argentina and then moved to Europe, where he found recognition as a writer as well as an outspoken opponent of the expansion of U.S. power in the Western Hemisphere. Ugarte combines an account of his travels through the United States, Mexico, Central America, and South America in the early 1920's with observations on the origins of and challenges posed by the United States, which he called the "New Rome," the new imperial power of the twentieth century. His judgments about the United States are not all negative. He expresses admiration for the energy and organizational abilities of the people of the United States and sees their outward thrust as the natural outcome of these characteristics. Ugarte was one of the first commentators to understand the innovative and flexible forms of U.S. domination, which generally avoided direct annexation in favor of political and diplomatic pressure and economic penetration, reinforced by military interventions and the threat of such interventions. He also points out the weaknesses of the Latin American nations in their inability to develop stable governments. This instability undermined efforts to assemble a cohesive opposition to the intrusions of the United States. Students will find Ugarte's book to be a challenging statement of anti-imperialist ideas.

Wesson, Robert, and Heraldo Muñoz, eds. *Latin American Views of U.S. Policy*. New York: Praeger, 1986.
Recognizing the lack of Latin American writing in English on inter-American relations, editors Wesson and Muñoz put together this volume of seven essays written by scholars from Argentina, Chile, Venezuela, and Mexico. The book appeared in 1986, at a time when U.S. policy in Central America brought on much leftist criticism. These authors write from moderate to conservative positions in which Marxism and other radical ideologies had little influence. They do include criticisms of the Reagan Administration's policies. For example, Muñoz faults the United States for its "obsession" with security concerns in Central America to the neglect of the problems of international debt and economic development. Roberto Bouzas examines U.S. policies on trade and investment, and other authors cover the inter-American political system and U.S. relations with Central America, Mexico, Brazil, Argentina, and Chile. Each article includes helpful footnotes, and editor Wesson provides a concluding essay.

Latin American Immigration

Brimelow, Peter. *Alien Nation: Common Sense About America's Immigration Disaster*. New York: Random House, 1995.
Brimelow, an immigrant from Great Britain who became a citizen of the United States, raises serious questions about U.S. immigration policy since 1965 and its consequences for the well-being of the nation. Brimelow is convinced that the United States has lost control of its borders, by which he means that immigrants are arriving at a much faster rate than the U.S. economic, social, and political institutions can absorb. He cites statistics to show that the foreign presence in the U.S. population (immigrants and their children) is on the rise, from 17% in 1970 to a projected 27% around the year 2035. Brimelow places Latin American immigration near the top of his list of concerns—especially the movement of undocumented migrants across the border with Mexico. Two of his main theses are that these large numbers of newly arrived people do not contribute to the productivity of the economy and cannot be accommodated in a nation that is already facing the

stresses of ethnic tensions, inefficient welfare programs, and the consequent pressures on the political system. His recommendations include the replacement of the Immigration Act of 1965 with laws that require higher levels of skills and education for immigrants. Perhaps the most controversial of Brimelow's contentions is that the arrival of non-European people threatens the cultural traditions and political stability of the United States. These and others of the author's assertions are controversial and should be balanced with reading in other books mentioned in this section.

Cardoso, Lawrence A. *Mexican Emigration to the United States, 1897-1931: Socio-economic Patterns.* Tucson: University of Arizona Press, 1980.
The migration of Mexicans to the United States has its origins deep within the internal histories of these countries. Cardoso covers both sides of immigration in impressive depth. He describes the harsh conditions of debt peonage, the breakup of village-owned lands, and the painful rise of food prices for landless peasants during the dictatorship of Porfirio Díaz (1876-1911). At roughly the same time, railroad construction in Mexico tied the two countries together. Railroad jobs in northern Mexico attracted landless peasants, many of whom rode the rail lines they helped to build into the southwestern United States, where landowners recruited them to harvest vegetables and cotton crops on recently irrigated lands. This pattern of migration continued during the first decade of the Mexican Revolution. Many Mexicans sought refuge in the United States from the violence, social disruptions, and economic uncertainty that continued into the 1920's. Cardoso examines the policies of the Mexican government, which generally discouraged emigration and also attempted to establish legal protection for Mexicans who had migrated to the United States. The book concludes with a short chapter on the beginnings of repatriation in the early 1930's, when local and state governments in the United States began to expel Mexicans after nearly half a century of recruitment and immigration. Cardoso's footnotes and bibliography have valuable suggestions for further research.

Chomsky, Aviva. *West Indian Workers and the United Fruit Company in Costa Rica, 1870-1940.* Baton Rouge: Louisiana State University Press, 1996.
Not all immigration in Latin America involves the movement of people to the United States. Chomsky's detailed examination of the migration of West Indian (mainly Jamaican) workers to the Caribbean coastal

area of Costa Rica is an important example of the impact of a large U.S.-based multinational corporation—the United Fruit Company—on the lives of immigrants. Chomsky discusses the company's recruitment of these workers and emphasizes the motives of the approximately twenty thousand Jamaicans who moved to Costa Rica. High wages paid in the banana industry in the early twentieth century and the opportunity to own small plots of land were the overriding motives in this migration. The second point was especially appealing to Jamaicans who were descendants of slaves and wanted to achieve the independence associated with land ownership. Chomsky uses West Indian immigrants' newspapers published in the coastal city of Limón and the archives of the Costa Rican government to study the struggles of these Afro-Caribbean peoples to survive and to find their place in the predominantly Hispanic nation of Costa Rica. The author also examines various policies of the United Fruit Company: health care in this disease-prone region of Costa Rica; labor relations; with emphasis on the banana workers' strikes of 1910 and 1934; and arrangements with the independent banana-producing farmers. Throughout the text, Chomsky stresses the capacity of the West Indian immigrants to create their own institutions, such as churches and newspapers, as a means of preserving their culture. The depth of Chomsky's research on this unique topic gives this study special importance in immigration history.

Cose, Ellis. *A Nation of Strangers: Prejudice, Politics, and the Populating of America*. New York: Morrow, 1992.
Cose places the immigration of the 1980's in a historical context that stretches back to the 1780's. The first one-third of the book deals with the evolution of U.S. immigration policy from the early national period to World War II. In the remaining two-thirds of the text, Cose presents in-depth coverage of the Cold War period, when questions of political ideology (a tendency to favor refugees from Communist countries) and ethnic origins (the revival of concerns about the arrival of large numbers of immigrants with non-European backgrounds) became prominent issues not only in policy discussions but also in political campaigns. He gives considerable attention to questions concerning Mexican, Cuban, and Haitian immigrants and provides a succinct analysis of the Simpson-Mazzoli (or Immigration Reform and Control) Act of 1986.

Daniels, Roger. *Coming to America: A History of Immigration and Ethnicity in American Life*. New York: HarperCollins, 1990.

This college-level survey text provides broad coverage of two very large topics: the history of immigration and government immigration policy, and the efforts of various immigrant ethnic groups to blend into the mainstreams of U.S. national culture, society, and politics. Daniels gives balanced discussions of the colonial and Revolutionary War eras, the early national period, and the nineteenth century. His commentary on Latin American immigration has the greatest depth in the last one-third of the book, which is focused on the period since 1921. Daniels includes sections that deal with Puerto Ricans, Cubans, Haitians, and other Caribbean islanders, as well as Mexicans and Central Americans. His analysis tends to place immigration and ethnic relations in the larger contexts of national politics and international diplomacy. The footnotes and bibliography are of much value in the location of additional published material on these topics.

Galarza, Ernesto. *Farm Workers and Agri-business in California, 1947-1960.* Notre Dame, IN: University of Notre Dame Press, 1977.
Many Mexican immigrants to the United States found their jobs in the fruit, vegetable, and cotton fields of California, where low wages and arduous working conditions were common. Galarza's book reflects his own experiences in attempting to organize farmworkers under these conditions. He writes with clearly stated sympathies for the workers and a highly critical attitude toward the landowners who, in his terms, formed the "agri-business" sector of California's booming economy. Once aware of the author's point of view, the reader can find much useful information and many valuable insights on the struggle to organize migrant farmworkers, the legal and political power of California's agribusiness, and the reasons for the ultimate failure to establish a viable, inclusive union in the late 1950's. The ten-page annotated bibliography includes numerous published books and articles available in many college and some larger public libraries.

Gutiérrez, David G., ed. *Between Two Worlds: Mexican Immigrants in the United States.* Wilmington, DE: Scholarly Resources, 1996.
Mexican immigration to the United States has stirred political and academic debate for several generations. Editor Gutiérrez has assembled a revealing sampling of some of the best writing on this subject, covering topics from the mid-nineteenth to the late twentieth century. These essays include an analysis of Anglo-American perceptions of and prejudice against Mexican Americans and an article on the evolution of Mexican views of the role of the border in the lives of those who had crossed it as temporary residents and those who became U.S.

citizens. One essay offers a convenient historical survey of the bracero program, under which Mexicans worked for U.S. businesses to meet labor shortages during World War II and succeeding decades. A remarkably perceptive study deals with the impact of U.S. popular culture—especially Hollywood films and advertising—on adolescent Mexican American females growing up in U.S. cities from the 1920's through the 1940's. Four of these selections deal with the complex, multisided debate regarding Mexican immigration from the 1970's to the 1990's.

_____. *Walls and Mirrors: Mexican Americans, Mexican Immigrants, and the Politics of Ethnicity.* Berkeley: University of California Press, 1995.

This book addresses an important but frequently overlooked or slighted topic in immigration history. Even among the best informed observers of ethnic politics and culture in the United States, the shifting relationship between Mexican Americans (people of Mexican origin who are U.S. citizens) and Mexican immigrants is a topic that is seldom fully appreciated. Gutiérrez traces this relationship from the era of Manifest Destiny in the 1840's and 1850's, when established Mexican communities in Texas and California became parts of the expansionist United States, to the heated discussion of the 1990's, when multiculturalism and immigration became controversial issues in state, national, and international politics. The author examines the successive waves of Mexican immigration and the responses of Mexican Americans to the new arrivals from south of the border. Gutiérrez provides an unusually perceptive and nuanced account of attitudes and actions within the Mexican American communities of the United States. The historical institutions and trends discussed include LULAC (League of United Latin American Citizens), a prominent Mexican American organization that began in Texas in the 1920's and stressed the importance of U.S. citizenship and involvement in mainstream U.S. culture and politics. Gutiérrez also studies a contrasting trend in the Chicano movement of the 1960's and 1970's; that movement focused on the struggling immigrant workers (many without proper documentation) who toiled in the fruit orchards and vegetable fields of the Southwest and came to symbolize an ardent ethnic awareness among many Mexicans and Mexican Americans. In general, this well-written text gives the reader a thoughtful, dispassionate overview of a subject that is often complicated by strongly held opinions.

Jones, Richard C. *Ambivalent Journey: U.S. Migration and Economic Mobility in North-Central Mexico*. Tucson: University of Arizona Press, 1995.

International migration often is a family and community phenomenon. Individuals, usually young males, decide to leave their families and communities to earn more money or to find a better way of life. Jones addresses the question of whether this type of migration benefits the family and community left behind. His study concentrates on two regions in Mexico: central Zacatecas, an area troubled by economic stagnation, and northern Coahuila, a relatively prosperous area located on the border with the United States. Jones uses geographical, histori-cal, and economic perspectives along with survey data and interviews to describe the conditions in these two regions that motivated young males—usually recently married, with children—to seek employment in the United States. The author's main concern is the economic impact of this migration on families and communities. In the case of central Zacatecas, families use the migrants' income to improve their eco-nomic conditions at home. Jones cites Zacatecas' expanding commer-cial peach orchards as an example of how migrants' income is put to productive use. In northern Coahuila, by contrast, the migrants' income tends to be used to purchase consumer items and is not invested in productive activities. These case studies give the reader specific exam-ples of the meaning of migration in these Mexican communities. Jones also includes a sophisticated discussion of the main trends in world-wide immigration studies and how central Zacatecas and northern Coahuila fit into these patterns.

McWilliams, Carey. *North from Mexico: The Spanish-Speaking People of the United States*. 1949. Reprint. New York: Greenwood Press, 1968.

The original publication of this book in 1949 marked a breakthrough in the recognition of the importance of the Mexican people of the southwestern United States. Its republication in 1968 (with a new introduction by the author) established McWilliams' work as a classic historical, sociological, and legal study of the troubled relations be-tween Anglos and Mexicans in the area that stretched from California to Texas. McWilliams covers the historical dimension from the Coro-nado expedition that explored the region from 1540 to 1542 for the Spanish viceroy in Mexico City to the hypocrisy in the fiestas cele-brated by so-called Californios of the 1940's, in which no persons of Mexican origin took part. The author combines the research of U.S. historians Herbert Eugene Bolton and Walter Prescott Webb with the findings of Mexican anthropologist Manuel Gamio, New Mexican educator-historian George Sánchez, and several other contemporary commentators. McWilliams' focus is on incidents in which the difficulties between Hispanics and Anglos are paramount, such as the 1942 Sleepy Lagoon murder case, in which seventeen Mexican American defendants were victimized by a prejudiced Los Angeles court, and the 1943 zoot-suit riots in downtown Los Angeles, involving Mexican Americans, local Anglos, servicemen stationed in the area, and law enforcement officials. The author also discusses the more peaceful blending of Hispanic and Anglo cultures and the chances for harmonious relations.

Miller, Jake C. *The Plight of the Haitian Refugees.* New York: Praeger, 1984.
Several thousand Haitian "boat people" made the perilous crossing from their homeland to Florida in the early 1980's, dramatizing their decision to migrate to the United States. Miller's book explains both the conditions in Haiti that drove them to this risky venture and their generally unfriendly reception in the United States. The repressive government of François Duvalier ("Papa Doc") from 1957 to 1971 and his son and heir Jean-Claude Duvalier from 1971 to 1986 did not allow serious political debate, much less meaningful opposition. Haiti's limited natural resources and lack of industry meant few jobs for a nation of impoverished peasants and workers. Miller points out that many Haitians sought refuge from poverty and repression in other nearby nations, such as the Dominican Republic, Cuba, Jamaica, and the Bahamas, in addition to making their highly publicized migration to the United States. He also describes the condition of their detention centers, often located in jails and former military bases. The purpose of Miller's book is clear: to provide his readers with a sympathetic account of the plight of the Haitian migrants, who faced extreme hardships not of their own making.

Portes, Alejandro, and Alex Stepick. *City on the Edge: The Transformation of Miami.* Berkeley: University of California Press, 1993.
Miami became one of the world's preeminent international cities in the 1980's. An essential part of its internationalization was the growth in size, political influence, and economic strength of its Cuban population. Portes and Stepick present a clearly written sociological analysis of this decade, beginning with the Mariel boat lift of 1980, in which newly arrived immigrants from Cuba (including a small but prominent number of criminals and drug addicts) caused controversy between the city's Cuban and native white populations and contributed to the rise

of a unified Cuban community in both Miami and Florida politics. The authors also include considerable information on the historical background of the Cuban community in Florida and the pressure of other national and ethnic groups—specifically Haitians, Nicaraguans, and U.S. African Americans. Although the authors stress the resilience of cultural diversity, they conclude by noting early signs of convergence among the several distinctive populations of the city.

Reimers, David M. *Still the Golden Door: The Third World Comes to America.* 2d ed. New York: Columbia University Press, 1992.
Immigration from Third World areas—mainly Latin America and East Asia—became the subject of increasing controversy in the United States in the 1980's and 1990's. Reimers' timely book is a much-needed, careful, and dispassionate study in recent history that discusses the legal basis for U.S. immigration policies and their actual impact on the flow of Third World peoples into the United States in the years since 1945. Latin America is a prominent part of this study. Reimers' analysis of Mexican immigration identifies a pattern in which the movement of migrants seeking jobs has been a constant phenomenon in spite of several changes in U.S. immigration law. He also examines the influences of the Cold War in the immigration from Cuba after the rise of Fidel Castro's Communist government in the 1960's. The text gives thorough discussions of immigration law and the political debates surrounding various laws, including the Immigration Act of 1965, the Immigration Reform and Control Act of 1986, and the often neglected Immigration Act of 1990. The footnotes are informative and include citations of several important specialized studies.

Rieff, David. *The Exile: Cuba in the Heart of Miami.* New York: Simon and Schuster, 1993.
Rather than discussing politics, ideology, and guerrilla warfare, this book gives an essentially personal and family-centered portrait of the sense of separation that troubles many of the Cuban residents of Miami. Rieff looks into the angry responses to the editorial and news coverage policies of the *Miami Herald* by the Cuban-American National Foundation led by Jorge Mas Canosa, but at the center of this book is the experience of a married couple, Raúl and Niñón Rodríguez, and their son, Ruly. Raúl, an architect, receives much criticism from Miami's Cubans because of his frequent visits to his homeland. Rieff sensitively examines Raúl's feelings of disconnectedness and the huge gap between growing up in Havana and living his adult years in Miami. Havana is much closer geographically to Miami than the homelands

of immigrants from Asia and even Mexico are to their new dwellings, but among the Cuban exiles of Miami, this small spatial distance is multiplied by the trauma of their sudden exodus, the lingering presence of Fidel Castro, and the growing realization that assimilation into the culture of the United States has become an important factor for their children.

Ueda, Reed. *Postwar Immigrant America: A Social History*. New York: St. Martin's Press, 1994.
This book contains a convenient synthesis of research on a topic of much political, journalistic, and academic interest in the 1980's and 1990's. Ueda explains some of the basic concepts in immigration history, such as push (the reasons that lead people to decide to leave their homeland) and pull (the attractions that draw immigrants to their destination). The author also gives brief, comprehensible discussions of both the U.S. Immigration Act of 1965 and the Immigration Reform and Control Act of 1986, along with the place of these laws in the flow of immigration into the United States. The author pays considerable attention to Mexico and the Caribbean in this process. Ueda also discusses the place of immigrants in U.S. society, including economic opportunity, social mobility, language and cultural assimilation, and marriage/family patterns. The last portion of the book deals with the interaction of immigration and politics. Ueda identifies several problem areas, including the appearance of nativism (anti-immigration attitudes and organizations) in the 1970's and 1980's. In general, he is more optimistic on the issues of assimilation, economic opportunity, and stability than is Brimelow (see his book annotated in this section).

Popular Culture and the Mass Media

Black, George. *The Good Neighbor: How the United States Wrote the History of Central America and the Caribbean*. New York: Pantheon, 1988.
The intimate relationships between the United States and the nations of Central America and the Caribbean include news coverage, tourism, academic analysis, fiction, and film as well as diplomacy, trade, and military interventions. Black has assembled an entertaining collection of photographs, newspaper cartoons, motion picture stills and posters, and quotations from books, essays, and songs that reveal the mixture of idealism, materialism, cynicism, and propaganda that has characterized the complex image of this region in the U.S. media. Readers

should not dismiss the illustrations as mere entertainment. In many cases, they contain telling commentary not only on native peoples and local environments but also on those who created the illustrations and took the photographs. Black's book covers the Spanish-American War, military interventions in the first three decades of the twentieth century (especially the pursuit of Augusto César Sandino in Nicaragua), the Good Neighbor Policy and World War II, and Fidel Castro, Che Guevara, and Daniel Ortega in the Cold War. Advertisements for the tourist trade and U.S.-made exports to the region are interspersed throughout the text.

Dorfman, Ariel. *The Empire's Old Clothes: What the Lone Ranger, Babar, and Other Innocent Heroes Do to Our Minds.* New York: Pantheon, 1983.
Popular culture's manifestations in comic books, magazines, films, and television programs are among the most conspicuous exports of the United States in the twentieth century. Chilean novelist/social critic Dorfman examines the content of page and screen to determine how these images reflect the power of governments and corporations and the passivity of the mass audience in the United States and the Third World—particularly Latin America. His commentary includes Babar (the elephant in children's books), Walt Disney's Mickey Mouse and Donald Duck, and popular heroes of comic books, radio, and television, such as the Lone Ranger and Superman. He also presents an extended examination of the *Reader's Digest* in which he concludes that this magazine's underlying assumptions regarding the rewards to common sense and virtuous behavior, much like the justice dispensed by the Lone Ranger and Superman, create a set of beliefs that encourage passivity and reinforce the existing power structure that rests on the unequal relationship between the United States and Third World nations. Clark Hansen's translation conveys the pungent prose and sharp critiques in Dorfman's text.

Fortner, Robert S. *International Communications: History, Conflict, and Control of the Global Metropolis.* Belmont, CA: Wadsworth, 1993.
This pathbreaking textbook covers a field that has grown dramatically in importance since the 1950's. Fortner's writing style is clear, and his explanation of key terms is thorough and easy to understand. The book begins with chapters on the general background of communications history, communications theory, and the technology involved in the field. Most of the book is a chronologically arranged study of the evolution of international communications systems from telegraphy to

radio to television, with strong emphasis on the role of propaganda in World War I, the rise of Fascism, World War II, and the Cold War. Fortner also discusses recent trends in technology and public diplomacy. Although he does not have an extended section devoted exclusively to Latin America, Fortner brings the region into his examination of the "Periphery Versus Core in the Global Metropolis" as a part of his study of the flow of news and propaganda between developing countries and the industrial powers in the years since 1945. The footnotes and bibliography list valuable sources for additional studies of international communications in Latin America.

Johnson, John J. *Latin America in Caricature*. Austin: University of Texas Press, 1980.

The strengths of this unusual book are both simple and profound. Johnson, a veteran Latin American historian, assembled 131 editorial cartoons as they appeared in the U.S. press, almost all of them from the 1890's to the 1970's. The profundity becomes evident in the author's arrangement of these cartoons to illustrate several themes that reflect serious points of concern in U.S.-Latin American relations. These themes include the simplistic depiction of Latin American nations as a monolith, the use of a light-skinned female to symbolize the entire region, and the use of other convenient images, such as quarrelsome children and stereotypical black people (including obviously racist drawings). Johnson also includes cartoons that render judgments on militarism and social reform. His commentary should be read carefully because it adds significantly to an understanding of the attitudes and ideas behind the cartoons.

King, John. *Magical Reels: A History of Cinema in Latin America*. London: Verso, 1990.

The author provides a sophisticated, sympathetic survey of the uneven evolution of motion pictures in Latin America. King employs a chronological approach, moving from the silent era of the early twentieth century to the arrival of the innovative "New Cinema" of the 1960's to the divergent tendencies of the 1980's. Within this chronology, he gives succinct interpretive discussions of individual nations, with emphases on Argentina, Mexico, Cuba, Chile, and Brazil. King is particularly adept in exploring apparent contradictions. For example, he points out that the technology of motion pictures—camera, film, and projector—is the product of modern industry generally associated with external economic domination and imperial power, but, once in the hands of Latin American directors, writers, technicians, and performers, it becomes a tool for the expression of national themes that often turn squarely against external domination. The influence of the United States is pervasive in the international culture of film and often manifests itself in unexpected ways, as during World War II, when Washington bolstered the Mexican film industry as a rival to that of apparently pro-Axis Argentina (which had enjoyed considerable success in Latin America and Europe through the tango films of Carlos Gardel). The huge presence of Hollywood films is discussed throughout the book. One of King's central themes is the continuing debate among Latin American filmmakers concerning their acceptance or rejection of the Hollywood model in their work. The intellectual importance of film in Latin America is indicated by numerous quotations from leading literary figures such as Carlos Fuentes, Manuel Puig, Jorge Luis Borges, and Gabriel García Márquez.

King, John, Ana M. López, and Manuel Alvarado, eds. *Mediating Two Worlds: Cinematic Encounters in the Americas*. London: British Film Institute, 1993.
This exceptional collection of twenty-three essays focuses on a central theme in this section—the interaction of Latin America and the United States (as well as Europe) through the medium of film. Essay topics include the work of directors Luis Bunuel and Sergei Eisenstein, the images of native American tribal societies in U.S. feature films, ethnicity in the Hollywood films of the 1930's and 1940's, and an analysis of Hollywood's depiction of Central America in the 1980's. More than half the book consists of essays on the development of film in Latin America, with discussions of cinema in Mexico, Argentina, Brazil, Colombia, and Cuba. Topics explored in depth include the role of governments in film production and the portrayal of gender issues, ethnicity, cultural nationalism, and modernity. In most of these essays, the authors express concerns about the looming presence of the U.S. film and television industries.

Klein, Alan M. *Sugarball: The American Game, the Dominican Dream*. New Haven, CT: Yale University Press, 1991.
Baseball entered the Dominican Republic in the 1890's and in the early decades of the twentieth century to become an immensely popular sport among players and fans alike. It was often played by young males who worked in or near sugar refineries (hence the book's title). Generally lacking in formal organization, amateur, semiprofessional, and professional teams created their own set of legends that gave baseball on this island nation a uniquely national character. Klein's scholarly

study concerns the connections between Dominican baseball and the professional leagues in the United States. Beginning in the 1950's, it appears that U.S. professional baseball exercised a kind of colonialism over the Dominican Republic by recruiting its best players to participate in the tightly organized version of the game played in North America. Klein, however, sees a broader pattern in which Dominican fans, scouts, managers, and players make full use of this channel of opportunity into the center of the dominant culture and material wealth in the United States. Klein examines the roles of Dominicans such as highly regarded scouts Ralph Avila and Epy Guerrero in this process.

Oleksak, Michael, and Mary Adams Oleksak. *Beisbol: Latin Americans and the Grand Old Game.* Grand Rapids, MI: Masters Press, 1991.
The long and eventful history of Latin American baseball is summarized in an engaging fashion in this much-needed synthesis. The Oleksaks' direct prose style and the biographical and anecdotal content of their text tends to hold the attention of both fans and general readers. The authors offer interesting sketches of Cuba's pioneer big league pitcher of the 1920's, Adolfo Luque; the Washington Senators' premier scout in Havana in the 1940's, Joe Cambria; and Mexico's Pasquel brothers' challenge to the American and National Leagues with their rival league of the late 1940's. Approximately two-thirds of the text deals with the achievements of Latin American players in the big leagues from the 1950's to the 1980's; these players include Roberto Clemente, Luis Aparicio, Juan Marichal, and Orlando Cepeda in the early years of this period. The authors also discuss winter baseball and the Caribbean World Series, including brief descriptions of these games and their Latino and Anglo players. The book's appendices provide listings and the cumulative statistical records of Latin American big leaguers and the year-by-year records of twenty stars.

Pike, Fredrick B. *The United States and Latin America: Myths and Stereotypes of Civilization and Nature.* Austin: University of Texas Press, 1992.
Since the early 1800's, many important U.S. writers, artists, and political leaders have attempted to explain Latin America in their essays, novels, poems, paintings, speeches, and other media. Pike, a remarkably well-read and innovative historian, examines the varying and often conflicting perceptions of Latin America that have appeared in the United States. He cites the themes of civilization and nature as focal points around which the likes of Andrew Jackson, Franz Boas, Theodore Roosevelt, Waldo Frank, and Stuart Chase have tended to

view the cultural and material contrasts between Latin America and the United States. Pike discusses several topics, such as the frontier, imperialism, racism, and progress, as integral parts of the uneasy relationship between civilization and nature. One of his most suggestive insights is the identification of a long-standing counterculture among U.S. writers and artists, who saw the rough edges and innate energy of native Americans, African Americans, and people of mixed ancestry in Latin America (including the U.S. West) as a healthy and, in many ways, admirable counter (or balance) to the dominant rigidities, restrictions, and materialism of urban North America. Pike traces the counterculture from the 1830's to its reemergence in the 1920's and 1930's and again in the 1960's, and he notes that it provided stimulating if sometimes overwrought commentary on the people and politics of the Latin American nations and their relations with the United States. Pike's footnotes give additional insights as well as a wealth of other sources on the images of Latin America in the United States.

Roberts, John Storm. *The Latin Tinge: The Impact of Latin American Music in the United States*. New York: Oxford University Press, 1979. Music is one of the most fluid and subtle elements in culture. The influence of Latin American music in the United States is perhaps underappreciated, and Roberts makes a major contribution to the correction of this misunderstanding. He provides a well-researched and persuasively written exploration of this often neglected topic. The rhythms of the Caribbean—especially Cuba—and Mexico began to penetrate into the United States in the nineteenth century. Luis Moreau Gottschalk, a New Orleans pianist and composer, incorporated Afro-Cuban themes into his performances and compositions in the 1850's. At about the same time, the Mexican *corrido* (a long ballad usually telling a story in great detail) began its contributions to the soon-to-be popular cowboy songs of the U.S. Southwest. Roberts relates in interesting detail the successive waves of music that originated in Latin America and swept across the United States in the twentieth century as popular music became a huge commercial enterprise. He discusses the arrival of the Argentine tango in 1913, the explosion of interest in the Cuban rumba and conga as popularized by Xavier Cugat and Desi Arnaz, jazz trumpeter Dizzy Gillespie's collaboration with Cuban Chano Pozo in the 1940's, the arrival of the mambo in the 1950's, and the enthusiastic reception of the Brazilian bossa nova introduced by João Gilberto in the 1960's. Roberts is especially concerned with the connections between Latin American music and U.S. jazz, a theme that he pursues from New Orleans of the early twentieth century to the international complexities and nuances of the 1960's and 1970's.

Ruck, Rob. *The Tropic of Baseball: Baseball in the Dominican Republic*. Westport, CT: Meckler, 1991.

By the 1980's, the Dominican Republic had become a hotbed for the cultivation of baseball talent for the major leagues in the United States. Ruck examines how baseball took hold in the Dominican Republic through a largely biographical and narrative approach (in contrast to the social science approach used by Alan M. Klein in his book on the same subject annotated in this section). Like Klein, Ruck dates the beginning of baseball in the Dominican Republic from the 1890's, but he also sees 1914 as a turning point because in that year, local teams challenged and defeated teams made up of U.S. Marines and sailors who were part of the intervention force then stationed in the island nation. According to Ruck, baseball was not an imposition of U.S. imperialism but instead grew as an integral part of Dominican popular culture while offering to young men with the necessary talent the opportunity to find success on the professional baseball fields of the United States. Ruck's biographical portraits of Tony Peña, Juan Marichal, Rico Carty, the Alou family (Felipe, Mateo, Jesús, and Moises), Alfredo Griffin, and George Bell, among others, provide readers with examples of the rise of Dominicans in the major leagues. He also explains the informal but intense atmosphere of San Pedro de Macorís, the small city that has produced a large number of big leaguers.

Sharbach, Sarah E. *Stereotypes of Latin America, Press Images, and U.S. Foreign Policy, 1920-1933*. New York: Garland, 1993.

Latin America often appeared on the front pages of U.S. newspapers in the 1920's. The coverage generally focused on controversial issues such as U.S. military intervention in Nicaragua or revolutionary conditions in Mexico, but Sharbach's absorbing analysis reveals that racist stereotypes and cultural prejudices frequently dominated the content of articles, essays, and books in the U.S. print media. She introduces this subject in a well-written chapter directed at the general reader. The remainder of her text deals with a series of themes and events in U.S.-Latin American relations in which ethnic and cultural attitudes were crucial. Her discussion of the pronouncements of U.S. State Department personnel indicates that disdain for Latin America was prevalent among diplomats and Foreign Service officers. In contrast to such prejudice, she cites journalist Carleton Beals and minister/activist

Samuel Guy Inman, who wrote with sympathy for the nations and people of the region and usually railed against Washington's interventions. Sharbach also includes a discussion of the clumsy, inept journalism of William Randolph Hearst, whose newspapers published forged documents in a futile effort to discredit the Mexican government and its sympathizers in the U.S. Senate. Throughout the book, Sharbach examines the assumptions concerning Latin America's racial, cultural, and economic inferiority as a fundamental component of the justifications for the United States' policies of intervention and domination in the Western Hemisphere. This book's footnotes contain a listing of many valuable publications in the popular press from the 1920's and early 1930's.

Slatta, Richard W. *Cowboys of the Americas*. New Haven, CT: Yale University Press, 1990.

Cowboys played important roles in the histories of several Western Hemisphere nations. They went by several different names: the gauchos of Argentina, the *huasos* of Chile, the *llaneros* of Venezuela, the *vaqueros* of Mexico, and the cowboys of the United States and Canada. As Slatta reveals in his smoothly written text, the various types of cowboys, although differing in language, culture, and other factors, tended to share the challenge of herding cattle across vast grasslands while astride powerful horses. This book is comparative history at its best. The author presents frequent comparisons and contrasts in discussions of "bronco busting," cattle drives, life on the ranch, folk games, relations with native Americans, and the decline of open ranching. Slatta emphasizes that much of the more general cowboy culture came from a blending of the Spanish heritage with the native American way of life. The cowboys of the United States absorbed many of these traditions over the last half of the nineteenth century in the formerly Mexican territory from Texas to California. Slatta also covers the enduring image of the cowboy in literature and mass culture, including Hollywood films and popular music. This book is exceptionally well illustrated, and the footnotes are extensive, with many valuable suggestions for additional reading.

Wells, Alan. *Picture-Tube Imperialism? The Impact of U.S. Television on Latin America*. Maryknoll, NY: Orbis Books, 1972.

Television was a new medium of communication in Latin America when Wells researched and wrote this pioneering study. Wells, a sociologist by training, directs his attention to the pattern of television programming, the structure of the television industry, and the likely impact of this new technology and its messages on Latin American society. The prevalence of U.S. influence is evident throughout the text. The author points out that most television stations in Latin America follow the format of entertainment programs accompanied by commercials for consumer products such as automobiles and soft drinks. U.S. advertising agencies are active in the development of Spanish- and Portuguese-language commercials throughout the region. Wells also describes the role of the United States Information Agency (a branch of the U.S. government) in the promotion of U.S. propaganda abroad. A central theme in Wells's book is the imposition of U.S. commercial culture in this rapidly growing mass medium in Latin America.

Woll, Allen L. *The Latin Image in American Film.* Los Angeles: UCLA Latin American Center, 1980.

This survey text intended for the college classroom furnishes a brief introduction to a complex and often controversial subject. Woll uses a chronological framework that begins with silent films and concludes with the early 1970's. He covers the brief film career of Mexican rebel Pancho Villa, the negative images of Mexicans and other Latin Americans in early silent films, biographical sketches of major stars Ramon Novarro and Dolores del Rio, the more positive image of Latin America in Hollywood films of the 1930's and 1940's, and the enduring impacts of films such as *Juárez* (1939), *Viva Zapata!* (1952), and *Salt of the Earth* (1954).

Protestantism in Latin America

Baldwin, Deborah J. *Protestants and the Mexican Revolution: Missionaries, Ministers, and Social Change.* Urbana: University of Illinois Press, 1990.

Mexico's tumultuous decade of violent revolution (1910-1920) disrupted community life and national politics, but it also provided Protestant missionaries with numerous opportunities to acquire influence and converts. Baldwin's book is based on careful research in Mexican and U.S. archives and a perceptive understanding of the role of religious movements in times of crisis. She discusses the early struggles of Protestant missionaries from the middle of the nineteenth century to the outbreak of the revolution. Although Protestants constituted a very small proportion—probably less than 1%—of the Mexican population, they played important roles in the revolution. Protestant missionaries gave much of their energy to the establishment of schools as a way to expand their influence in local communities. Many Mexicans who attended these schools became active participants in the revolution. Samuel Guy Inman, prominent in the missionary movement, was close to Venustiano Carranza, a revolutionary leader who (though not a convert to a Protestant church) relied on Protestant support. In 1914 and 1915, the surge of Mexican nationalism led many missionaries to pull back into the United States, but this shift was only temporary. In the last half of the decade, Protestant influence in the revolution assumed larger proportions. Inman and other Protestants often defended the revolution against its critics in the United States and actively opposed U.S. military interventions. Baldwin's study gives a readable portrait of the religious, ideological, and political impact of Protestant ministers and missionaries in a crucial decade in Mexican history.

Bastian, Jean-Pierre. "The Metamorphosis of Latin American Protestant Groups: A Sociohistorical Perspective." *Latin American Research Review* 28, no. 2 (1993): 33-61.
The rapid growth of evangelical Protestantism—especially in Brazil, Chile, and Guatemala—in the decades after 1960 has stimulated an outpouring of scholarly studies. Bastian's important essay incorporates the findings of Latin American, European, and U.S. writers on this subject in a perceptive analysis. He argues that the Protestant missionaries who arrived in the late nineteenth and early twentieth centuries brought with them the values and attitudes of Presbyterian, Methodist, and Baptist churches, which included religious freedom, public education, popular participation in politics, and social reform. Bastian contrasts this liberal Protestantism with the recent wave of evangelism (often Pentecostal), which is based on oral, often nonliterate, traditions and emphasizes messianic movements, charismatic leaders, and authoritarian community and political structures. In short, Bastian concludes that the "metamorphosis" of Protestantism had brought a return to the hierarchical system of Latin America's past (but clearly outside the Catholic church) and away from the open society advocated by the earlier Protestant missionaries.

Colby, Gerard, and Charlotte Dennett. *Thy Will Be Done: The Conquest of the Amazon: Nelson Rockefeller and Evangelism in the Age of Oil.* New York: HarperCollins, 1995.
This sweeping 830-page study reveals the many connections among religion, politics, and multinational corporate enterprise in the intrusion of U.S. power and culture into the homelands of the native

American peoples. To a large extent, this book contains parallel biographies of Nelson Rockefeller, the well-known grandson of John D. Rockefeller of Standard Oil and a national political figure in his own right, and William Cameron Townsend, the devoted linguist-evangelist who founded the Wycliffe Bible Translators, an organization committed to the translation of the Christian Bible into every language on the face of the earth. Rockefeller used his immense personal wealth and his political influence to acquire access to and, in some cases, control of petroleum and other resources in Central and South America, whereas Townsend used his exceptional energy and impressive skill as a linguist to reach the native American communities in the same areas. Colby and Dennett conducted extensive research in the papers of their two principal subjects in addition to interviews of dozens of individuals who worked with the organizations that Rockefeller and Townsend led. Rockefeller used his position as President Franklin D. Roosevelt's Coordinator of Inter-American Affairs during World War II to develop a grand vision of private enterprise as the driving force in the economic development of the Amazon and other isolated, resource-rich areas in Latin America. At about the same time, Townsend established his bases of operation in Mexico and Guatemala, which eventually became consolidated under the name of the Summer Institute of Linguistics. The authors trace the impact of the activities of these two influential individuals through the middle decades of the twentieth century. Their work extended throughout Latin America (especially the Amazon basin) and continued beyond their deaths (Rockefeller died in 1979 and Townsend in 1982) to bring, in the view of Colby and Dennett, disruption, despoliation, and death to the native Americans caught up in these twin sources of rapid socioeconomic change—evangelism and economic development. The authors condemn these aggressive actions as contributing to a type of holocaust for the inhabitants of previously isolated regions of the Americas. The conclusions and some of the information in this study will be controversial for many readers. Colby and Dennett provide sixty-five pages of footnotes to indicate their sources. For other perspectives on Townsend's work, see the book by James and Marti Hefley annotated in this section. The works by David Stoll (also mentioned in this section) tend to support the conclusions of Colby and Dennett.

Garrard Burnett, Virginia. "God and Revolution: Protestant Missions in Revolutionary Guatemala, 1944-1954." *The Americas* 46 (October, 1989): 205-233.

In this brief but thought-provoking article, Garrard Burnett summarizes the experiences of several groups of Protestant missionaries in Guatemala during a decade of government-directed revolutionary change. The missionaries, including Presbyterians and small contingents of Pentecostals, concentrated not only on conversions but also on schools and learning. The Guatemalan government, at the same time, began to expand its public school system. The author traces the shift from friendly cooperation between missionaries and public officials under the presidency of Juan José Arévalo (1945-1950) to the onset of rivalry and, in some cases, hostility during the administration of President Jacobo Arbenz Guzmán (1950-1954). This article reveals the ever changing, sometimes tense relationship between Protestant missionaries and governments that was typical of Guatemala and many Latin American nations.

Hefley, James, and Marti Hefley. *Uncle Cam: The Story of William Cameron Townsend, Founder of the Wycliffe Bible Translators and the Summer Institute of Linguistics.* Milford, MI: Mott Media, 1981.
William Cameron Townsend was one of the most influential U.S. missionaries to work in Latin America in the twentieth century. He began his endeavors among the Cakchiquel Indians of Guatemala in 1917 at the age of twenty-one. In 1934, he established the Summer Institute of Linguistics in Mexico for the training of linguists who would disperse throughout Latin America to study native American languages and translate the Bible into these languages. Townsend established a close relationship with Mexico's President Lázaro Cárdenas (1935-1940) and continued the practice of conferring with Latin American heads of state thereafter. By the 1960's, Townsend's organization extended throughout Latin America and had reached Africa and Asia. The authors' account of Townsend's life is highly sympathetic to their central subject. For criticisms of the Summer Institute of Linguistics, see the two books by David Stoll and the study by Gerard Colby and Charlotte Dennett that are discussed in this section.

Howard, George P. *Religious Liberty in Latin America?* Philadelphia, PA: Westminster Press, 1944.
Howard, an Argentine citizen who was the son of U.S. citizens living in that South American nation, uses this book to argue for an end to barriers against the expansion of the Protestant missionary effort in Latin America. The reader should be careful in consulting Howard's text, but the content is quite valuable in assessing the state of Protestantism in Latin America in the 1940's. Howard discusses the opposi-

tion of many Catholic leaders to the work of Protestant missionaries in the region and then develops his own critique of the Catholic church, which in his view failed to maintain the respect and loyalty of large numbers of Latin Americans. One of the most interesting aspects of this book is the author's use of several dozen interviews and published quotations from prominent citizens of many Latin American nations who favor the growth of Protestantism. Among those quoted are Peruvian politician and social critic Luis Alberto Sánchez, Chilean poet Gabriela Mistral, and Argentine anti-imperialist Alfredo Palacios. Howard selects quotations that support the case for Protestantism and, therefore, reinforce the central purpose of the book. For balance on this issue, the reader should consult the works by Gerard Colby and Charlotte Dennett, J. Lloyd Mecham, David Martin, and David Stoll discussed in this section.

Lee, John. *Religious Liberty in South America with Special Reference to Recent Legislation in Peru, Ecuador, and Bolivia.* Cincinnati, OH: Jennings and Graham, 1907.
The colonial legacy of three hundred years of Spanish rule in the Americas generally included a legal monopoly on religious activity for the Catholic church. As of the 1890's, existing laws in Peru, Ecuador, and Bolivia gave Protestant ministers no opportunities to perform marriages and other functions usually associated with the ministry. Lee's book discusses the origins of a movement in Chicago in 1894 to open these three nations to Protestant missionaries. Lee's text includes quotations from U.S. President William McKinley (1897-1901); his Secretary of State, John Hay (1898-1905); Pope Leo XIII (1878-1903); and many other leaders—both Catholic and Protestant—who favored legal rights for Protestantism in these countries. Lee's writing style tends to be calm, but the content of the text and its many quotations makes clear that the issue involved considerable controversy. The reader should also consult the works by J. Lloyd Mecham, David Martin, and David Stoll discussed in this section.

Mackay, John A. *The Other Spanish Christ: A Study in the Spiritual History of Spain and Spanish America.* New York: Macmillan, 1932.
Mackay, a Presbyterian missionary in Peru in the 1920's and a leading advocate for an aggressive Protestant campaign for converts in Latin America, wrote this provocative study as a part of that campaign. The author concentrates on Spanish South America, with numerous references to Argentina, Chile, and Peru. He presents quotations from leading intellectuals, such as social commentator Ricardo Rojas of

Argentina and poet Gabriela Mistral of Chile, who criticize several
aspects of Catholicism as practiced in South America. Mackay praises
the sixteenth century Dominican priest Bartolomé de las Casas as a
worthy proponent of a vigorous Christianity but laments the decline of
his influence in later years. The author advocates an extensive missionary campaign supported by Protestants in the United States as a
solution for the region's religious malaise as he perceives it. This book,
though stimulating and well written, is a document of the 1930's and
should be consulted along with more recent studies such as those by
Gerard Colby and Charlotte Dennett, J. Lloyd Mecham, David Martin,
and David Stoll discussed in this section.

Martin, David. *Tongues of Fire: The Explosion of Protestantism in Latin
America*. Boston: Basil Blackwell, 1990.
The erosion of Catholicism in Latin America beneath the recent flood
of Protestant (especially Pentecostal) expansion may constitute a major
turning point in the history of the Western Hemisphere. Martin's
wide-ranging historical survey places this phenomenon in a large
cultural context. He contrasts the origins of Latin American Catholicism in Spain and Portugal of the 1500's and 1600's with the origins
of British North American Protestantism in approximately the same
time period. Martin next examines the successes of Methodism, first
in North America of the 1700's and 1800's and then in its missionary
extensions in Latin America in the late nineteenth and early twentieth
centuries. He also includes the work of Presbyterians and Baptists, but
the center of his attention is the rapidly expanding Pentecostals. The
book contains discussions of several countries, including Brazil, Chile,
Argentina, El Salvador, Guatemala, and Mexico. Statistics on conversions vary greatly from country to country, but Martin indicates that
the number of Pentecostals has increased dramatically from a few
thousand in the nineteenth century to about forty million in the 1980's.
This study goes beyond statistics and narrative to a sociological explanation of how and why Protestantism has been able to make such
inroads in a region that for more than four centuries was, at least on
the surface, a stronghold of Catholicism. Martin's explanation is too
nuanced and sophisticated to be summarized here, but two significant
points stand out: The rapid growth of Protestantism is a part of the
spread of the cultural and economic values of the United States, and
this transformation is most extensive among working-class people who
have recently migrated from the countryside to the city.

Mecham, J. Lloyd. *Church and State in Latin America: A History of Politico-Ecclesiastical Relations.* 2d ed. Chapel Hill: University of North Carolina Press, 1966.

The often troubled relationship between Latin American governments and the Catholic church spawned political debates, civil strife, and revolution in the nineteenth and twentieth centuries. Mecham covers the Spanish and Portuguese colonial backgrounds in his first 87 pages. The remaining 340 pages are devoted to country-by-country surveys of church-government relations in the independent Latin American nations. Mecham gives little direct attention to Protestantism, but one of his main themes ties into explanations of how missionaries from the United States were able to acquire significant numbers of converts beginning in the 1960's. This theme centers on the decline of Catholicism's status as the only legally established church in many Latin American countries. Granted an official monopoly on religious practices by the colonial governments, the Latin American Catholic church lost this privileged position as the result of a variety of liberal and radical movements during the early and middle decades of the twentieth century. Mecham provides a calm and comprehensive discussion of this controversial process. During this time, Protestant missionary leaders such as George Howard, John Lee, and John Mackay began to call for a greater missionary effort in the region (see their books mentioned in this section).

Pike, Fredrick B. *The Politics of the Miraculous in Peru: Haya de la Torre and the Spiritualist Tradition.* Lincoln: University of Nebraska Press, 1986.

Víctor Raúl Haya de la Torre (1895-1979) was Peru's most dynamic political personality of the early twentieth century. From the 1920's to the 1960's, Haya and his political party, APRA (Popular Revolutionary Alliance of America), campaigned to win control of the Peruvian government in order to bring the lower and middle classes into the mainstream of that nation's history. Haya never attained the presidency, but his highly popular campaign methods stimulated the religious values and political awareness of the native Americans and their relatives of mixed Indian and European ancestry. An important part of Haya's appeal was his presentation of a Protestant approach to individual redemption that eventually would result in a transformation of society in general and the correction of inequities in the political and economic structure of the nation. Pike carefully explains the intellectual influences on Haya, including Presbyterian missionary John Mackay, who employed the young Peruvian as an instructor in the missionary boys' school in Lima in 1920 (see Mackay's book discussed in this section). Haya did not convert to Protestantism, but his spiritualist approach and his insistence on social reform drew favorable responses from the Peruvian masses that were indicative of a weakness in the Catholic church's standing with the general population of that nation and an opening for a more intensive Protestant evangelism in later years. Pike's extensive footnotes provide valuable insights for additional study on this theme.

Stoll, David. *Fishers of Men or Founders of Empire? The Wycliffe Bible Translators in Latin America*. London: Zed Press, 1982.
The Wycliffe Bible Translators, a group of highly trained linguist-missionaries (also referred to as the representatives of the Summer Institute of Linguistics), carried out their chosen task of translating the Bible into the many native American languages of the Western Hemisphere from the 1930's to the last decades of the twentieth century. Their founder, William Cameron Townsend, was an influential figure known by presidents and cultural leaders from Washington, D.C., to Bogotá, Colombia, to Lima, Peru. Although Stoll gives attention to these achievements, much of his text discusses the wave of criticism that engulfed the Wycliffe Bible Translators in the 1970's. Many Latin American commentators argued that these translators brought with them the cultural values and ideologies of the modern industrial society of the United States, which had the potential to disrupt the native Americans' traditional ways of life. For a more positive assessment of Townsend's work, see his biography by James and Marti Hefley discussed in this section.

_____. *Is Latin American Turning Protestant? The Politics of Evangelical Growth*. Berkeley: University of California Press, 1990.
Stoll's study is a stimulating retrospective on the impact of religious and political change on international relations in the 1980's. That decade saw a loud and lengthy debate on the rise of the Sandinista government of Nicaragua to a position of prominence in the Western Hemisphere and on the methods employed by the administration of President Ronald Reagan (1981-1989) to undermine that leftist government. Stoll connects this classic Cold War struggle to the less publicized growth of evangelical Protestantism in Central America and throughout much of Latin America. He discusses the conservative fundamentalist outlook of most evangelical leaders and the influence in Central America of U.S. television evangelists such as Pat Robertson, Jimmy Swaggart, and Jerry Falwell. He emphasizes the regime of

born-again Protestant President Efraín Ríos Montt of Guatemala (1982-1983), who used a rigidly repressive policy against the leftist guerrilla movement in his own country. Stoll's challenging analysis also considers the potential for the evangelical movement to become a vehicle for the expression of the grievances of the lower classes against governments and corporations: in other words, a shift from the right to the left along the ideological spectrum. This book has a useful bibliography for students seeking additional sources in English.

Willems, Emilio. *Followers of the New Faith: Culture Change and the Rise of Protestantism in Brazil and Chile*. Nashville, TN: Vanderbilt University Press, 1967.
As Protestant churches began to win significant numbers of converts in Latin America in the 1960's, social scientists began to examine why this process was taking place in a region known for its tradition of Catholicism. Willems, an anthropologist with a special interest in cultural change, carried out extensive fieldwork in Brazil and Chile to determine what led to the growth of U.S.-based Protestant groups: Baptists, Methodists, Presbyterians, and Pentecostals. Willems presents an analysis of his fieldwork integrated with the findings of other social scientists. The author concludes that extensive cultural and social change may create a situation in which many Catholics convert to one of the Protestant churches. Such changes include migration from relatively isolated rural areas where wealthy landowners and the Catholic church tend to dominate local communities to a large city where an urban industrial environment contains more opportunities for individual choice and less hierarchical structure. Furthermore, Willems finds that whereas Baptists, Methodists, and Presbyterians have experienced some growth, Pentecostals are the most rapidly expanding movement because of their appeal to the lower classes.

The Environment in International Perspective

Anderson, Anthony B., Peter H. May, and Michael J. Balick. *The Subsidy from Nature: Palm Forests, Peasantry, and Development on an Amazon Frontier*. New York: Columbia University Press, 1991.
The main purpose of this nicely written, well-illustrated book is to point out an economically viable alternative to the rapid deforestation of the Amazon region and the imposition of cattle ranching as the main land use pattern. The authors provide a thorough examination of the ecological setting, biological development, and economic functions of

the babassu, a tree-sized palm that thrives in the Amazon. This book includes analyses from the disciplines of biology, anthropology, geography, and economics to present a full picture of the potential of the versatile babassu. For the local market, this palm provides charcoal, edible oils, and construction materials for baskets and structures. The authors also discuss the processing and sale of babassu extracts for use as a vegetable oil and in soaps and cosmetics in the national Brazilian consumer market. A key point is that the babassu is a naturally occurring plant that flourishes in the Amazon when spared the devastation of massive forest clearing. This book includes several useful charts and maps and a useful list of references for further study.

Balée, William. *Footprints in the Forest: Ka'apor Ethnobotany—The Historical Ecology of Plant Utilization by an Amazonian People*. New York: Columbia University Press, 1990.

This highly specialized study deals with the intricate, harmonious way of life of a small group of native Americans who face the threats of deforestation and advancing commercial agriculture. Balée focuses on the Ka'apor of the eastern Amazon basin. The disciplines of anthropology, biology, linguistics, and history intersect in this examination of the Ka'apor and their use of native plants as crucial sources of food and shelter. The Ka'apor are semisedentary, in that they migrate within a limited geographical area to gather such food sources as manioc, various nuts, bananas, and other tropical edibles (Balée identifies more than 170 different plant food sources) in addition to fish and wild game. Balée also examines the Ka'apor language and mythology as they reflect these people's concern for the plant life around them. He also gives a brief discussion of the arrival of the Brazilian national government and commercial agriculture in the Ka'apor region after 1928, on pages 42-48. This text also contains several appendices with extensive botanical and linguistic information.

Cleary, David. *Anatomy of the Amazon Gold Rush*. Iowa City: University of Iowa Press, 1990.

The Amazon basin witnessed one of the world's greatest gold rushes in the 1980's. On closer examination, as Cleary reveals, there were several gold rushes in at least eight different locations, from the state of Maranhão on the Atlantic to Mato Grosso in the interior to the Venezuelan border in the north. Cleary concentrates on two of the major fields: Gurupí in Maranhão and Serra Pelada in the neighboring state of Pará. His emphasis is on the *garimpeiros*, the independent Brazilian miners who form a type of gold field community in order to organize the digging and processing of the ore while holding arguments and violence to a minimum. Cleary indicates the importance of the Brazilian gold strikes of the 1980's by pointing out that the annual production of gold reached ninety tons (perhaps more), placing the Amazon gold rush ahead of the fabled California gold rush of 1848-1856 and the Klondike rush of 1896-1900. Only the South Africa gold rush of the 1880's exceeded the tonnage produced in Brazil. The environmental consequences of this event for the Amazon are significant. The huge number of *garimpeiros*—estimated to be between 150,000 and 200,000—implies great pressure on the region's often fragile ecology. Through numerous interviews, first-person observations, and extensive research, Cleary provides an in-depth study of the social structure and economic practices of the *garimpeiros*. He also includes incisive chapters on the role of Serra Pelada as a national political issue as well as the environmental repercussions of these massive undertakings, including the residue of poisonous mercury (used to separate gold from impurities in the ore) in the animal and plant life of the region.

Crosby, Alfred W. *Ecological Imperialism: The Biological Expansion of Europe, 900-1900.* Cambridge, England: Cambridge University Press, 1986.

This study combines history and biology in a unique and stimulating fashion to explain the impact of European expansion on plant and animal life around the world, primarily from the 1490's to 1900. Crosby defines his terms with care and specificity. He uses the expression "Neo-European" to refer to those colonies in which the European part of the population became dominant: Canada, the United States, lower South America (southern Brazil, Uruguay, and Argentina), Australia, and New Zealand. He explores the results of European arrival in these areas in three main categories of effects on plant and animal life. He calls one the introduction of "weeds," by which he means plants that spread rapidly when introduced into a new area (white clover and wild artichoke are examples). The second category includes introduction of animals such as pigs (an often underrated element in colonial diets) and the more highly celebrated types such as cattle and horses. A third category involves the germs of infectious diseases, such as smallpox, that devastated large segments of the native populations. Of all the components in the European biological expansion, in Crosby's carefully considered judgment, human beings were the most harmful to the environments that they entered because of their efficient use of weapons and their wholesale introduction of technologies that ushered in rapid change. Europeans, however, also created highly productive farms and ranches that produced large food surpluses for export back to Europe and to other parts of the world. Crosby's footnotes identify several valuable sources for in-depth research, most of which are in English.

Davis, Shelton. *Victims of the Miracle: Development and the Indians of Brazil.* Cambridge, England: Cambridge University Press, 1977.
Davis directs the reader's attention to the rush for economic development in Brazil's vast Amazon basin and the tragic consequences for the native Americans who inhabit the region. They are the "victims" of a "miracle" in an ironic sense. The "miracle," in the author's view, is actually a disaster for the Indians who had to abandon their villages and their ways of life in response to the construction of modern highways, the expansion of the cattle industry, and intermittent inundations of gold seekers. Davis identifies several culprits in this process, including Brazil's military government from 1964 to the mid-1970's (the military government remained in power until 1985) and multinational corporations. He discusses two types of corporations, based mainly in the United States: enterprises involved directly in timber, cattle, and other Amazon undertakings, and the international lending institutions that make loans to support such enterprises. He also criticizes the Brazilian National Indian Federation for its promotion of rapid development without plans to help the native Americans. In his unequivocal criticisms of these institutions, Davis introduces a wide array of factual descriptions and statistics to support his argument. Readers who may disagree with his conclusions nevertheless can find much valuable material in this study.

De Onís, Juan. *The Green Cathedral: Sustainable Development of Amazonia.* New York: Oxford University Press, 1992.
The polemical controversies spawned by the economic development of the Amazon in the 1970's and 1980's dominated most of the books and articles about this region. De Onís, a veteran journalist who covered Latin America for *The New York Times*, attempts to place some of these controversies in a broader perspective. His central purpose is to find a set of government policies and private sector practices that would bring about "sustainable development," or a balance between economic growth and environmental protection. He points out several of the problems that plague the Amazon region, including excessive violence and a general lack of social and political stability because of frequent migrations. De Onís also notes the absence of a generally

accepted formula for land use in the Brazilian Amazon as well as the portions of the basin in the bordering countries of Bolivia, Peru, Ecuador, Colombia, and Venezuela. In spite of these problems, the resource base continues to draw corporations and individuals to the area. He gives considerable attention to the timber industry, the great potential for mining of minerals such as iron and manganese as well as gold, and energy sources such as petroleum, biomass, and hydro-electricity. The author refrains from giving a specific formula for economic development, but his effort to find a balance between environmental principles and material gain is an interesting approach.

Margolis, Mac. *The Last New World: The Conquest of the Amazon Frontier.* New York: Norton, 1992.
The Amazon basin contains a variety of frontiers that promise economic opportunities for a wide range of ambitious, imaginative, and, in many cases, greedy people. Margolis uses a low-keyed, entertaining writing style to survey these frontiers and the people affected by these enterprises. Prominent among those whom he praises is Cândido Mariano da Silva Rondon, the early twentieth century Brazilian explorer who became a defender of the native Americans whose ways of life were (and are) threatened by economic development. Margolis concentrates on the 1980's, when three major groups faced off in a conflict: private corporations and individuals who favor rapid development, ecologists who protest against this approach, and the Brazilian government, caught between these two groups and also caught up in the transition from military to civilian leadership. Margolis provides a convenient survey of the enterprises involved in the economic growth of the region: iron mining, lumber, gold mining, cattle ranching, and government construction projects such as roads, bridges, and dams. The author has a succinct chapter on the internationally known Brazilian rubber tapper, Chico Mendes, who stood up to the cattle industry and in 1988 fell victim to assassination—an act that added fuel to the fiery confrontations about the Amazon and its future. This book also discusses how the natives of the rain forest and peasant settlers, previously pawns in the power struggle, began to speak out in their own defense.

Place, Susan E., ed. *Tropical Rainforests: Latin American Nature and Society in Transition.* Wilmington, DE: Scholarly Resources, 1993.
This exceptionally useful book of readings includes thirty carefully selected articles and portions of books that offer the reader an interesting cross section of perspectives on the processes of deforestation, the

justifications for rain forest preservation, and alternatives for the development of tropical resources within an ecologically responsible framework. Although the focus is on Brazil's Amazon region, these readings also cover Central America, Colombia, Peru, and ecological dynamics in general. Place's brief introduction gives a coherent overview of the larger issues. Several of these selections include footnotes (or references) that give the reader some guidance for additional sources, and Place's annotated bibliography is an excellent place to begin a search for more published work.

Schmink, Marianne, and Charles H. Wood. *Contested Frontiers in Amazonia*. New York: Columbia University Press, 1992.
This tightly focused book has implications for many of the larger issues surrounding the environment and economic development. Schmink and Wood concentrate on the southeastern portion of the Brazilian state of Pará, which is located in the eastern part of the Amazon basin. The organizational framework is based on a series of frontiers where outsiders begin to exploit certain resources. The native population responds to these intrusions with protests and other forms of resistance. The authors examine this process of challenge and response over the years from 1976 to 1991. During the first part of this period, the military government of Brazil usually encouraged large-scale development such as cattle ranching and mining. Many of these enterprises encountered peasant farmers organized to express their opposition to local, state, and national government officials. Another of these conflicts involved the mining of Serra Pelada, where, after a long struggle, the small independent miners won access to rich gold deposits over larger corporate interests (see the book by David Cleary discussed in this section for more details on Serra Pelada). By the end of the 1980's, the policy of encouraging large-scale development in Pará and throughout the Amazon region came into question. The authors include a useful bibliography that covers not only Pará but also frontier and ecological studies in general.

Shoumatoff, Alex. *The World Is Burning: Murder in the Rain Forest*. Boston: Little, Brown, 1990.
The murder of Chico Mendes in December, 1988, set off reverberations in the environmental movement, government offices, and corporate boardrooms from Brazil to the United States and around the world. Shoumatoff explores the causes and consequences of Mendes' death in this book, which relies heavily on the author's interviews. Shoumatoff also readily admits that many of his conclusions are based on

carefully considered conjecture in the absence of hard evidence. Mendes, the son of immigrants who moved from Brazil's drought-prone northeast to the western state of Acre in the Amazon basin, rose from the lowly status of peasant to international symbol of the environmental movement. Mendes was a rubber tapper, whose job was to cut into the bark of the Amazon's scattered rubber trees to drain the latex, which he sold for a small profit. He and several thousand other rubber tappers maintained a modest existence in the rain forest until the rain forest began to be cleared to make way for cattle ranches, highways, and other intrusive enterprises. Mendes organized protests against the arrival of these outside businesses. Shoumatoff places the rubber tappers in their ecological, political, and economic contexts as he explains the circumstances surrounding the Mendes murder. This book does not contain the definitive account of these events, but it does capture the complex interplay of idealism, poverty, greed, violence, and mystery that characterized the Amazon region in the 1980's.

Stone, Roger D. *Dreams of Amazonia*. New York: Viking, 1985.

The author, a veteran journalist with many years of experience in Brazil, provides a very readable, nontechnical discussion of the ecological evolution of the Amazon basin. Stone begins with an account of his trip up the Rio Negro in the northwest Amazon region in 1983. Next, he presents a conventional survey of early European explorations of the river and its tributaries, including the expeditions of French scientist Charles-Marie de la Condamine in 1744 and British naturalist Alfred Russel Wallace in 1852. Stone's main concern is what he calls the "development impulse" of the twentieth century, which includes Henry Ford's futile effort in rubber production along the Tapajós River in the 1920's. Four of the book's nine chapters discuss the more recent drive for development and the resulting ecological crisis. These chapters feature an overview of several studies of the endangered balance of flora and fauna, a balance heavily affected by gold mining, cattle ranching, and the Brazilian government's highway construction project. The bibliography lists several relevant publications in English.

Wallace, David Rains. *The Quetzal and the Macaw: The Story of the Costa Rican National Parks*. San Francisco, CA: Sierra Club, 1992.

The main environmental battleground of the late twentieth century is the Amazon region, but advocates of rain forest preservation have achieved some of their greatest victories in Costa Rica. Wallace, an experienced writer for the Sierra Club, gives the reader an informal portrait of how naturalists influenced and cooperated with the Costa

Rican government in the 1960's and 1970's to establish a series of national parks that preserve rain forests and other areas rich in animal and plant life. The parks are located on both the Caribbean and Pacific coasts as well as in the interior. The largest, La Amistad, is on the border with Panama, and the Cabo Blanco Absolute Biological Reserve is on the southern tip of the Guanacaste Peninsula. The title of this book contains references to birds that dwell in many of these protected areas: the green and scarlet Quetzals and the colorful, squawking Macaws. Wallace is enthusiastic about Costa Rica's national parks, particularly their emphasis on biological concerns and nature preservation over recreational tourism. He sees the Costa Rican approach as a model for other countries seeking to cope with the challenges of rapid economic development.

The International Drug Trade

Duzán, María Jimena. *Death Beat: A Colombian Journalist's Life Inside the Cocaine Wars.* New York: HarperCollins, 1994.
The front line in the war between drug smugglers and law enforcement during the 1980's and early 1990's was in Colombia. Duzán's account is not only a narrative of crime, disorder, and the Colombian government's attempts to deal with perpetual crisis in that violence-torn nation's recent past; it is also a first-person testimony of a reporter who used her pen as a weapon against the drug lords. Duzán was a reporter for Colombia's *El Espectador*, a long-established newspaper that faced threats from the cocaine mafia because of its aggressive coverage. The drug barons bombed Duzán's home in 1982 and blew up *El Espectador*'s office building in 1989. Duzán's sister Sylvia also was an investigative journalist, specializing in documentary films. She fell victim to assassination by the drug barons in 1990. Duzán weaves her own personal traumas into the larger fabric of the complex struggles involving the press, honest Colombian leaders such as President Virgilio Barco (1986-1990) and head of internal security Miguel Maza, and the notorious Medellín cocaine organization led by Pablo Escobar and Jose Gonzalo Rodríguez Gacha. She also documents the peasant production of coca paste in the Colombian village of El Raudal and the cruel urban environment that produces *sicarios*, the teenage assassins hired by the cocaine mafia to eliminate its enemies. Much of her information is based on interviews with Colombians caught up in this conflict. She lists forty-six informants, but many of her sources are not

listed in order to protect their personal safety. The translation by Peter Eisner conveys the low-keyed, determined journalism of the author.

Eddy, Paul, Hugo Sabogal, and Sara Walden. *The Cocaine Wars*. New York: Norton, 1988.

Researched and written at the time that the flow of smuggled cocaine reached a huge volume in southern Florida, this book is a fast-moving journalistic account of U.S. law enforcement's efforts to come to grips with the international criminal empires that prospered on this trade. The trio of authors interviewed key figures in law enforcement, such as Lewis Fernández and Preston Lucas of the Miami police force; Luis García (also known as "Kojak"), a drug dealer turned informant; and U.S. Senate investigator Jack Blum. They also incorporate biographical sketches of some of the leading members of the Colombian drug smuggling operations, notably Jorge Ochoa and Carlos Lehder. Their judgments on law enforcement efforts at the local level in Miami and Dade County and at the national level on the "task force" approach of the administration of President Ronald Reagan are sympathetic but also frequently critical. The reader can benefit from the twenty-six-page section titled "Notes and Sources," which gives the names of people interviewed and some citations of printed sources.

Ehrenfeld, Rachel. *Narco-terrorism*. New York: Basic Books, 1990.

This provocative and controversial book attempts to show a widespread connection between Marxist governments and revolutionary movements, on one hand, and the international drug trade, on the other. According to Ehrenfeld, terrorists following Marxist-Leninist strategy engage in the drug trade to generate revenue to support their violent actions against non-Communist governments and, at the same time, to boost the spread of drug addiction within capitalist countries as another device to weaken their social and moral fabric. Most of this book deals with Latin America. Colombia is the center of attention in the chapter titled "The Superstate of Narco-terrorism." Ehrenfeld also discusses the practices of the Castro government in Cuba and of the Sandinistas in Nicaragua, as well as the spread of coca cultivation and its implications for Peru and Bolivia. Critics argue that the importance of Marxist-Leninist strategy is overstated in this analysis, but the author provides important information and an interesting argument.

Gagliano, Joseph A. *Coca Prohibition in Peru: The Historical Debate*. Tucson: University of Arizona Press, 1994.

In the furor stirred by the rapid spread of cocaine addiction in the United States in the 1970's and 1980's, many observers adopted the false assumption that this problem was unique to the last decades of the twentieth century. In contrast to that view, Gagliano's careful, thoughtful research shows that the use of the coca leaf triggered debates in the Spanish Empire as early as the sixteenth century. Peruvian Indians chewed the leaf even before the arrival of the Spanish in the 1530's. The continuation of this practice by natives involved in heavy labor in mining and agriculture caused some church and government officials to condemn coca consumption as harmful, often because of the non-Catholic religious practices associated with it. Other officials replied that the coca leaf helped the natives to endure the hunger and hardships associated with their work. Those who favored prohibition of use of the leaf lost this debate. In the late 1800's, the debate resumed, based on the accumulation of medical evidence that grew out of the use of cocaine (or refined coca) in Europe and the United States. A United Nations study in 1949 called on the Peruvian government to attempt to end coca production and use, and Peru soon moved in that direction. These efforts were not successful, however, and by the 1980's, production had increased sharply in Peru as a result of the growth of international demand and the rise of the Colombian drug organizations. Gagliano's book provides a much-needed historical perspective on Peru's experience with the coca leaf.

Gugliotta, Guy, and Jeff Leen. *Kings of Cocaine: Inside the Medellín Cartel—An Astonishing Story of Murder, Money, and International Corruption.* New York: Simon and Schuster, 1989.

Gugliotta and Leen trace the rise of the cocaine smugglers based in and near Medellín, Colombia, from their early years as petty criminals to the late 1980's, when their operations had become multibillion-dollar enterprises. The authors' approach tends to be biographical, with portraits of Medellín "cartel" leaders Carlos Lehder, Jorge Ochoa, and Pablo Escobar, and the struggle of Colombian President Belisario Betancur (1982-1986) to cope with their expanding wealth and power and their violent methods. The authors also discuss the role of U.S. Drug Enforcement Agency informant Barry Seal, who provided valuable information concerning the activities of the smugglers, and the work of Jaime Ramírez, the chief of Colombian law enforcement's antinarcotics unit who directed the 1984 raid on Tranquilandia, a huge cocaine processing plant. The text also includes an account of the trial and conviction of Lehder in U.S. federal court in Tampa, Florida.

Lee, Rensselaer W. *The White Labyrinth: Cocaine and Political Power.* New Brunswick, NJ: Transaction Books, 1991.

Lee gives the reader a broad synthesis of the cocaine business, from the peasant coca cultivators in the Andean nations of Peru and Bolivia through the powerful, violent dealers of Colombia. He documents the political influence of producers and dealers in their local communities and on their national governments. He also explores the remarkably large financial profits in the cocaine trade, which grew to billions of dollars in the 1980's. The connection between narcotics traffickers and leftist guerrilla movements in strife-torn Colombia forms an important element in this study. The chapter titled "The Enforcement Picture" gives a clear-cut assessment of the problems concerning international efforts to combat the large and well-equipped drug smuggling operations. Lee makes a cautionary evaluation of the possibilities for direct military participation in such actions. His final chapter has sensible judgments about U.S. policy options, from eradication of coca cultivation to legalization of cocaine use.

McClintick, David. *Swordfish: A True Story of Ambition, Savagery, and Betrayal.* New York: Pantheon, 1993.

The U.S. government's efforts to stem the flow of illegal drugs took an unusual and dramatic turn in the 1980's in the form of "Operation Swordfish," a joint venture of the Drug Enforcement Agency and the Department of Justice. Journalist McClintick concentrates on personalities and policy issues in this detailed examination of the undercover work that ultimately penetrated the secretive world of banks and corporations that handled the illicit profits of Colombian drug baron Carlos Jader Alvarez. The two main characters in McClintick's volume are Swordfish's infiltration agent, Robert Darius, a Cuban-born, CIA-trained veteran of the ill-fated Bay of Pigs invasion of 1961; and the Jader Alvarez organization's Marlene Navarro, a Colombian-born linguist and money manager who directed the flow of drug profits out of the United States. Darius' risky work resulted in Navarro's arrest and conviction, but some U.S. officials believe that this type of undercover approach has little if any impact on the actual flow of cocaine and other harmful drugs into the United States. McClintick, however, concludes that this operation was a major blow against the Jader Alvarez-Navarro group and indicates a promising direction for the war against drug smuggling. McClintick uses interviews and court records for much of his information, as indicated in the book's extensive footnotes.

MacDonald, Scott. *Dancing on a Volcano: The Latin American Drug Trade*. New York: Praeger, 1988.

This book contains a convenient country-by-country survey of the international drug trade. In addition to a lengthy chapter on Colombia, MacDonald includes a succinct summary of the historical background of cocaine use and then provides coverage of Bolivia and Peru, Mexico, Jamaica, Belize, and what the author terms the "transit states" of the Bahamas, Panama, and the Turks and Caicos Islands. There is also a chapter that delves into the roles of the leftist governments of Cuba and Nicaragua in the drug trade. The last chapter is a well-organized examination of a variety of policies that were debated in the 1980's. The author covers both economic and political factors, along with a focus on biography and law enforcement that is typical of most writing on this subject. MacDonald's text is thoroughly footnoted, giving the reader an informative listing of additional books as well as citations for newspaper and newsmagazine articles.

McWilliams, John C. *The Protectors: Harry J. Anslinger and the Federal Bureau of Narcotics, 1930-1962*. Newark: University of Delaware Press, 1990.

This well-written biography traces Anslinger's career from detective for the Pennsylvania Railroad to head of the U.S. government's Federal Bureau of Narcotics. McWilliams' thorough research in Anslinger's papers and his reading of contemporary documents and other published sources establishes a firm factual basis for this study of a man whose public image was determined largely in the 1930's by his high-profile, alarmist campaign against the alleged evils of marijuana. McWilliams concedes that Anslinger exaggerated the threat of marijuana to the U.S. public, but the author also points out Anslinger's more responsible work, for example, his investigation of the "Mafia" at a time when J. Edgar Hoover of the Federal Bureau of Investigation refused to take such initiatives. Anslinger was also a capable administrator who understood the nuances of bureaucratic politics in Washington. His determination to enforce and to expand antinarcotics laws was an important factor in the U.S. pattern of responses to the drug trade, as discussed in the studies by William O. Walker and David Musto mentioned in this section.

Mermelstein, Max. *The Man Who Made It Snow*. New York: Simon and Schuster, 1990.

Brooklyn is more than two thousand miles from Medellín, Colombia, but Mermelstein made the lengthy transit from his home city to the center of the international drug trade by becoming a key operative in the organization controlled by the Ochoa family and Pablo Escobar. From 1981 to 1985, he was responsible for guiding the drug smugglers' airplanes and boats into Florida and dispersing their cocaine cargos among dealers in the United States. Mermelstein claims that he arranged for the shipment of fifty-six tons of cocaine into the United States, earning more than $300 million for the Colombian organization. After his arrest and indictment, Mermelstein became an informant on drug smuggling for U.S. law enforcement and entered the government's witness protection program. Interviewers/writers Robin Moore and Richard Smitten present his story in a well-organized text that explores this insider's point of view on the workings of the Medellín cocaine smuggling operations. Mermelstein earned the confidence of the powerful leaders of the drug mafia and visited the Ochoa family estate in Colombia. He also knew pilots, "shooters" (hit men), money launderers, and drug dealers at the lower levels of the smuggling business. This book can be placed in a broader perspective by consulting the studies of Rensselaer W. Lee and Scott MacDonald discussed in this section. It also offers interesting contrasts to the books by Paul Eddy, Hugo Sabogal, and Sara Walden and by Guy Gugliotta and Jeff Leen on the antidrug campaign of the 1980's because of the point of view of Mermelstein from within the operations of the Colombian drug organization.

Musto, David F. *The American Disease: Origins of Narcotics Control.* 2d ed. New Haven, CT: Yale University Press, 1988.

This highly respected study concentrates on government efforts in the United States to control the distribution and use of narcotic substances—mainly opium, cocaine, and marijuana—from the 1890's through the 1930's. The Harrison Act of 1914 is the focal point of Musto's examination of law enforcement because it provided the legal basis for the closing of the narcotics clinics that had, in the early years of the twentieth century, treated drug addicts through maintenance programs supervised by physicians. Musto also discusses the international aspects of the drug trade. He connects the waves of legitimate concern and exaggerated fear that swept through the U.S. public and had large impacts on politicians and policymakers from 1919 to the late 1930's. In particular, he notes the tendency to blame the spread of narcotics use on foreigners, such as the association of marijuana with Mexican immigrants. Chapter 9, on the Federal Bureau of Narcotics, is especially informative. The 1988 edition of this book has a new chapter on the 1980's that updates the original 1973 edition. Musto's footnotes contain important explanatory material in addition to numerous citations of earlier studies in medical science as well as politics and the law.

Nahas, Gabriel G. *Cocaine: The Great White Plague*. Middlebury, VT: Paul S. Erikson, 1989.

Nahas, a medical doctor, gives much of his attention to the scientific questions surrounding cocaine use as well as political, social, and cultural issues. His writing style is informal and includes extended quotations from his conversations with figures in science (such as Timothy Leary) and government as well as his own expert testimony in court. Nahas explores the disagreement between pharmacologist Ludwig Lewin and psychoanalyst Sigmund Freud concerning the effects of cocaine use on the human body. He also gives a brief history of efforts to regulate cocaine use in the United States from the early 1900's to the 1980's. He condemns the permissive attitudes of the 1960's in the general public and in the scientific community. Chapters 18 to 23 describe his collaboration with French ecologists/oceanographers Jacques and Jean-Michel Cousteau in their investigation of cocaine production and use in Peru. Nahas is quite explicit in his conclusions, which call for the prohibition of the use and sale of cocaine and the eradication of its production. The footnotes include scientific references in addition to studies in politics, history, and sociology.

Painter, James. *Bolivia and Coca: A Study in Dependency*. Boulder, CO: Lynne Rienner, 1994.

Painter's work is of special value because of the three South American nations most active in the international drug trade, Bolivia is not as well studied as Colombia and Peru. The primary producing region in Bolivia is in the Chapare lowlands to the east of the capital city of La Paz. A lightly settled area before the cocaine boom, its population more than doubled in the 1970's and 1980's. The international cocaine boom came at the same time that the Bolivian economy was hit by drought, declining prices for tin, and a decline in much of its industry and commerce. Although it is difficult to measure accurately the income from coca leaf sales, Painter's research indicates that from 1960 to 1985, Bolivian farmers' returns from the sale of coca leaves increased at an annual rate of 11 percent, whereas the market value of the potato crop actually declined. Painter points out reliable estimates that approximately 180,000 Bolivians, or 10%, of the nation's workforce was employed in the coca leaf and cocaine business in 1990. U.S. government pressure on the Bolivian government to use military and law enforcement personnel against coca leaf and cocaine production placed the nation's leaders in a difficult situation because of the widespread importance of this crop in the economy, especially among peasant farmers. Painter's analysis indicates that alternative forms of economic development (to replace coca leaf production with coffee, bananas, and dairy farming) is a more promising policy than military or police interdiction. This book includes several helpful charts and graphs and extensive footnotes.

Shannon, Elaine. *Desperados: Latin Drug Lords, U.S. Lawmen, and the War America Can't Win.* New York: Penguin, 1989.
Although most of the press and public attention on cocaine smuggling during the 1980's concentrated on Florida, Shannon emphasizes the flow of illegal drugs through Mexico. She examines in depth the circumstances surrounding the 1985 murder of U.S. Drug Enforcement Agency investigator Enrique Camarena near Guadalajara, Mexico. Much of the text concerns what Shannon calls the "Guadalajara cartel," a loose grouping of narcotics dealers who used this Mexican city as their base of operations. One of the central figures in this group was Rafael Caro Quintero, who amassed a fortune from selling marijuana before his 1988 conviction. The author also discusses Colombian cocaine dealers and the penetration of cocaine traffic into Mexico in the 1980's. She is critical of the policies of Ronald Reagan's administration (1981-1989) and uncovers several implications of corruption in the middle and upper echelons of the Mexican government, particularly in the Camarena murder. Thirty-two pages of footnotes at the end of the text provide the reader with valuable newspaper citations.

Thornton, Mark. *The Economics of Prohibition.* Salt Lake City: University of Utah Press, 1991.
Central in the war on drugs are prohibitions of the sale and consumption of cocaine and marijuana. In this comparative study, economist Thornton examines the history of U.S. prohibition policies, including the effort in the 1920's to outlaw alcoholic beverages as well as the outlawing of cocaine, heroin, and marijuana over more extended time periods. The results of these policies, according to Thornton, are counterproductive. Prohibition makes social and medical problems associated with the use of these substances even worse because the enforcement of prohibition increases prices and makes smuggling more profitable. With greater income, those selling the prohibited products can afford to bribe corrupt officials and to spread the use of

the prohibited substance. Thornton's analysis is based on economics and is supported by extensive research, documented in footnotes. He devotes a large portion of his text to the cocaine issue and favors the replacement of prohibition by the free market (not a government distribution system). Many readers may find Thornton's analysis disturbing, but his points deserve a fair hearing.

Toro, María Celia. *Mexico's "War" on Drugs: Causes and Consequences.* Boulder, CO: Lynne Rienner, 1994.
This brief book (seventy-two pages) covers an important subject in considerable depth. Toro begins her historical section with the early years of the twentieth century, when the Mexican government agreed to assist the United States in trying to block the movement of illegal drugs (mainly marijuana) across the border. The flow of marijuana into the United States continued, however, in spite of the efforts to block it. This illegal traffic received sporadic public attention until the 1970's and 1980's, when the consumption of illicit drugs in the United States rose rapidly. Marijuana production in Mexico rose sharply, particularly among small farmers. Heroin production (introduced into Mexico in the 1910's and 1920's) also expanded rapidly in the 1970's. Mexico does not produce cocaine, but, according to Toro's analysis, Mexico became a major transit stop for Colombian producers on the way to the U.S. market. This increase in the movement of illegal drugs from Mexico to the United States and the murder of U.S. Drug Enforcement Agency investigator Enrique Camarena in Mexico in 1985 resulted in Washington's shift from bilateral cooperation to intrusive antismuggling operations that often took U.S. federal agents and laws across the border into Mexico. Toro emphasizes that these policies have had little success in decreasing drug consumption in the United States but have created serious strains in U.S.-Mexican relations. Toro's twenty-one pages of footnotes and bibliography contain many useful sources in English.

Tullis, LaMond. *Unintended Consequences: Illegal Drugs and Drug Policies in Nine Countries.* Boulder, CO: Lynne Rienner, 1995.
The expansion of the international drug trade in the 1980's and early 1990's produced extraordinary revenues for the underground empires that controlled it, with estimates running as high as $150 billion to $300 billion. The Colombian drug dealers, pioneers in this area, retained profits of $39 billion to $66 billion from 1975 to 1989. Tullis provides the reader with a much-needed synthesis on this important but often elusive topic. His survey includes Colombia, Peru, Bolivia, and Mex-

ico as well as the Asian nations of Pakistan, Thailand, Laos, and Burma, and the state of Kentucky in the United States. He examines the production, processing, distribution, and sale of cocaine, opium, heroin, and cannabis. Although illegal drug production fell in certain countries for certain periods, in general, the amount of drugs in the international market seems to be rising steadily as producers open new markets or adopt new products. For example, Colombia's Cali group opened new markets in Europe in the early 1990's, and Mexican dealers moved into opium production during the same time period. According to Tullis, the antidrug campaigns of the United States and other world powers have not worked very well. He concludes that supply reduction strategies (the destruction of the crop in the field) do not have a lasting impact. Tullis emphasizes the unintended consequences of the struggle between law enforcement and the dealers: violence, corruption, social dislocation, and a growing contempt for authority. The author gives careful consideration to several strategies for reducing the harmful effects of the international drug trade. His thoughtful conclusions deserve careful reading. In general, he advocates a gradualist approach in which consuming countries (mainly the United States and the West European nations) reduce demand within their boundaries while the exporting countries move away from military/police suppression and try to find other sources of income for local producers of the illegal substances.

Walker, William O. *Drug Control in the Americas.* 2d ed. Albuquerque: University of New Mexico Press, 1989.

This excellent study of the United States' efforts to enforce its drug control policies in the Western Hemisphere from the early twentieth century to the 1980's is based on careful research and thoughtful analysis. The first edition of this book appeared in 1981, at a time when few people were concerned with the international drug trade. The second edition is augmented by the author's synthesis of studies on this subject that were published in the 1980's. The central theme throughout the text concerns the efforts of the United States to use diplomacy to establish a system of international controls on the drug traffic. Walker finds the origins of this effort in the U.S. Progressive movement from 1900 to 1917. The sudden concern about marijuana use in the United States in the 1930's led to pressure on Mexico and, in 1940, an agreement between the two countries to police this substance on both sides of the border. Thus, the United States established the pattern in its international efforts to control the movement of drugs that it continued to employ in later years. Walker's assessment of U.S. policies in the 1970's and 1980's identifies the continuation of this pattern of prohibition. The book has informative footnotes and a lengthy bibliography, with a "Bibliographical Update" in the new edition.

_____, ed. *Drugs in the Western Hemisphere: An Odyssey of Cultures in Conflict.* Wilmington, DE: Scholarly Resources, 1996.
The illegal traffic in drugs has inspired a large volume of academic and journalistic writing as well as numerous government reports. Walker, a pioneering specialist in the history of the international drug trade, has assembled an excellent collection of readings on this important topic. The selections include essays on the social origins and medical consequences of the use of cocaine, the early phases of cocaine and heroin smuggling in the 1920's and 1930's (including U.S. State Department reports from Mexico and Honduras), a 1947 speech by U.S. antidrug official Harry J. Anslinger on opium production in Mexico (see John C. McWilliams' biography of Anslinger annotated in this section), and several selections on the growth of illegal drug smuggling from the 1960's to the 1990's. This volume also includes several general articles by scholars such as Bruce Bagley, Richard Craig, and editor Walker that give the reader much-needed overviews of the relationships between the smugglers and law enforcement throughout the Americas. Each scholarly article is reprinted with its original footnotes, and Walker provides a useful annotated bibliography.

The North American Free Trade Agreement

Barry, Tom, Harry Browne, and Beth Sims. *The Great Divide: The Challenge of U.S.-Mexican Relations in the 1990's.* New York: Grove Press, 1994.
This broad survey of relations between the two countries concentrates on issues that came into prominence in the early 1990's. The section titled "The Economic Connection" devotes 112 pages to an extended discussion of the positive and negative aspects of NAFTA for both the United States and Mexico. Barry and his coauthors stress that President Carlos Salinas de Gortari (1988-1994) saw the free trade agreement as a means of attracting U.S. investment capital to Mexico in addition to expanding trade in manufactured and agricultural goods. The authors also cover other issues such as migration, the drug trade, environmental regulation in the border region, and diplomatic relations between the two governments. The extensive footnotes provide additional informa-

tion and list articles published in newspapers and magazines as well as books. Most citations are to works published in English.

Camp, Roderic. *Politics in Mexico*. New York: Oxford University Press, 1993.

Although NAFTA is based on international economics, it is also the product of government decision making in response to various political pressures. This book provides valuable background material on Mexican politics at the time that NAFTA emerged as an important issue. Camp's concise, clearly written text is a convenient synthesis of the history, culture, and values that make up Mexican politics as well as a penetrating analysis of the governmental system. He examines the nature of political leadership and the structure and function of influential groups in Mexico, including business organizations, labor unions, and outspoken dissenters. Chapter 7 provides a sharply focused analysis of the decision-making process in the Mexican government. Chapter 9 presents an evaluation of the early years of the administration of President Carlos Salinas de Gortari (1988-1994), one of the chief architects of NAFTA.

Castañeda, Jorge. *The Mexican Shock: Its Meaning for the U.S.* New York: The New Press, 1995.

The celebration of the creation of NAFTA soon ended in the abrupt collapse of the Mexican peso and large sectors of the Mexican economy in late 1994 and 1995. Mexican political scientist Castañeda provides one of the first comprehensive analyses of these traumatic events. His intent is to reach readers in the United States who were, he insists, sadly misinformed by overly optimistic reporting on the administration of President Carlos Salinas de Gortari (1988-1994) and his well-publicized campaign for NAFTA. Castañeda, an outspoken critic of this administration, points out that many Mexicans at various levels of society were skeptical about the impact of NAFTA on the nation. He argues that the basic causes of the economic disaster are in the interconnections of NAFTA, the Mexican political system, and the nation's traditional culture. A central problem is the persistent rejection of democratic practices by the nation's political elite, led by Salinas and the powerful Party of the Institutional Revolution or PRI. This avoidance of openness and accountability enabled the doomed Salinas Administration to cover its corruption and mistakes in judgment (such as the refusal to adjust the value of the peso to a realistic level in NAFTA's first year) until the collapse of the peso. Castañeda also gives the reader a critical look at the Salinas Administration's promotion of

NAFTA as a solution to the nation's problems; the violent, disruptive presidential election of 1994; the unrepresentative and, according to the author, deceptive victory of the PRI in that election; and the first few nightmarish months of President Ernesto Zedillo's tenure.

Hufbauer, Gary C., and Jeffrey J. Schott. *NAFTA: An Assessment*. Rev. ed. Washington, DC: Institute for International Economics, 1993.
This book is an explanation and evaluation of the North American Free Trade Agreement as signed by the United States, Mexico, and Canada in December, 1992. In this revised edition, the authors include discussions of the additional agreements reached by the three nations in 1993 on environmental standards, labor conditions, and the regulation of import surges (rapid increases in imports of specific products). The authors explain their views of the likely outcomes of NAFTA in the areas of automobile manufacturing, textiles, agriculture, financial services, transportation, and telecommunications. The section titled "An Evaluation of NAFTA" examines the larger impacts of the agreements on the economies of the three signatory nations. The original version, published in March, 1992, and the revised edition, released in February, 1993, are both typical of the optimistic views widely held by economists, political scientists, and politicians before the Mexican government's devaluation of the peso in December, 1994, and the economic crisis that followed.

Jenkins, Barbara. *The Paradox of Continental Production: National Investment Policies in North America*. Ithaca, NY: Cornell University Press, 1992.
The attraction of foreign investors to domestic industry has long been a concern in Mexico. The administration of President Carlos Salinas de Gortari (1988-1994) was energetic in its pursuit of foreign investment and its promotion of international trade before and during the negotiation of NAFTA. Jenkins' book (which appeared just as the agreement was signed in 1992) examines this approach in a broad framework. The word "paradox" in the title refers to the continued importance of national markets and domestic politics in spite of the "continental" agenda of NAFTA. Although she recognizes the importance of private-sector enterprises in international economics, Jenkins argues that governments will continue to play an important role in regulating the movement of investments across national boundaries in order to counteract the low points in business cycles and to balance large trends in private investment strategies. Jenkins draws attention to noneconomic factors, including the influence of domestic politics,

labor unions, and nationalism. The book considers the United States and Canada as well as Mexico and provides some useful comparisons of their respective policies toward foreign investments.

Langley, Lester. *Mexico and the United States: The Fragile Relationship.* Boston: Twayne, 1991.

Intended for the general public as well as the college classroom, this book offers a concise survey of the history of the relations between the two nations from the early 1800's to the late 1980's. Langley places diplomacy in a larger context that includes political, social, and economic history on both sides of the border. A central point in his analysis is the inevitable trend toward closer relations between the two countries. He gives special attention to economic development since World War II, the impact of Mexican immigration in the United States, Mexico's petroleum policy in the 1970's, that nation's financial and debt crises of the 1980's, and other sources of tension and cooperation in the relations between Washington and Mexico City. This text is an informative background study to NAFTA because of the author's discussion of the growth of economic and political connections between the two countries. These conclusions are supported by extensive footnotes that direct the reader to several important scholarly and journalistic studies published in English.

Lustig, Nora. *Mexico: The Remaking of an Economy.* Washington, DC: Brookings Institution, 1992.

At the time that this book appeared, optimism was on the rise in Mexico as a result of that nation's apparent recovery from the economic crisis of 1982. In addition, Mexico, the United States, and Canada were moving rapidly in the negotiation of NAFTA, which seemed to have the potential for stimulating further economic growth. Lustig's book conveys the sense of confidence typical of government officials, business leaders, and academics in all three countries that Mexico had made good use of the tools of deregulation (removing government controls on private corporations), careful budgeting of government resources, and the reduction of tariffs and other barriers to international trade. Lustig's account emphasizes the breadth and depth of improvement in the Mexican economy during this period. In several ways, this text captures the high point of optimism before Mexico's severe monetary and economic crisis of the mid-1990's.

Maxfield, Sylvia. *Governing Capital: International Finance and Mexican Politics.* Ithaca, NY: Cornell University Press, 1990.

Mexico's economic crisis of the early 1980's set the stage for President Carlos Salinas de Gortari's drive to establish NAFTA. Maxfield's careful study of the government's nationalization of Mexico's banks in 1982 gives important depth for understanding NAFTA. In particular, she traces the history of one of the most important private-sector financial groups, the bankers' alliance made up of the leaders of private-sector banks and industries that favored limited government regulation and laissez faire economics. The bankers' alliance was hostile to and distant from the radical programs of the administration of President Lázaro Cárdenas (1934-1940) but acquired considerable influence during subsequent administrations. Half of this book deals with the period from 1970 through the 1980's and concentrates on the internationalization of the Mexican economy and the importance of this process for the nation's banking institutions. Maxfield discusses the reaction of the bankers' alliance to the government's nationalization of Mexico's banks in 1982 and the means by which private bankers retained considerable control of the nation's financial resources even after this highly controversial decision. She is critical of the Mexican government in the 1980's because of its emphasis on monetary stability (stabilizing the exchange rate of the peso and the dollar) and its failures to use currency exchange controls and to restrict capital flight (the movement of financial assets outside Mexico). The last chapter consists of a revealing comparative analysis of Mexico, Argentina, Brazil, and Chile in their efforts to deal with the internationalization of financial institutions and policies after 1970.

Pastor, Robert A., and Jorge Castañeda. *Limits to Friendship: The United States and Mexico.* New York: Vintage, 1988.
The authors of this book collaborated in a unique format. They selected eight major issues in the relations between Mexico and the United States; each one analyzes these issues from his nation's point of view. Pastor took the U.S. perspective, and Castañeda presents the Mexican point of view. In terms of the developments leading to NAFTA, this book contains an extended discussions of what the authors term "sliding toward economic integration" on pages 195 to 241. Pastor explains the U.S.-Mexican "Framework Agreement" of 1987, under which the two countries began to accelerate the elimination of barriers to trade. Castañeda explores the Mexican ambivalence toward increased economic integration in the early and middle 1980's. Other topics in this volume include the foreign policies of the two governments, the problems along the border, and the issues surrounding Mexican immigration to the United States.

Ramírez, Miguel. *Mexico's Economic Crisis: Its Origins and Consequences.* New York: Praeger, 1989.

Although the economic crisis analyzed in this volume took place in the early 1980's, a decade before NAFTA, the root causes of this crisis continued to plague Mexico into the 1990's. Ramírez provides what many nonspecialists interested in economics and business seek but often cannot find—a brief, clearly written survey of the economic and historical forces that led to these problems. Ramírez begins with the economic surge during the dictatorship of Porfirio Díaz (1876-1910), the impact of the Mexican Revolution, and the nation's success with import substitution industrialization (1940-1970), in which local factories began to manufacture products such as steel that previously had been imported. Ramírez emphasizes that the crisis of the early 1980's began with the exhaustion of the possibility for continued growth in import substitution industrialization. In order to go beyond this form of industrialization, the Mexican economy relied increasingly on capital borrowed from foreign sources—especially the United States. At the same time, many wealthy Mexicans continued to place their savings in banks and stocks in the United States and Europe. These two problems, reliance or foreign capital and the "capital flight" of domestic wealth, indicate basic trends that continued to trouble the Mexican economy in the 1990's as in the 1980's.

Weintraub, Sidney. *A Marriage of Convenience: Relations Between Mexico and the United States.* New York: Oxford University Press, 1990.

Weintraub's assessment of the economic relations between these two countries is a clear, well-organized summary of the trends that led to the formation of the North American Free Trade Agreement (NAFTA). This book does not mention NAFTA explicitly because the author completed his writing before the negotiations began, but he does make a case that the movement toward Mexican-U.S. economic integration had achieved the status of inevitability by the late 1980's. The debt and financial crises of the 1980's forced Mexico's political leaders to make profound changes in their policies. Weintraub examines this troubled decade through chapters on trade and tariffs, shifts in patterns of industrialization, petroleum prices and productivity, the debt crisis, the border region, and migration from Mexico into the United States. The author advocates "managed integration" by which the governments of Mexico and the United States would attempt to maximize benefits for their respective peoples in the integration process. The author's twenty-six-page bibliography is a comprehensive listing of books and articles published in the 1970's and 1980's on this theme.

Chapter 5
NATIONS AND DIPLOMACY

Mexico

Andrews, Gregg. *Shoulder to Shoulder? The American Federation of Labor, the United States, and the Mexican Revolution, 1910-1924.* Berkeley: University of California Press, 1991.

Although diplomats, politicians, and business executives usually were the most active participants in U.S. foreign relations, labor union leaders also had a deep interest in the Mexican Revolution. Andrews presents an absorbing portrait of Samuel Gompers, who, as head of the American Federation of Labor (AFL), closely observed the rise to power of the Regional Confederation of Mexican Workers. Gompers used his influence to support this labor union and Alvaro Obregón, who was president of Mexico from 1921 to 1924. Gompers helped the Obregón Administration obtain favorable publicity in the U.S. press and arranged for a show of unity involving Mexican and U.S. workers at the AFL convention in El Paso, Texas, in 1924. In spite of this sense of common purpose, however, Gompers and the AFL used their influence to stifle the radicalism of the Mexican labor movement and to keep the Mexican economy under the domination of U.S. business interests. Andrews emphasizes that the impact of the AFL in Mexico was to direct the energy of the working class toward U.S.-style unionization within the framework of a free enterprise economy. According to Andrews, the AFL served to undercut some of the more radical aspects of the Mexican Revolution.

Britton, John A. *Ideology and Revolution: The Image of the Mexican Revolution in the United States.* Lexington: University Press of Kentucky, 1995.

The Mexican Revolution had a significant impact on journalists, academics, and other serious observers in the United States from its outbreak in 1910 through its constructive phase in the 1920's and 1930's. The author identifies several types of observers by ideological groupings—from anarchists, Communists, and socialists on the far left, to liberals in the center, to conservatives on the far right—and proceeds to explain their responses to the crucial phases of the revolution. The text emphasizes the widespread enthusiasm among many leftists and

146

liberals in the early 1920's and their disillusionment with the actions of Plutarco Elías Calles as president (1924-1928) and as a power behind the scenes (1928-1934). He also explores the wide range of responses to the Lázaro Cárdenas presidency (1934-1940), when conservatives believed that they saw a Communist beachhead in the Americas, liberals and many leftists praised the Mexican president, and a few sympathetic critics such as Columbia University historian Frank Tannenbaum detected signs of excessive governmental power. Britton argues that, during the Cold War, U.S. intellectuals and policymakers forgot or ignored this Mexican experience to concentrate on Communism and its offshoots as the basis for understanding revolution. The author includes the responses of several well-known writers, such as John Reed, Herbert Croly, Katherine Anne Porter, Stuart Chase, Ernest Gruening, Lesley Byrd Simpson, John Steinbeck, and Anita Brenner. The footnotes and bibliographical essay mention several publications in English by these and other writers.

Brown, Jonathan. *Oil and Revolution in Mexico*. Berkeley: University of California Press, 1993.

The discovery of Mexico's vast reserves of petroleum in the early part of the twentieth century coincided with the demise of the dictatorship of Porfirio Díaz and the outburst of political and social strife known as the revolution of 1910. The intensification of this revolution from 1910 to 1920 formed the environment in which foreign entrepreneurs—mainly Edward Doheny of the United States and Weetman Pearson of Great Britain—located the oil deposits, erected drilling equipment, and entered into the highly profitable and highly erratic business of pumping, refining, and selling petroleum on the international market. Brown presents this fascinating era in an exceptionally well-organized and clearly written study. His research in archives in Mexico, the United States, Great Britain, and The Netherlands gives impressive depth in the technical, diplomatic, and political aspects of a rare episode in business history: a large-scale international business boom that occurred in the midst of a violent social revolution. Brown gives particular attention to the exploits of rebel leader Manuel Peláez, who became famous (to many, infamous) for his raids in the oil zone along the Caribbean coast near Tampico. This book also contains a revealing discussion of working conditions for laborers in the oil fields, the early stages of labor unrest, and the formation of labor unions. Brown's text contains historical photographs, extensive footnotes, and a useful bibliography with many sources in English.

Cronon, E. David. *Josephus Daniels in Mexico*. Madison: University of
Wisconsin Press, 1960.

Daniels was U.S. ambassador to Mexico from 1933 to 1942, a period
in which relations between the two countries were strained close to the
point of rupture. A North Carolina newspaper editor and a longtime
member of the Democratic Party, Daniels arrived at his post in Mexico
City with a large mark against him—he had ordered the military
occupation of the port of Veracruz in 1914 while he was Secretary of
the Navy. As Cronon's well-written text makes clear, Daniels overcame
that initial disadvantage to become an effective ambassador who
earned the respect and trust of Mexican government officials as well
as the Mexican citizens. Daniels had to deal with a range of problems,
including the tense political transition from former president and
power broker Plutarco Elías Calles to the new and popular President
Lázaro Cárdenas, an international dispute concerning Mexico's plans
for socialist education, the expansion of land reform and its impact on
U.S. property owners, and, most difficult of all, President Cárdenas'
nationalization of foreign-owned petroleum lands. Cronon's careful
research and talent for good writing give this book an enduring value
in spite of the research and publication in this area since 1960.

Delpar, Helen. *The Enormous Vogue of Things Mexican: Cultural Relations Between the United States and Mexico, 1920-1935*. Tuscaloosa:
University of Alabama Press, 1992.

Given the dominance of the United States over Mexico in many areas
since the 1840's, many readers may be surprised by the main thesis of
this excellent study. Delpar documents the growing influence of Mexican culture in the United States during the decade and a half when
artists and writers from south of the border began to attract critical as
well as popular acclaim in the United States. Muralists Diego Rivera
and José Clemente Orozco led the way, with novelists, anthropologists,
and philosophers also attracting attention. In addition, Delpar examines the travels of U.S. novelists, poets, artists, art critics, social
scientists, and historians to Mexico, where they not only witnessed the
cultural effervescence in art and letters but also investigated the vitality
of native folklore, the nation's centuries-old history, and the innovations associated with revolutionary change. Among the leading commentators on Mexican affairs were Katherine Anne Porter, Frank
Tannenbaum, and Alma Reed. Delpar effectively brings together
higher culture and popular culture as expressed in motion pictures and
journalism. Researchers can find much helpful commentary on articles
and books written in the 1920's and early 1930's.

Eisenhower, John S. D. *Intervention! The United States and the Mexican Revolution, 1913-1917*. New York: Norton, 1993.
Military and naval actions were central features in U.S.-Mexican relations from 1913 to 1917. John Eisenhower, the son of U.S. President Dwight Eisenhower (1953-1961) and himself a retired Army general, presents a fast-moving account of these events that is intended for the general public as well as for college students. Drawing on previously published academic studies, Eisenhower covers in interesting detail the Veracruz intervention of 1914; rebel activity along the border, including Pancho Villa's raid on Columbus, New Mexico; the mobilization of U.S. forces in that area; and the 1916 punitive expedition led by General John J. Pershing into northern Mexico in search of Villa. The strengths of this text are in the author's readable explanations of the military maneuvers and engagements and his nicely focused biographical sketches of military and political leaders on both sides. Well-chosen photographs and maps enhance the text.

Gilderhus, Mark. *Diplomats and Revolution: U.S.-Mexican Relations Under Wilson and Carranza*. Tucson: University of Arizona Press, 1977.
This scholarly study provides an in-depth examination of President Woodrow Wilson's policies toward Mexico from 1913 to 1921, a period in which General Victoriano Huerta seized power and lost it (1913-1914), and in which Venustiano Carranza struggled for and finally succeeded in the establishment of a constitutional government, which he headed from 1917 to 1920. Wilson ordered two armed interventions intended to bring stability to Mexico, the first in Veracruz in 1914 and the second in northern Mexico in 1916. Neither intervention achieved this central goal. Gilderhus covers these controversial interventions and also presents an impressive analysis of Wilson's frustrated responses to Mexico's decisions to regulate and to restrict the operations of foreign-owned oil corporations through its revolutionary programs. The author's examination of the ideas and personality traits that guided Wilson's decisions gives excellent insights into the origins and conduct of the United States' policies toward Mexico in these years.

Hall, Linda. *Oil, Banks, and Politics: The United States and Postrevolutionary Mexico, 1917-1924*. Austin: University of Texas Press, 1995.
Hall's detailed examination of this crucial period in U.S.-Mexican relations offers to the reader the advantage of nicely etched biographical portraits of key figures and impressive analyses of important

historical trends. She concentrates on four types of U.S. leaders: Presidents Woodrow Wilson (1913-1921) and Warren G. Harding (1921-1923), bankers such as Thomas W. Lamont of the Morgan bank, oil company executives such as Edward Doheny, and other politicians, including governors and senators. Chapter 3 is an illuminating portrait of Albert Fall, the Senator from New Mexico who led a highly publicized investigation intended to discredit the Mexican government and to protect oil company properties. Hall also provides balanced coverage on Mexican leaders, including Presidents Venustiano Carranza (1917-1920) and Alvaro Obregón (1920-1924), rising politicians such as Adolfo de la Huerta, and revolutionary peasant chieftains such as Manuel Peláez. Hall guides the reader through the complexities of the troubled early 1920's, when the United States applied pressure on the new Obregón Administration by withholding diplomatic recognition. President Harding and his Secretary of State, Charles Evans Hughes, finally extended normal diplomatic recognition in 1923, to a large extent because Obregón established a strong central government and mastered the violence and chaos that had characterized the previous decade. Obregón and other Mexican leaders used this same government to extend the nation's control over its oil reserves, much to the dismay of the U.S. corporations. Hall concludes that Mexico's assertions of nationalism frustrated U.S. policymakers. Diplomatic intimidation and the threat of military interventions that had enabled Washington to dominate the smaller Central American and Caribbean nations did not bring the expected results in Mexico.

Hall, Linda, and Don Coerver. *Revolution on the Border: The United States and Mexico, 1910-1920*. Albuquerque: University of New Mexico Press, 1988.

The two-thousand-mile border between the United States and Mexico was the scene of both military and civilian activity during this violent decade. Hall and Coerver examine Pancho Villa's New Mexico raid and General John J. Pershing's military expedition into Mexico in response to that raid. The authors also provide careful assessments of the disruptive impact of the revolution on economic activities in mining and oil production in this region. These economic disruptions, the revolutionary violence, and the general uncertainties of life throughout Mexico stimulated a large immigration to the United States (both legal and illegal) that passed through the border region. The authors present a statistical and narrative account of immigration, with considerable attention to San Antonio, Texas. Hall and Coerver get the maximum value from their sources in an innovative chapter on the boom in border commerce, which emphasizes smuggling—especially the shipment of arms and ammunition from the United States to Mexico. This book contains an excellent selection of photographs of the border region during this decade.

Hart, John Mason. *Revolutionary Mexico: The Coming and Process of the Mexican Revolution*. Berkeley: University of California Press, 1987. This stimulating account of the origins and course of the Mexican Revolution includes a large role for the United States. Hart's book shows how the histories of the two countries were deeply interwoven from the late 1800's to 1924, through the interactions of U.S. politicians, diplomats, and corporate leaders first with the political and business elite of the dictatorship of Porfirio Díaz and, after 1910, with the dominant groups in the revolution. The uprising that began in 1910 ultimately included peasants, workers, the middle class, and some members of the elite who reacted against the acquisition of large tracts of land and large numbers of oil wells and mines by U.S. business interests. These same business interests used their influence with President Woodrow Wilson to support military intervention in Veracruz in 1914. This intervention, according to Hart, left significant quantities of arms and ammunition in warehouses to be used by the forces under Venustiano Carranza and Alvaro Obregón. These two leaders were in favor with many prominent figures on Wall Street and in Washington. Carranza, who was president from 1917 to 1920, and Obregón, who was head of state from 1920 to 1924, guided the national government away from the demands of peasants and workers and in the direction of the more moderate reforms favored by U.S. investors and property owners in Mexico.

Katz, Friedrich. *The Secret War in Mexico: Europe, the United States, and the Mexican Revolution*. Chicago: University of Chicago Press, 1989. The revolutionary upheaval in Mexico triggered a series of policy decisions in the United States, Great Britain, France, and Germany that, for much of this period, amounted to a multidimensional rivalry for diplomatic, strategic, and economic advantage in the strife-torn nation south of the Rio Grande. This nation was crucial to the United States because the two nations shared a long unfortified common border and because Mexico held heavy U.S. investments. The British, French, and Germans, who in 1914 entered the brutal combat of World War I, used their presences in Mexico to try to gain some leverage against their opponents and in their dealings with the United States. Katz's impressive research carried him deep into the archives of all five nations, and his text weaves together stories of diplomacy, espionage, military combat, and revolutionary action from the rise of Francisco Madero in 1910 to the fall of Venustiano Carranza in 1920. Katz's text contains a wealth of detail on the European efforts in Mexico that underscores the strategic importance of that nation in the era of the revolution and World War I. It also provides valuable insights on the international aspects of the revolutionary careers of Victoriano Huerta, Pancho Villa, Madero, and Carranza.

Knight, Alan. *U.S.-Mexican Relations, 1910-1940: An Interpretation*. La Jolla: Center for U.S. Mexican Studies, University of California, San Diego, 1987.
This brief study of U.S.-Mexican relations presents a challenging view of what most historians have considered a period of sharp disagreements and deep antagonisms in the relations between the two countries. Knight argues that Mexican xenophobia (antiforeign attitudes and actions) was seldom directed against U.S. citizens and that Mexican economic nationalism, although growing in these years, reached the stage of being a major international issue only briefly in the mid-1920's and again on a larger scale in the late 1930's. In general, Mexican attitudes toward the United States followed the traditional pattern associated with political patriotism in response to U.S. military interventions and were not the result of revolutionary extremism. Under these conditions, according to Knight, Mexico and the United States were able to work out their differences through standard diplomatic methods during these revolutionary years.

Langley, Lester. *MexAmerica: Two Countries, One Future*. New York: Crown, 1988.
This book provides an excellent example of how the relations between two countries can be shaped as much by ordinary people and their culture as by diplomats and corporate executives. Langley, a historian by profession and a traveler by abiding curiosity, takes the reader through an exploration of what he terms "MexAmerica," the vast expanse that stretches from Chicago, Illinois, to Mexico City, Mexico, and includes urban centers such as Los Angeles, California, and Guadalajara, Mexico. One of Langley's main points is that this region has become an arena in which U.S. and Mexican cultures are interacting but not necessarily blending, as the typical melting-pot experience might lead one to expect. Connected to their national and ethnic roots by the ease and frequency of migration across the border, and reflecting the rapidly growing Mexican presence in the United States, many

immigrants of Mexican origin have retained a firm identity with their homeland. Langley combines a first-person account of his 1986-1987 travels through cities, towns, and countrysides with historical and sociological interpretations of this huge region and its component parts, from the Rio Grande Valley to the world's largest metropolis, Mexico City. Students will enjoy his descriptions of roadside restaurants, inexpensive hotels, and interesting characters, and how they relate to the main themes in this book.

MacLachlan, Colin, and William Beezley. *El Gran Pueblo: A History of Greater Mexico*. Englewood Cliffs, NJ: Prentice Hall, 1994.
This innovative textbook focuses on Mexican history from 1821 to the 1990's, with an appropriate concentration on the flow of immigrants, goods, investments, and culture across the border between the two countries. The nineteenth century coverage includes the independence of Texas in the 1830's, the war between Mexico and the United States (1846-1848), and the arrival of U.S. investments during the dictatorship of Porfirio Díaz (1876-1911). The Mexican Revolution is the main feature of the section on the early decades of the twentieth century. The authors explore in considerable depth its origins and early phases, through the uprisings of peasants and workers and the actions of leaders such as Francisco Madero, Pancho Villa, and Emiliano Zapata. MacLachlan and Beezley view the two decades from 1917 to 1937 as the period in which presidents such as Alvaro Obregón and Lázaro Cárdenas attempted to carry out reforms to satisfy the revolutionary goals. The authors also consider the importance of Mexican immigration to the United States and the tensions between the two nations caused by the revolutionary policies. After 1937 (about halfway through the Cárdenas presidency of 1934-1940), the Mexican government began to turn to large-scale projects for economic and political modernization and moved away from the original revolutionary goals. The last one-fourth of the text deals with the nation's uneven performance in the quest for economic growth from the 1940's to the 1990's and the expansion of ties with the United States. The footnotes and bibliography provide the reader with a broad selection of books and articles for additional research.

Meyer, Lorenzo. *Mexico and the United States in the Oil Controversy, 1917-1942*. Austin: University of Texas Press, 1972.
Mexico's large reserves of petroleum along its Caribbean coast attracted heavy investments from U.S. corporations in the early years of the twentieth century. With the eruption of the Mexican Revolution in

1910 and, in particular, the writing of the Constitution of 1917, the two countries experienced a series of crises concerning the status of U.S. investments in Mexican oil lands. Meyer discusses the early phases of the oil industry, the origins and application of the controversial Article 27 of the Constitution of 1917 (which established the Mexican government's control of subsurface resources such as petroleum), and the periodic controversies that involved the U.S. government, large international oil companies, and the Mexican government. These disputes continued into the late 1930's, when President Lázaro Cárdenas (1934-1940) faced a challenge to his authority by these corporations and responded by nationalizing their oil properties. Meyer covers the subsequent diplomatic negotiations leading to the compromise settlement of 1943, by which the oil companies received financial compensation. Meyer places this confrontation in the context of the struggle between an industrial power and a developing nation—the type of conflict that became increasingly evident in world politics in subsequent decades. The translation by Muriel Vasconcellos conveys the clarity of Meyer's writing style.

Quirk, Robert. *An Affair of Honor: Woodrow Wilson and the Occupation of Veracruz*. New York: Norton, 1967.
U.S. responses to the Mexican Revolution followed a complex and often confusing pattern from 1910 to 1940. Historian Quirk's book cuts through much of this complexity by focusing on a single dramatic event—the U.S. military occupation of the port of Veracruz in April, 1914. Tensions between the two countries were high because of the mistaken arrest and brief detainment of some U.S. sailors in the port of Tampico. At the same time, President Wilson was eager to undermine the government of Victoriano Huerta, a military dictator. Wilson used the Tampico incident and the impending arrival of a shipment of arms for Huerta as reasons to order the invasion of Veracruz and the seizure of the customs house. Quirk's fluid prose provides an engrossing narrative of events in unusual depth, including biographical sketches of politicians, diplomats, soldiers, and sailors as well as a detailed account of the unexpected bloodshed resulting from the invasion.

Raat, W. Dirk. *Mexico and the United States: Ambivalent Vistas*. Athens: University of Georgia Press, 1992.
The historical relationship between Mexico and the United States had its beginnings in the colonial era, when native Americans began to compete with people from Spain and Great Britain for land and

resources in the vast area that now constitutes the Southwest of the United States and the northern part of Mexico. Raat pulls together these strands of history from the distant past to the twentieth century and weaves them into a readable textbook. He moves from the colonial period to the Anglo-American settlement of Texas, the Mexican-American War, the export-oriented economic development of the dictatorship of Porfirio Díaz (1876-1910), the outbreak of the Mexican Revolution, and the promises and disappointments of the presidencies of Plutarco Elías Calles (1924-1928) and Lázaro Cárdenas (1934-1940). Raat devotes his last two chapters to the period since 1940, when the two countries grew closer through diplomatic and business relationships but also experienced tensions resulting from Mexico's foreign debt, the immigration issue, and the international drug trade. This book has extensive footnotes (including many references in English) and a helpful bibliographical essay.

_____. *Revoltosos: Mexico's Rebels in the United States, 1903-1923*. College Station: Texas A&M University Press, 1981.
Many of the important events in the Mexican Revolution had their origins and even their base of operations in the United States at least for several months, some for a few years. Raat examined archives on both sides of the border to bring to light several episodes that had been shrouded in exaggeration and myth. This book discusses the Flores Magón brothers and their anarchist followers, who used bases of operations as far north as St. Louis, Missouri (but mainly in Southern California), in their unsuccessful efforts to overthrow Porfirio Díaz. Francisco Madero led the revolt that toppled Díaz in 1910-1911, a revolt that had its base in San Antonio, Texas. Raat provides a close examination of the work of the United States government and private detective agencies to track the *revoltosos*. Ricardo Flores Magón endured arrest, trial, conviction, and incarceration in the United States. Raat includes a valuable bibliographical essay with many books and articles in English.

Richmond, Douglas W. *Venustiano Carranza's Nationalist Struggle, 1893-1920*. Lincoln: University of Nebraska Press, 1983.
Carranza emerged as the leader of the Mexican Revolution in 1914-1915, during its most violent phase. He became the nation's first president under the revised Constitution of 1917, which codified some of the movement's basic goals in the areas of land reform, labor legislation, and public education. Although he was not a radical of the far left, Carranza was an ardent nationalist who stood firmly for his

nation's control over its land and resources. Richmond's clearly written study recounts Carranza's hostile responses to the U.S. intervention in Veracruz in 1914 and General John Pershing's unsuccessful pursuit of Pancho Villa in northern Mexico in 1916. The author also examines Carranza's nationalistic policy (the Carranza Doctrine), which rejected the idea that the United States or any other foreign power had the right to intervene in Mexico's internal affairs in order to collect debts or to protect foreign investments. Carranza also asserted that Mexican law, rather than laws or practices imposed by foreign powers, was the basis for business operations in that nation. Richmond's archival research adds much depth to this important book.

Riding, Alan. *Distant Neighbors: A Portrait of the Mexicans.* New York: Random House, 1984.

Riding, a respected journalist and former bureau chief for *The New York Times* in Mexico City, made many of his observations for this book in the early 1980's, when the reverberations of Mexico's debt and financial crises were quite strong. Readers will find his topical approach easy to follow. He has chapters on the political system, corruption, the economy, the special place of oil in the economy, social problems, and life in Mexico City. The last three chapters contain observations on the relations between Mexico and the United States. One of Riding's main points is that in spite of the obvious connections between the two countries—whether political, social, cultural, or economic—there remains a very profound ignorance in the United States regarding its neighbor to the south.

Schmitt, Karl. *Mexico and the United States, 1821-1973: Conflict and Coexistence.* New York: Wiley, 1974.

This survey offers a convenient summary of the history of U.S.-Mexican relations, with more than half of the text dealing with the period from 1910 to the early 1970's. Schmitt emphasizes the conflicts of the two nations, in the three decades after 1910, over Mexico's determination to break up large estates and redistribute agricultural lands to peasant farmers, as well as the government's decisions to regulate (and in 1938 to expropriate) foreign-owned oil properties. Using the basic concept that the United States and Mexico engaged in the policies typical of relations between a world power and a smaller, less powerful nation, the author examines the means by which Mexico was able to carry out some of its revolutionary projects in spite of the United States' opposition. Chapters 7 and 8 cover the more placid years from 1945 to 1970. The ten-page annotated bibliography gives the reader some valuable ideas for further reading, mainly in books and articles published in the 1950's and 1960's.

Shafer, Robert J., and Donald Mabry. *Neighbors—Mexico and the United States: Wetbacks and Oil.* Chicago: Nelson Hall, 1981.
This college-level text has much to offer the student as well as the general reader. The authors present their material in straightforward, nontechnical language. They emphasize twentieth century issues— particularly the ebb and flow of Mexican migration into the United States and the impact of Mexican petroleum on the economic and political affairs of both nations. Chapter 7 deals specifically with the growing importance of the Mexican-American community within the United States. Chapter 9 consists of thoughtful, often provocative generalizations that span the history of U.S.-Mexican relations and provide the reader with some useful ideas on the larger themes in the diplomacy, politics, and economics of these two nations.

Smith, Robert Freeman. *The United States and Revolutionary Nationalism in Mexico, 1916-1932.* Chicago: University of Chicago Press.
The violence of revolutionary strife began to give way to the policies of revolutionary nationalism in this critical phase of U.S.-Mexican relations. Smith directs much of his attention to Mexico's Constitution of 1917 and the administration of President Venustiano Carranza (1917-1920), both of which posed challenges to the watchful Woodrow Wilson, who, as president of the United States (1913-1921), attempted to push the Mexican Revolution in a direction less threatening to U.S. interests. The Constitution of 1917 gave the Mexican government the authority to regulate and even to expropriate the holdings of foreign-owned corporations. Wilson and his successors in the White House— Warren G. Harding (1921-1923), Calvin Coolidge (1923-1929), and Herbert Hoover (1929-1933)—relied on the advice and negotiating skills of Wall Street bankers to reach agreement with Mexico. For example, President Plutarco Elías Calles (1924-1928) appeared to be determined to enforce the Constitution of 1917 against the U.S.-owned oil companies until banker-turned-diplomat Dwight Morrow exerted his skills and influence. Smith combines archival research with a talent for compact narrative to explain how the United States responded to Mexico's outbursts of revolutionary nationalism.

Vázquez, Josefina Zoraida, and Lorenzo Meyer. *The United States and Mexico.* Chicago: University of Chicago Press, 1985.

This concise, intelligent synthesis of Mexican-U.S. relations covers the period from the 1820's to the early 1980's and provides the student with valuable insights on this relationship from the points of view of two internationally respected Mexican historians. The calm, factual approach employed by Vázquez and Meyer reinforces their succinct summaries of major events in the subtitled sections of each chapter. This book follows a chronological organization that includes the Mexican-American War of 1846-1848, which cost Mexico the northern half of its national territory; the rise, consolidation, and overthrow of the dictatorship of Porfirio Díaz (1876-1910); the struggle between Mexico's revolutionary nationalism and U.S. imperialism from 1910 to 1940; and the establishment of a more stable diplomatic relationship after 1940, when issues relating to Mexico's economic development became increasingly important. The authors' clear, direct style is captured effectively in the translation by Gloria Benuzillo and Magda Antebi.

Central America as a Region

Arnson, Cynthia. *Crossroads: Congress, the Reagan Administration, and Central America*. New York: Pantheon, 1989.
The administration of President Ronald Reagan (1981-1989) decided to place a barrier against the spread of what it perceived to be the spread of international Communism in Central America and thereby triggered a decade of acrimonious debate in Washington and the nation as a whole. Arnson's study of that debate reveals the depth of the divisions in the United States on the military-economic campaign against the Sandinista government in Nicaragua and the leftist rebels in El Salvador. Arnson argues that this debate was unique in the recent history of U.S. foreign policy because neither the Reagan Administration nor its congressional opponents could build a popular consensus in support of their respective positions. The United States' unfortunate experience in Vietnam in the 1960's and 1970's was a looming presence in this debate. Important personalities in this period were Representative Edward Boland, House Speaker Tip O'Neill, Salvadoran politicians José Napoleón Duarte and Roberto D'Aubisson, CIA Director William Casey, and Reagan Administration official Oliver North.

Bulmer-Thomas, Victor. *The Political Economy of Central America Since 1920*. Cambridge, England: Cambridge University Press, 1987.

The economic history of Central America often has been depicted in U.S. popular culture in terms of bananas and other tropical fruits. Bulmer-Thomas takes his readers beyond this stereotype to examine what he terms export-led economic growth. This book does cover the importance of bananas, along with coffee, timber, and mining, but Bulmer-Thomas places the Central American economies in the international context, in which monetary policy, currency exchange rates, and banking are often essential in understanding stagnation and decline as well as growth. This exceptionally readable economic history text employs a decade-by-decade approach in which the author establishes the main characteristics of each period. For example, in the 1960's, the Central American nations formed a common market and attempted an industrialization strategy grafted onto a traditional export-led economy. The experiment failed, however, as inflation, international debt, and lower prices for exports damaged the Central American economy in the 1970's. The United States encountered a challenge to its economic and political hegemony in the region from the Sandinista regime in Nicaragua in the 1980's. The text includes helpful footnotes, statistical tables, and bibliographical references.

Chace, James. *Endless War: How We Got Involved in Central America—And What Can Be Done.* New York: Vintage, 1989.
This brief book (144 pages) is a sharply focused attack on U.S. policy in Central America. Chace, an experienced journalist with a special interest in foreign policy, provides a historical summary of U.S. influence in the region, but his main point is that the administration of President Ronald Reagan (1981-1989) failed to understand the nature of both the Sandinista movement that came to power in Nicaragua in 1979 and the rebel movement in El Salvador of the 1980's. According to Chace, these rebel movements resulted from local causes and had little connection to international Communism. Chace insists that the credibility of the United States was in doubt, but not in terms of military power or national will. Rather, Chace argues that a negotiated settlement to these conflicts is preferable to continued military and economic pressure exerted from Washington. This work can be contrasted with some of the less polemical studies mentioned in this section.

Coatsworth, John. *Central America and the United States: The Clients and the Colossus.* New York: Twayne, 1994.
The controversies surrounding U.S. involvement in Central America in the 1980's often blurred the actual events of that decade and the essential background to those events in recent history. Coatsworth uses

a straightforward conceptual framework to organize this study of U.S. relations with the six nations of modern Central America (Guatemala, El Salvador, Honduras, Nicaragua, Costa Rica, and Panama). The "clients" in the title are these small nations, which exist under the economic and strategic hegemony of the United States, which is "the colossus." Coatsworth provides a synthesis of the numerous academic and journalistic publications on Central America that appeared in the 1980's and early 1990's. The result is a coherent critique of U.S. policy in the region, with emphasis on the Cold War period (1945-1989). The United States tended to ignore the Central American nations in the 1970's, only to be caught by surprise with the leftist Sandinista rebels' victory in Nicaragua in 1979. The Reagan Administration (1981-1989) overreacted to its perception of the spread of Communist-inspired leftist radicalism in the 1980's and deployed its economic, diplomatic, and political might only to bring "destruction and disarray" to the region. In spite of its superior military and economic power, the United States during the Reagan Administration, according to Coatsworth, failed to achieve its main objectives. The author includes an excellent annotated bibliography that will benefit those readers who want to do additional research on this subject.

Findling, John E. *Close Neighbors, Distant Friends: United States-Central American Relations*. Westport, CT: Greenwood Press, 1987.
This well-written textbook offers a balanced historical survey of the complex relationship between the United States and the nations of the Central American isthmus from 1800 to the 1980's. The six chapters that form the heart of this book are organized around coherent themes. For example, Chapter 2 covers the period from 1800 to 1850 and is organized around the themes of diplomatic recognition of the new Central American nations by the United States and the development of transportation links between North and Central America. The next chapter deals with U.S-British rivalry for dominance in the region from 1850 to 1900. Chapters 4 and 5 focus on the issues of revolution, intervention, and dictatorship in the early decades of the twentieth century. Chapters 6 and 7 explain the rise of nationalism and radical-ism—especially in Nicaragua, El Salvador, and Guatemala—as an essential element in understanding the arousal of security concerns in the United States and the consequent international conflicts of the 1980's. Findling's chapter footnotes include many useful references in English, and his appendix has a listing of the chief U.S. diplomatic representatives to the Central American nations since the early nine-teenth century.

LaFeber, Walter. *Inevitable Revolutions: The United States in Central America*. New York: Norton, 1984.

In this scholarly textbook intended for the college classroom, veteran diplomatic historian LaFeber surveys a century of troubled relations between the United States and the Central American nations. The reader can quickly grasp the layout of this book through the detailed table of contents. According to LaFeber, the United States established a system of diplomatic, strategic, and economic dominance of the isthmian region in the 1880's. The phrase "inevitable revolutions" refers to the internal imbalances between wealthy landowners and business leaders (often allied with U.S. interests) and the struggling majority made up of peasants and workers who, periodically and inevitably, rebel against the burdens of this power structure. LaFeber traces the international dimensions of this system from its establishment in the era of Secretary of State James G. Blaine in the late 1800's through the turmoil of the time of Augusto César Sandino in the 1920's to the dramatic challenges to the system in the 1970's and 1980's with the rise to power of the Sandinista rebels in Nicaragua in 1979. The author's extensive footnotes and brief bibliographical essay provide additional reading in this subject area.

Leonard, Thomas M. *Central America and the United States: The Search for Stability*. Athens: University of Georgia Press, 1991.

The often explosive debate concerning U.S. intervention in Central America in the 1980's created an atmosphere in which polemical, one-sided commentary on regional affairs became quite common. Leonard's convenient one-volume summation of nearly two centuries of history is notable for its calm tone and its understated interpretations. Leonard divides his text into three sections. The first covers the period from the 1820's to 1903, during which U.S. interest fluctuated from the neglect of the early years to the interventions led by private citizens such as William Walker in the 1850's. The second section begins in 1903, when the Panama Canal established Central America as an essential component in U.S. commercial and strategic concerns. During World War II, Central America was important strategically because Nazi penetration in the Western Hemisphere was a threat. After World War II, the Cold War competition between the United States and the Soviet Union often confused and entangled Central American struggles for social justice with Communist intrigues in the region. Leonard gives special attention to the 1948 civil war in Costa Rica, CIA intervention in Guatemala in 1954, and the heated debates concerning

U.S. policies toward Nicaragua and El Salvador in the 1980's. The text is fully footnoted and also has a twelve-page bibliographical essay.

Salisbury, Richard V. *Anti-Imperialism and International Conflict in Central America, 1920-1929*. Wilmington, DE: Scholarly Resources, 1989.
After World War I, the former European rivals of the United States— Great Britain, Germany, and France—were severely weakened by the carnage and destruction of the battlefields, but policymakers in Washington continued to encounter challenges to their projections of hegemony over the Central American isthmus. Mexico, caught up in its revolutionary nationalism, and Spain, the mother country, began to exert their distinctive forms of influence from Guatemala to Costa Rica. They found fertile ground, especially among the growing number of Central American anti-imperialists who took bold stands in opposition to U.S. dominance. Salisbury's excellent combination of his own archival research with previous scholarly studies portrays this anti-imperialism as a political and intellectual movement led by Costa Ricans Alejandro Alvarado Quirós and Joaquín García Monge, Salvadoran José Gustavo Guerrero, Honduran Froylán Turcios, and Peruvian Víctor Raúl Haya de la Torre (who discussed Central America in broad hemispheric terms). Salisbury also discusses the anti-imperialist activities of Augusto César Sandino, whose forces fought against U.S. Marines in his homeland of Nicaragua.

Schoonover, Thomas. *The United States in Central America, 1860-1911: Episodes of Social Imperialism and Imperial Rivalry in the World System*. Durham, NC: Duke University Press, 1991.
The United States began to build its dominating influence in Central America in the late nineteenth century through what Schoonover calls "social Imperialism." He defines this process as the extension of U.S. trade and investment into the region, as a way of attempting to solve domestic problems in the United States such as unemployment and low prices for agricultural products—crises that afflicted workers and farmers from New York to California. Schoonover explains how U.S. entrepreneurs found Central American *compradors* (local business/political people who collaborated with the foreign corporations) to establish their operations in the region. The text also contains discussions of the activities of Confederate blockade runners during the Civil War, the pathbreaking effort of George M. Williamson to promote trade between Central America and the U.S. gulf coast, and the activities of President Theodore Roosevelt in the 1903 Panamanian revolt for

independence against Colombia. A major strength of this outstanding study is the careful examination of German and French business promoters and diplomats who were serious rivals to their U.S. counterparts in Central America. Schoonover's explanation of these rivalries is based on his extensive pioneering research in German and French archives. This book enables the student to grasp the economic forces involved in the eventual U.S. domination of the isthmian region.

Van den Haag, Ernest, and Tom J. Farer. *U.S. Ends and Means in Central America: A Debate.* New York: Plenum Press, 1988.

The public debate about the Reagan Administration's policies in Central America reached its peak in the late 1980's. Van den Haag (a prominent conservative and a scholar at the Heritage Foundation) and Farer (a liberal formerly connected with the Council on Foreign Relations) discuss this issue from their respective perspectives. The book is divided into five parts in which van den Haag argues in favor of U.S. intervention and Farer explains his opposition to this approach. For example, in the first section, Farer argues that U.S. support of the contra rebels who were trying to overthrow the Sandinista government of Nicaragua only added to the instability in the region, thereby making matters worse. He insisted that the Contadora negotiations (initiated by Colombia, Venezuela, Mexico, and Panama) were following the more promising path of peaceful diplomacy. Van den Haag replies with the assertion that the international law that would support such a settlement was based on unrealistic assumptions and therefore offered little hope for meaningful peace. Both debaters consider the establishment of stable democratize institutions as an appropriate goal, but they disagree on what the United States should do in order to reach this goal.

Williams, Robert C. *Export Agriculture and the Crisis in Central America.* Chapel Hill: University of North Carolina Press, 1986.

The political turmoil in Central America of the 1970's and 1980's had many of its roots in the transformation of the region's economy in the quarter century after World War II. Economist Williams examines the booms in the production of cotton and beef for export to the international market, then explains how this boost to the region's short-term prosperity actually weakened the traditional strengths of the local economies in coffee and bananas as well as products such as corn, vegetables, and livestock produced for consumption in peasant and worker homes. With the sharp rise in oil prices in the early 1970's and the consequent disruption of international trade and credit patterns, the economies of the Central American nations suffered extensive damage. Under these conditions, displaced peasants and unemployed workers turned to radical movements—especially in Nicaragua, El Salvador, and Guatemala. Williams' study complements the work of Thomas Schoonover and Victor Bulmer-Thomas (mentioned above) in the area of international economics and its impact on the region.

Woodward, Ralph Lee. *Central America: A Nation Divided.* 2d ed. New York: Oxford University Press, 1985.
Central America has a long and colorful history. The past five centuries include the Spanish conquest, a period of extensive economic growth and social change in the 1700's, the disruptions of the independence movements in the early 1800's, and great expectations for material progress based on tropical enterprises such as the United Fruit Company in the early twentieth century—all before the troubled 1970's and 1980's, when the region experienced painful, disruptive conflicts in the last stages of the Cold War. Woodward, the dean of historians of Central America, gives the reader a cogent, well-organized survey of this unique area based on voluminous reading and his own extensive archival research. This book explains the underlying historical forces that set the stage for the crises of the 1970's and 1980's: the frequent and inevitably frustrated attempts to unite the region as a single nation, the persistent social imbalances between the rich and the poor, and the dominant and deeply resented presence of the United States. Woodward's fifty-three-page bibliographical essay is a treasure trove of sources, many of which are published in English, and his twenty-three-page chronology of important events runs from 1501 to 1984.

Individual Central American Nations

Costa Rica

Ameringer, Charles. *Democracy in Costa Rica.* New York: Praeger, 1982.
Costa Rica is unique in Central America because of its well-established traditions of democratic government. Ameringer examines the historical, institutional, and social bases for this democracy in a text that is written for the introductory student. Chapter 2 covers the evolution of government and politics in Costa Rica from the nineteenth century to the 1970's. Chapter 3 discusses the structure and functions of the government, and Chapter 4 explores how Costa Rica's "shirtsleeve democracy" works. Ameringer argues that a lack of elitism and a

commitment to carefully supervised elections account for much of this nation's success in maintaining democratic practices. Chapter 5 examines Costa Rican foreign relations, with a heavy emphasis on interactions with the United States. Ameringer examines how Costa Rica and the United States have often worked together, particularly in the troubled times from the 1950's to the 1970's. The author gives considerable attention to the most influential international leaders from Costa Rica, especially José Figueres (president from 1953 to 1958 and from 1970 to 1974), who had close ties to the United States during these years.

Bell, John Patrick. *Crisis in Costa Rica: The 1948 Revolution*. Austin: University of Texas Press, 1971.

Costa Rica has a well-deserved reputation for democratic government, but its political system experienced serious problems in the 1940's. The reformist government of President Francisco Calderón Guardia (1940-1944) established a social security program and an advanced labor code, and it made an alliance with the Costa Rican Communist Party. Over the next four years, however, the usually reliable electoral process began to break down. Bell's superb study examines this crucial period in Costa Rican history. The Calderón Guardia party lost favor with the United States because of its ties with the Communists. Bell concentrates his analysis on José Figueres, who led the movement to overthrow the discredited Calderón Guardia regime, and, with the blessing of the United States, established a new government. Although Figueres appeared to be an anti-Communist conservative, his new government pursued more liberal, reformist policies that, in a sense, continued what Calderón Guardia had started, but within a democratic, non-Communist framework. One of the strengths of this study is that the author uses information from interviews of key figures in this period as well as Costa Rican archives.

Honey, Martha. *Hostile Acts: U.S. Policy in Costa Rica in the 1980's*. Gainesville: University Press of Florida, 1994.

Costa Rica's long tradition of harmonious relations with the United States met a severe test in the 1980's. Honey and her husband, Tony Avirgan, both experienced journalists, went to Costa Rica in 1983 to cover the conflicts in Central America from what they assumed was a safe haven. Their illusions about a peaceful environment were shattered when Avirgan narrowly escaped death in an apparent CIA-arranged bombing of a press conference held by the controversial rebel leader Eden Pastora in the village of La Penca on the banks of the San

Juan River, which forms the border between Costa Rica and Nicaragua. Honey describes this incident to introduce the reader to the main thesis of this book, that the growing CIA/military buildup in northern Costa Rica was an attempt to establish a "southern front" in the undeclared war against the Sandinista government of Nicaragua. Reagan Administration official Oliver North was prominent in this operation. This "southern front" posed a threat to Costa Rica's practice of restricting military power and emphasizing civilian government. Oscar Arias Sánchez, a mild-mannered conservative politician and President of Costa Rica from 1986 to 1990, negotiated a peace settlement to the Central American fighting in 1987, against the objections of the United States, and won the Nobel Peace Prize in the process. Honey's book contains a wealth of footnotes and a useful bibliography.

El Salvador

Bonner, Raymond. *Weakness and Deceit: U.S. Policy and El Salvador.* New York: Times Books, 1984.

El Salvador abruptly became an issue not only in U.S. foreign policy but also in U.S. domestic politics in the early 1980's. Bonner, an experienced journalist, covered El Salvador in these turbulent years and compiled this book from his firsthand observations, interviews with officials in El Salvador and the United States, and declassified U.S. government documents. He concludes that U.S. policy in El Salvador was based on "weakness and deceit." The weaknesses appeared in the consistent failure of U.S. officials to pressure the Salvadoran military to end its repression of peasant and worker movements. This failure was, in part, an outgrowth of Washington's assumption that these movements were not internal or domestic in origin, but rather resulted from the meddling of Communist agitators from Nicaragua and Cuba. The deceit in U.S. policy arose when the administration of President Ronald Reagan told the U.S. public that its military strategy was to defeat Communist aggression in Central America when, according to Bonner, the Salvadoran rebels were acting mainly on their own in a struggle against brutal military repression. Bonner also includes much information on the Salvadoran Catholic church's outspoken support for peasants and workers and its opposition to the military and the government. A central event in this civil strife was the 1980 killing of four churchwomen from the United States by right-wing vigilantes. Bonner includes footnotes and a bibliography as guides for further reading.

Duarte, José Napoleón. *Duarte: My Story*. New York: Putnams, 1986.
El Salvador was torn apart by civil strife in the 1980's. Radical leftists demanded massive socioeconomic changes to benefit the impoverished peasantry, and wealthy coffee planters and their allies in the Salvadoran army used military force to oppose this movement. Duarte's book (written in collaboration with Diana Page) is a first-person account of his work as the leader of the moderate reformist party, the Christian Democrats, to find a middle ground in El Salvador in order to bring an end to the fighting. A graduate of the University of Notre Dame and fluent in English, Duarte became an important figure in efforts to end the fighting in his homeland of El Salvador, to reduce international tensions in Latin America, and to bridge the gap between his country and the United States. Finally elected to the presidency of El Salvador in 1985, Duarte wrote this book to explain to the U.S. public his personal and political struggles in these years and his plans for his administration. Unfortunately, Duarte contracted debilitating cancer before he could achieve his goals, but this book remains a valuable source on his work in a crucial period in U.S.-Salvadoran relations.

Montgomery, Tommie Sue. *Revolution in El Salvador: Origins and Evolution*. Boulder, CO: Westview Press, 1982.
The focus of this book is on the clash between the right-wing government of El Salvador and that nation's leftist guerrilla movement in the early 1980's. President Ronald Reagan's administration argued that this revolutionary movement was connected with international communism. Montgomery expressed her disagreement by presenting the historical background to this clash in two chapters that survey the economic and political trends in El Salvador from the colonial era (the 1520's to the 1820's) into the 1970's. She emphasizes the expansive power of the oligarchy, made up of a few families of wealthy coffee plantation owners, and of the Salvadoran army, which began to play an especially prominent role in the nation's politics in the 1970's. These powerful conservative allies faced the determined revolutionaries known as the FMLN (the Farabundo Martí Front for National Liberation, named for the leader of an unsuccessful peasant uprising in 1932). Montgomery sees the origins of the FMLN in the decades of exploitation of peasants and workers by the coffee planters and their military supporters. She is critical of the U.S. government's aid to the Salvadoran government, which in her view was working to defeat the FMLN in order to maintain the imbalanced economic system.

Guatemala

Dosal, Paul J. *Doing Business with Dictators: A Political History of United Fruit in Guatemala, 1899-1944*. Wilmington, DE: Scholarly Resources, 1993.

The operations of private businesses seldom receive the close scrutiny of historians because of the general unavailability of corporate records. Dosal's remarkable study of the United Fruit Company (UFCO) in Guatemala is an unusual case. Dosal, a resourceful historian, gained insight into the internal operations of UFCO through the records of the U.S. Department of Justice, which prosecuted an antitrust suit against this U.S.-based corporation in the 1950's. Dosal's text reveals the extent of UFCO's power and wealth and its immense impact on Guatemalan history. The company owned more than half a million acres of land and employed fifteen thousand workers, making it by far Guatemala's largest corporation. UFCO maintained close relationships with Guatemalan dictators Manuel Estrada Cabrera (1898-1920) and Jorge Ubico (1931-1944) and extended its control into the nation's railroad and port systems. North American entrepreneurs Minor C. Keith and Samuel Zemurray figure prominently in this study. In the 1930's, UFCO used its trade with Nazi Germany as leverage to fend off regulation by the U.S. and Guatemalan governments. By the time of the collapse of the Ubico dictatorship in 1944, U.S. officials and Guatemalan reformers were aware of the lopsided nature of the nation's economic development, in which UFCO, the dictators, and the small local elite took huge rewards while the native workers endured a very low standard of living.

Gleijeses, Piero. *Shattered Hope: The Guatemalan Revolution and the United States, 1944-1954*. Princeton, NJ: Princeton University Press, 1991.

The story of Guatemala from 1944 to 1954 is one of the most important chapters in the history of the Cold War in the Western Hemisphere. Gleijeses emphasizes the enigmatic personality and eclectic ideology of Jacobo Arbenz Guzmán, the former Guatemalan army officer who became president of his country from 1950 to 1954. The author, who based much of this assessment of Arbenz on interviews with his widow in the 1980's, argues that for the last two years of his presidency he was a determined Communist who wanted to convert his nation to a form of agrarian socialism through a massive land reform program. The U.S. State Department and CIA had an accurate perception of Arbenz in these years: They saw him as a Communist (although many of their evaluations of radicalism in Guatemala in the late 1940's were exaggerated and unreliable). Gleijeses sees Arbenz's form of Communism as an outgrowth of his concerns about the Guatemalan peasantry and not the result of international intrigue promoted by the Soviet Union. The author faults the actions of the CIA in the overthrow of Arbenz. The coup's success owed much more to luck than to good intelligence and careful planning. Many of Gleijeses' conclusions about Arbenz are at odds with the findings of Jim Handy, Richard Immerman, and Stephen Schlesinger and Stephen Kinzer in their books annotated in this section.

Handy, Jim. *Gift of the Devil: A History of Guatemala*. Boston: South End Press, 1984.
This textbook is a convenient, well-written summary of Guatemalan history from the arrival of the Spanish conquistadors in the 1520's to the civil strife of the early 1980's. The phrase "gift of the devil" is from a Mayan account of the conquest in which the native Americans express their dismay with and rejection of European religion. Handy uses this expression to refer to outside influences that have been imposed on the Guatemalan people. More than 200 of the text's 270 pages deal with the twentieth century, during which the United States became the primary source of outside influence through the operations of the United Fruit Company, the Central Intelligence Agency, and the U.S. Defense Department. Handy's sympathies are with the Guatemalan peasants who have carried the burdens of poverty and repressive government for generations. According to the author, their main breakthrough came in the "ten years of spring" (1944-1954), which brought land reform and education to the country people before the coup of 1954 ended these programs. This text has extensive footnotes that include numerous publications on Guatemalan history, many of which are in English.

Immerman, Richard. *The CIA in Guatemala: The Foreign Policy of Intervention*. Austin: University of Texas Press, 1992.
The 1954 overthrow of leftist President Jacobo Arbenz Guzmán (1950-1954) is one of the turning points in Guatemalan history and in the relations between that nation and the United States. Immerman examines the political, economic, and social background to this event, including the regime of conservative dictator Jorge Ubico (1931-1944), the 1944 revolution that toppled his government, and the reformist administration of Juan José Arévalo (1945-1950). According to Immerman, the U.S. State Department and CIA began to detect

increasing signs of Communist influence in the Arbenz administration—particularly in labor unions and the land reform program. At the same time, the United Fruit Company's public relations counsel, Edward Bernays, began to generate large amounts of publicity in the United States concerning the alleged expansion of the Communists in Guatemala. Under these conditions, President Dwight Eisenhower (1953-1961) elected to carry out the CIA plan to overthrow Arbenz. Immerman's version of these events and especially the extent of Communist influence in Guatemala contrasts with the conclusions drawn by Piero Gleijeses in his book annotated in this section.

Schlesinger, Stephen, and Stephen Kinzer. *Bitter Fruit: The Untold Story of the American Coup in Guatemala*. Garden City, NY: Doubleday, 1982.
The roles of the Central Intelligence Agency and the State Department in the administration of President Dwight Eisenhower (1953-1961) serve as the focal points in this study of the ouster of Jacobo Arbenz Guzmán from the presidency of Guatemala in 1954. Much like Richard Immerman's study, this book deals with the operations of the United Fruit Company and the limits as well as the strengths of the Communist Party in Guatemala in the 1940's and 1950's. Schlesinger and Kinzer tend to concentrate on the actions of U.S. Ambassador John Peurifoy, who served as coordinator for the State Department and the CIA during the planning and execution of the coup. Both this book and the Immerman study see the coup as an unfortunate consequence of the Cold War rivalry between the United States and the Soviet Union. Both books attribute less influence to Guatemalan Communists than does Piero Gleijeses' work. The Immerman and Gleijeses studies are annotated in this section.

Honduras

Acker, Alison. *Honduras: The Making of a Banana Republic*. Boston: South End Press, 1988.
This text is intended for the introductory student who has little or no background in Honduran or Latin American history. Acker begins with a discussion of foreign (mainly U.S.) perceptions of Honduras as an unstable, inhospitable "banana republic" and then proceeds to trace nearly five centuries of that nation's history, from the Spanish colonial era to the 1980's. Acker argues that Honduras has its own history that deserves a respectful reading. She emphasizes the economic impact of

U.S. corporations—especially the Standard Fruit and Steamship Company and the United Fruit Company—in the late 1800's and early 1900's. Nearly 50 of this book's 138 pages deal with the 1980's, when the United States launched its efforts to bring down the Sandinista government in neighboring Nicaragua. The presence of large numbers of troops and the arrival of large amounts of military/economic aid from the United States threw Honduran national politics and economic development into a state of serious imbalance. In general, Acker is highly critical of the U.S. influence in Honduras.

Morris, James. *Honduras: Caudillo Politics and Military Rulers.* Boulder, CO: Westview Press, 1984.

There are very few books in English on Honduras. Morris has made an important contribution to this short list with his brief, well-informed survey of that nation's history from the 1870's to the early 1980's. The main purpose of this study is to provide the introductory student with the basic political, economic, and social history of Honduras. The word "caudillo" in the title refers to the traditional man on horseback who often competed for political power by force and made a shambles of elections and governmental stability. Morris gives approximately two-thirds of this text to the period since 1972, in which the military dominated the nation's politics. He also discusses the brief and costly 1969 war with El Salvador. Throughout the text, Morris incorporates material on the U.S.-based banana exporting companies and the impact of U.S. foreign policy on Honduras.

Nicaragua

Bermann, Karl. *Under the Big Stick: Nicaragua and the United States Since 1848.* Boston: South End Press, 1986.

One of the assets of this book is that it traces U.S. relations with a single Central American country over an extended period of time. Bermann gives ample attention to William Walker's ambitious and fatal attempt to carry out a revolt to gain control of Nicaragua in the 1850's, the rise of nationalist José Santos Zelaya in the 1890's, and his 1910 overthrow, which had the support of the United States. Bermann's sympathies for anti-imperialist Augusto César Sandino of the 1920's and 1930's and the insurgency of the Sandinistas in 1979 are clear. He also includes a penetrating condemnation of the Somoza family that controlled Nicaragua from 1934 to 1979 and the Good Neighbor Policy, which helped the Somozas to build their power base. The last chapter is a critique of the early efforts of the Ronald Reagan Administration (1981-1989) to remove the Sandinistas from Managua. The author is a consistent critic of U.S. actions in Nicaragua, a perspective that can be placed in a wider context by consulting the less strident books by Tom Leonard and John Findling, as well as Ernest van den Haag's pointed defense (in his book with Tom J. Farer) of Reagan's policies—all of which are discussed in the previous section on relations of the United States with the Central American region as a whole.

Black, George. *Triumph of the People: The Sandinista Revolution in Nicaragua.* London: Zed Press, 1981.
Black's book was one of the first published accounts of the Sandinistas' rise to power. It appeared at a time of growing concern in the United States with Central American affairs. The text is divided into three parts. The first part gives the historical background, including a summary of Augusto César Sandino's legacy of resistance to U.S. intervention in the 1920's and 1930's and the excesses of the subsequent Somoza family dictatorship, which collapsed in 1979. The second part explains the early setbacks and eventual triumph of the Sandinistas, with emphasis on the years 1977 to 1979. The last and lengthiest part contains a detailed look at the first year of the Sandinista government. Black discusses the Sandinista economic plan, which calls for socialism in a mixed (or partially free enterprise) economy, the status of democratic practices, the beginnings of worker and peasant organizations, the government's education campaign, and the possibilities of counterrevolution, especially under the guidance of the United States.

Christian, Shirley. *Nicaragua: Revolution in the Family.* New York: Vintage, 1986.
Christian covers the last years of the Somoza dynasty, the rise of the Sandinistas and their seizure of power in 1979, and the first few years of the new government. Unlike many U.S. commentators on this era in Nicaraguan history, Christian tends to be critical of the Sandinistas and stresses the roles of Cuban and other international leftists in Nicaragua. A crucial break in the revolution was the rupture of the junta (or ruling committee) in which Daniel Ortega and the more radical leaders ousted Violeta Chamorro and other moderates. Christian argues that the contras (the rebels against the Sandinista government) drew their support from the Nicaraguan people as well as the U.S. Central Intelligence Agency. She concludes that a negotiated settlement between the United States and the Sandinista government was not in the best interest of Washington because such a settlement would solidify

the Nicaraguan government and reinforce the spread of its hostile attitude and policies.

Clark, Paul Coe. *The United States and Somoza, 1933-1956: A Revisionist Look*. Westport, CT: Praeger, 1992.
Relations between the United States and Latin American dictators often are controversial. Clark's revision of the standard view of U.S. policies toward the regime of Anastasio Somoza provides a stimulating analysis of the rivalries among policymakers in the State Department, the War Department (or Defense Department after 1947), and the presidential staff. Clark argues that the generally accepted historical view that the U.S. government supported the Somoza dictatorship as a convenient way to strengthen U.S. security in the Caribbean is an oversimplification. Instead, Clark points out that several State Department officials, including Arthur Bliss Lane, Philip Bonsal, and Spruille Braden, repeatedly criticized Somoza's authoritarian methods and urged that he be pressured to leave office. Clark sees Somoza as a clever and resourceful politician who identified his allies in Washington—usually in the military—and cultivated their support with considerable success. During World War II, Somoza was an enemy of Nazi influence, and during the Cold War he stood firm against the perceived Communist threat in leftward leaning Guatemala. Both positions won him friends in Washington. Clark's main thesis is that Somoza's capabilities as a clever and manipulative military strongman were more important to the endurance of his regime than was support from the United States. The author bases his findings on extensive research in U.S. government archives.

Kamman, William. *A Search for Stability: United States Diplomacy Toward Nicaragua, 1925-1933*. Notre Dame, IN: University of Notre Dame Press, 1965.
Few contemporary experts in hemispheric foreign policy grasped the long-term importance of Nicaragua for the United States until the 1920's. Kamman provides considerable detail on the workings of Nicaraguan politics, the 1925 withdrawal and the 1926 return of the U.S. Marines, the attempts of special emissary Henry Stimson to settle the strife in Nicaragua, and the work of U.S. armed forces and diplomats to deal with Augusto César Sandino and his rebel army in its campaign against the intervention. Kamman bases this study on research in the records of the U.S. State Department, the personal papers of Stimson and several other principals involved in the intervention, and books and newspapers published in both Central America and the

United States. A particular strength of this book is its presentation of the assessments by U.S. diplomats of conditions in Nicaragua during these years.

Kinzer, Stephen. *Blood of Brothers: Life and War in Nicaragua.* New York: G. P. Putnam's Sons, 1991.

Kinzer covered Nicaragua from 1976 to 1989, starting as a free-lance journalist and finishing his tour of duty as a correspondent for *The New York Times.* This book is a summation of his experiences as a journalist, including much firsthand information such as his interviews with Nicaraguan leaders Pedro Joaquín Chamorro, whose 1978 assassination helped discredit the Somoza regime; Tomás Borge, who was the tough-minded Sandinista military commander; and Daniel Ortega, who emerged as head of the Sandinista government in the 1980's. Kinzer presents this material in the context of the U.S. government's economic, diplomatic, and military campaigns against the Sandinista government. He also provides valuable insights on U.S. press coverage of Nicaragua. The last chapter is a discussion of the Sandinista defeat in the election of 1990 by a moderate coalition led by Violeta Chamorro, the widow of Pedro Joaquín Chamorro.

Lake, Anthony. *Somoza Falling.* Boston: Houghton Mifflin, 1989.

Lake served as director of policy planning for the U.S. Department of State during the presidency of Jimmy Carter (1977-1981). He was at the center of the policy debate during the decline and fall of the Somoza family dynasty in Nicaragua. One of the strengths of this book is the insider's view on these policy debates within the Carter Administration from the assassination of Nicaraguan newspaper editor Pedro Joaquín Chamorro on January 10, 1978, to the victory of the Sandinistas on July 20, 1979. Most of Lake's discussion focuses on the problem of how to remove Anastasio Somoza without creating a situation in which stridently anti-U.S. elements would take power. Lake expresses his disappointment with the results of U.S. policy and gives an extended critique of the policy-making process in the State Department and other branches of the U.S. government.

Macaulay, Neill. *The Sandino Affair.* 1967. Reprint. Durham, NC: Duke University Press, 1985.

The reprint of this classic study of Augusto César Sandino's 1927-1933 guerrilla war against the U.S. Marines and the Nicaraguan National Guard includes a new and insightful preface by the author (who served in Castro's rebel army in Cuba in 1959) that connects the events of the

1920's and 1930's with the 1980's. Macaulay presents in impressive detail the evolution of Sandino's guerrilla tactics from his bloody defeat by Marine dive bombers at Ocotal in 1927 to his use of camouflage and jungle canopy to carry out his hit-and-run raids in later campaigns. Sandino also used mountain terrain to avoid confrontation with larger Marine and National Guard units while he sent small rebel bands to raid supply centers and transportation routes. Although the Marines had the advantages of superior weapons and military aircraft (for reconnaissance, machine gunning, and dive bombing), they did not defeat Sandino because of his mobility and support from the Nicaraguan population. This text is supported by battlefield maps and extensive footnotes.

Miranda, Roger, and William Ratliff. *The Civil War in Nicaragua: Inside the Sandinistas*. New Brunswick, NJ: Transaction Publishers, 1993.
Much of the writing in the United States on the Sandinistas tends to be sympathetic to their revolution of 1979. This book, by contrast, is highly critical of their movement. One author, Miranda, was an official in the Sandinista Ministry of Defense from 1982 to 1987. He became disillusioned with the revolution. Ratliff is a senior research fellow with the Hoover Institution. The authors combine personal experiences, academic research, and ideological analysis to provide a broad condemnation of the Sandinista government (1979-1990). They see Daniel Ortega and other top Sandinistas as ambitious opportunists who overthrew the Somoza family dictatorship only to establish their own Marxist-Leninist-Castroite authoritarian regime. The Sandinistas' anti-United States speeches and policies made conflict with the United States inevitable. The authors also present an interesting—sometimes critical—analysis of the contras against the leftist government in Managua.

Pastor, Robert. *Condemned to Repetition: The United States and Nicaragua*. Princeton, NJ: Princeton University Press, 1987.
Pastor was national security adviser on Latin American affairs for President Jimmy Carter (1977-1981). He was involved in policy-making during the fall of the Somoza dictatorship and the rise of the Sandinistas; in many ways, this book parallels the later book by Anthony Lake mentioned in this section. Pastor gives important background information in the history of U.S.-Nicaraguan relations. According to Pastor, the memory of Fidel Castro's revolutionary successes seemed to haunt the thinking of Washington policymakers in the 1970's and 1980's. The bulk of this book concerns the complexities

and nuances of policy formulation in the Carter Administration. Another theme is Pastor's debunking of the myth that the Somoza dynasty existed for so long (1934-1979) because of support from the United States. In general, the author combines his personal memoirs with an analysis of Washington's responses to the Nicaraguan revolution. His coverage spans the Carter Administration and also examines the work of his successors in foreign policy in the first part of the Ronald Reagan Administration. He also makes thought-provoking recommendations for U.S. responses to other Third World revolutions.

Panama

Conniff, Michael. *Panama and the United States: The Forced Alliance.* Athens: University of Georgia Press, 1992.
 The history of Panamanian-U.S. relations is filled with schemes and intrigues, colorful characters, and dramatic confrontations. Conniff brings these stories to the printed page in a straightforward text suitable for the beginning researcher. The first three chapters cover the nineteenth century, including the "railroad era" of the 1850's and 1860's, when the narrow isthmus was a major point of transit for gold seekers bound for California. The author also provides an incisive account of the unsuccessful effort of the French to build a canal across the isthmus in the 1880's. Chapters 4 to 9 focus on the importance of the canal in Panamanian-U.S. relations, including the period of construction (1904-1914), the troubled 1920's and 1930's, the era of cooperation during World War II, and the growth of Panamanian nationalism during the Cold War. This text has solid coverage of the controversial negotiations of the 1977 Panama Canal treaties that allowed for the gradual turnover of the canal from the United States to Panama. Chapter 9 gives a fast-paced discussion of the rise and fall of the dictatorship of Manuel Noriega, including the U.S. invasion of Panama in December of 1989 that resulted in his capture and removal to the United States to stand trial. The footnotes and bibliography mention many valuable studies in both English and Spanish.

Dinges, John. *Our Man in Panama: The Shrewd Rise and Brutal Fall of Manuel Noriega.* New York: Random House, 1990.
 In 1988, attorneys for the U.S. government indicted Manuel Noriega (then head of the government of Panama) for his involvement in smuggling drugs into the United States. A U.S. invasion force of twenty-six thousand troops landed in Panama in December of 1989

and, within a few weeks, captured Noriega and brought him to Florida to face criminal charges. Dinges, an experienced foreign affairs journalist and a specialist in Latin America, points out that the United States had never before indicted a head of state of a foreign government on criminal charges and then invaded his homeland in order to bring him to trial. Dinges concentrates on Noriega's activities from 1984 to 1989, not only as a partner with Colombian drug smugglers but also as a paid intelligence informant for the CIA and a source of information on his rival drug smugglers in the Caribbean. The author focuses on Noriega's use of cunning and brutality in his rise to power in Panamanian politics. Like Frederick Kempe's book on Noriega (discussed below), this study is based on a large number of interviews with prominent figures in Panama and the United States.

Kempe, Frederick. *Divorcing the Dictator: America's Bungled Affair with Noriega*. New York: Putnam's, 1990.

Manuel Noriega came out of the shadowy world of international intelligence, counterinsurgency, and drug smuggling to become Panama's dictatorial head of state and a primary enemy of Presidents Ronald Reagan (1981-1989) and George Bush (1989-1993). The author uses the word "divorcing" in the title to make the point that for more than twenty years, Noriega was an accepted partner in U.S. operations against leftist movements in the Caribbean—particularly the Reagan Administration's campaign to unseat the Sandinista government of Nicaragua. Kempe's research indicates that although Noriega received payments from the United States for his work in intelligence, the Panamanian dictator also made lucrative business deals with Colombian drug lords who used Panama as a way station in their smuggling operations into North America. Kempe is critical of the Reagan and Bush administrations for allowing Noriega to continue his double-dealing until the high-risk invasion of Panama in December of 1989. Kempe worked as a foreign affairs journalist for many years and based much of this work on interviews with key figures in Panama and the United States.

LaFeber, Walter. *The Panama Canal: The Crisis in Historical Perspective*. New York: Oxford University Press, 1978.

During the presidency of Jimmy Carter (1977-1981), the United States and Panama negotiated a new treaty that allowed for the turnover of the Panama Canal to that small isthmian nation. Many people in the United States opposed this treaty. The debate involved politicians, academics, and the general public. LaFeber, a well-known expert in

U.S. diplomatic history, wrote this short and pointed study to explain the history and nature of U.S. control of the canal. He traces the diplomatic relations between the two nations and the various treaty revisions over the years in order to explain the legal and historical basis for the U.S. presence in the Canal Zone. LaFeber's interpretation is that the United States did not own (or have sovereignty over) the canal in the same way that it had sovereign control of Alaska. LaFeber argues that, in the absence of U.S. sovereignty and with the decline of the strategic importance of the canal after World War II, the Carter Administration followed the proper course in signing the treaty to allow for the eventual control of the canal by Panama.

Leonard, Thomas M. *Panama, the Canal, and the United States.* Claremont, CA: Regina Books, 1993.

Panama's domestic politics often have been heavily influenced by that country's relationship with the United States. Leonard explores these connections in this study written for students with little background in Panamanian history or U.S.-Latin American relations. The author uses readable prose and logical organization to present the complex and sometimes confusing story of Panamanian politics by devoting nearly half of the book to this topic. He explains the social and economic bases of Panamanian politics from the rise of the Arias brothers—Harmodio and Arnulfo—in the 1930's as spokesmen for the frustrated, nationalistic middle class to the military-populist dictatorship of Omar Torrijos (1968-1980) and the infamously corrupt and brutal dictatorship of Manuel Noriega (1980-1989). The story of U.S.-Panamanian relations constitutes the second half of this volume. Leonard surveys the role of the United States on the isthmus from its maneuverings with the French and the British in the nineteenth century to the machinations of Philippe Bunau-Varilla, Manuel Amador Guerrero, and Theodore Roosevelt in 1903 to gain control of the Canal Zone for the United States. He also covers the rise of nationalistic leaders such as the Arias brothers and Torrijos. The final chapter is a narrative and analysis of the U.S. invasion of Panama in 1989-1990, the capture of Manuel Noriega, and the travails of Guillermo Endara in the presidency in the early 1990's. Researchers can benefit from the twelve-page annotated bibliography. Maps and charts reinforce the main themes in the text.

Major, John. *Prize Possession: The United States and the Panama Canal, 1903-1979.* Cambridge, England: Cambridge University Press, 1993.

The Panama Canal occupied a central place in the strategic and economic concerns of the United States for most of the twentieth century. It was also the heart of the economy of Panama (geographically split by the Canal Zone) and was the dominant factor in the relations between these two nations. British historian Major provides a detailed survey of the history of the Panama Canal from the antics of President Theodore Roosevelt and French entrepreneur Philippe Bunau-Varilla in establishing U.S. control of the canal route in 1903 to the negotiations that led to "the reluctant handover" of the canal to Panama in 1979. Based on voluminous research in U.S. government archives and the private papers of key individuals such as engineer G. W. Goethals, this work contains an effective discussions of the Canal Zone's government, the labor practices within the zone (including the Gold and Silver system that discriminated against workers with darker skins), the operation of the Canal Zone Commissary (which controlled commerce within the zone), and the place of the canal in U.S. military planning and operations including World Wars I and II. This study also includes interesting photographs and an extensive bibliography.

The Caribbean as a Region

Knight, Franklin. *The Caribbean: Genesis of a Fragmented Nationalism.* 2d ed. New York: Oxford University Press, 1990.
  The islands of the Caribbean have a long and distinctive history from the arrival of the Spanish and their imperial conquest in the 1490's to the emergence of nationalism and social revolution in the 1960's and 1970's. Knight's study offers impressive depth on the background to the twentieth century in his examination of colonization, plantation agriculture, and slavery, with a special sensitivity to the multiethnic and multinational dimensions of the region. On many of the smaller islands, ranging from the Bahamas to Tobago, culture and language often transcend politics and government—a point captured in Knight's phrase "fragmented nationalism." The last third of the book assesses the importance of the United States in the region. Knight examines the varied attempts to develop national governments and national identities in the face of the expansion of the U.S. economy. He also devotes considerable attention to Fidel Castro's Cuban revolution and the regional aftershocks, particularly in Jamaica, Trinidad, and Puerto Rico.

Langley, Lester. *Struggle for the American Mediterranean: United States-European Rivalry in the Gulf-Caribbean, 1776-1904.* Athens: University of Georgia Press, 1976.

_____. *The United States and the Caribbean in the Twentieth Century*. Athens: University of Georgia Press, 1982.

Even the best-informed students of United States history often underrate the extent of U.S. involvements with the nations of the Caribbean and Central America. These two volumes combine the author's own wide-ranging archival research with a thorough knowledge of the publications of journalists and other academics. Langley weaves together the histories of the Central American nations and the Caribbean island countries of Cuba, Haiti, and the Dominican Republic with his analysis of U.S. policies in the region. The two volumes utilize a chronological framework that reaches from the era of the American Revolution to the turbulent decade of the 1970's. The main themes covered in the first volume are the U.S. push into the Gulf of Mexico with the Louisiana Purchase of 1803, the extension of its ambitions with the announcement of the Monroe Doctrine in 1823, U.S. rivalry with the French and British in Mexico and Central America into the middle and later years of the nineteenth century, and the causes and consequences of the Spanish-American War. In his volume on the twentieth century, Langley emphasizes U.S. domination and those who challenged it, from President Theodore Roosevelt (1901-1909) and the establishment of "the protectorate era" to the rise of Fidel Castro in the 1950's and 1960's. He also gives considerable attention to the U.S. intervention in the Dominican Republic in 1965 and the Sandinista overthrow of the Somoza dynasty in Nicaragua in 1979. The extensive footnotes in both volumes include numerous books and articles published in English.

MacDonald, Scott, Harold Sandstrom, and Paul B. Goodwin, eds. *The Caribbean After Grenada: Revolution, Conflict, and Democracy*. New York: Praeger, 1988.

The United States' invasion of the small island of Grenada in October, 1983, was a turning point in the recent history of the Caribbean. The radical tendencies in Grenada's government, the presence of Cuban workers on the island, and the growing conflict between leftist rebels and the U.S.-backed government in El Salvador created a situation in which the administration of President Ronald Reagan decided to make a firm stand against the spread of what it perceived to be Communism in the circum-Caribbean region. The editors of this unusually well-focused book of essays assembled some excellent commentary on the proximate causes and likely consequences of the intervention in Grenada. A second group of five essays examines the broad issues of revolution, democracy, and instability in Jamaica, Surinam, Haiti, and the Dominican Republic, as well as the French, British, and Dutch Antillean islands. The last section of this book deals with larger issues of geopolitics, including U.S., European, and Soviet influence in the Caribbean.

Martin, John Bartlow. *U.S. Policy in the Caribbean*. Boulder, CO: Westview Press, 1978.

The level of the United States' interest in the Caribbean varies considerably. When the author of this book served as U.S. ambassador to the Dominican Republic in the mid-1960's, Castro and the threat of spreading Communism gave the region a high priority in Washington. By the time Martin wrote this volume, a decade later, the Caribbean was a marginal area in U.S. foreign policy considerations. Martin's study covers the quarter century after 1950, with emphasis on the period of neglect in the early 1970's. Some of the general themes pursued by Martin are the importance of social and economic change throughout the Caribbean, its impact on politics, and, in Martin's view, the failure of U.S. policymakers to devise suitable responses to these transformations. Among the strengths of this volume are Martin's views of the Dominican Republic crisis of the 1960's, when he was directly involved in U.S. diplomacy. His critique of U.S. policies under the presidencies of Richard Nixon (1969-1974) and Gerald Ford (1974-1977) are provocative and deserve a serious reading.

Richardson, Bonham. *The Caribbean in the Wider World, 1492-1992*. Cambridge, England: Cambridge University Press, 1992.

Geography is one of the most indispensable academic disciplines for understanding the Caribbean. The prevalence of islands as the main type of landform accounts for much of the cultural diversity and many of the political divisions and economic weaknesses of the region. Richardson, a widely read geographer whose field research is reinforced by his capacity to absorb and explain the writing of historians, social scientists, and journalists, gives the reader a knowledgeable analysis of many aspects of Caribbean life. His central theme is the place of the Caribbean in the world economy. Chapters 3 and 5 examine the various elements in the region's dependency on outside markets for sugar and bauxite and on outside visitors for tourism. Chapter 4 is a valuable overview of the political and military dominance of the Caribbean by the United States, including the Grenada invasion. Chapter 6 covers migration, with emphasis on the movement of Caribbean natives to the United States. The phenomena of rebellion and social revolution (of great concern in the United States) are examined in Chapter 7. Throughout the text, Richardson reveals a perceptive awareness of the emergence of a sense of nationalism in many of the Caribbean countries.

Williams, Eric. *From Columbus to Castro: The History of the Caribbean, 1492-1969.* New York: Harper & Row, 1970.
    The long history of the Caribbean receives ample treatment in this 515-page text. Trained as a professional historian with a special interest in slavery and the plantation system, Williams rose to political prominence on the island of Trinidad in the 1960's and was the dominant political figure in that nation until his death in 1981. This background gave Williams a valuable perspective on the distant past as well as the political and economic challenges of the middle decades of the twentieth century. His book is an interesting mixture of academic research and political awareness expressed in a chronological framework that extends from the early Spanish voyages of discovery to the rise of the nationalist opposition to the remnants of European colonialism and the outburst of Fidel Castro's revolution in the 1950's and 1960's. Of the twenty-nine chapters in this text, the last ten discuss the growth of U.S. power in the Caribbean, first in the sugar industry of the 1800's, then in the Spanish-American War, and finally in the tensions of the early Cold War period. Students interested in Castro will find much of interest in Williams' critique of Cuba's economic performance in the 1960's.

Individual Caribbean Nations and Colonies

Cuba

Aguilar, Luis. *Cuba, 1933: Prologue to Revolution.* New York: Norton, 1974.
    Castro's 1959 revolution overshadowed an earlier radical movement that promised to deal with the stresses in Cuban society until it fell victim to its opposition. In the early years of the Depression, intellectuals, university students, and labor organizations joined with disaffected politicians to topple the government of dictator Gerardo Machado (1925-1933) and to begin a series of extensive reform programs under the leadership of President Ramón Grau San Martín. Aguilar's research clearly documents that U.S. officials—especially Ambassador Sumner Welles—did not like the new direction in Cuban politics. Welles used the participation of Cuba's small Communist

Party in the Grau San Martín government and the continuation of unrest in some localities on the island to convince the State Department that the new government was irresponsible and inept. In early 1934, after only four months in office, Grau San Martín resigned. The momentum for revolution was redirected under the government of Fulgencio Batista, who enjoyed the support of Welles and the State Department. Aguilar argues that the defeat of this revolutionary movement only postponed basic changes in Cuban society and contributed to the rise of Fidel Castro in the 1950's.

Benjamin, Jules R. *The United States and the Origins of the Cuban Revolution: An Empire of Liberty in an Age of National Liberation.* Princeton, NJ: Princeton University Press, 1990.
Geographical proximity and historical interaction have made Cuba and the United States intimate but unequal partners since the early 1800's. Benjamin's well-crafted survey weaves together Cuban and United States history in a smooth, highly readable form suitable for those unfamiliar with this story. The author uses extensive footnotes that contain numerous citations for those who want to read further on this theme. His nine chapters include discussions of the connections between the United States and Cuba as a colony of Spain from the 1820's to the 1890's, the role of the United States in Cuban independence and the Spanish-American War, and the troubled early decades of the twentieth century under the Platt Amendment. The author covers the rise of Fulgencio Batista in the 1930's and 1940's and his fall in the 1950's. The last three chapters assess Castro's revolution, which Benjamin views as a radical nationalistic rejection of the U.S. economic and political domination of the island.

Domínguez, Jorge I. *To Make a World Safe for Revolution: Cuba's Foreign Policy.* Cambridge, MA: Harvard University Press, 1989.
One of the main sources of friction between Cuba and the United States since 1959 has been the notion, widely held in Washington, that the Castro regime played a large role in fomenting revolution around the world. Domínguez examines this issue in a reasoned, dispassionate study. Although clearly not a pro-Castro advocate, the author discusses Havana's point of view on hemispheric and world events from the early phases of the revolution to the 1980's. The United States-sponsored Bay of Pigs invasion in 1961 and other attempts to overthrow and to assassinate Castro reinforced the Cuban government's decision to align itself with the Soviet Union and the cause of revolution in many Third World nations. Domínguez, however, also explores the friction be-

tween Moscow and Havana and makes a case that many Cuban operations in support of revolutionary movements in Latin America and Africa include considerable initiative from Castro. The former Portuguese colony of Angola on the west coast of Africa was a major commitment for Castro involving more than 200,000 Cubans in military and civilian capacities. Domínguez also discusses Cuban military and civilian support for movements in Guatemala, Grenada, El Salvador, and Nicaragua in the 1970's and 1980's and examines Castro's failures as well as his successes.

Gellman, Irwin F. *Roosevelt and Batista: Good Neighbor Diplomacy in Cuba, 1933-1945*. Albuquerque: University of New Mexico Press, 1973.
The name of Fulgencio Batista is most often connected with the inept dictatorship that collapsed under attack by Fidel Castro's 1958-1959 guerrilla movement. Historian Gellman examines Batista's early impact on Cuba when, as a shrewd sergeant in that nation's army, he exploited his opportunities to the fullest to rise to a position of dominance in the convulsive politics of the 1930's, then won election to a four-year presidential term in 1940. Gellman traces the relationship between the energetic Batista and President Franklin D. Roosevelt (1933-1945), who oversaw a restructuring of U.S. relations with Cuba as part of the Good Neighbor Policy. Roosevelt relied on U.S. ambassadors to Cuba in these years—especially Sumner Welles (April to December, 1933) and Jefferson Caffery (December, 1933, to August, 1937), both of whom worked closely with Batista. Gellman perceptively concludes that although the Roosevelt Administration gave up the right to intervene in Cuba under the Platt Amendment in 1934, Washington's policies brought the Cuban economy even further under the domination of the U.S. market for sugar and tobacco and U.S. sources for investments and loans.

Higgins, Trumbull. *The Perfect Failure: Kennedy, Eisenhower, and the CIA at the Bay of Pigs*. New York: W. W. Norton, 1987.
The failure of the CIA-organized Bay of Pigs invasion of Cuba in April of 1961 was a humiliation for the new administration of President John F. Kennedy and remains as one the major defeats for the United States in the Western Hemisphere. Higgins' study looks closely at the politics of policy-making in various branches of the U.S. government—especially the CIA—to determine how and why this ill-fated mission took place. Several factors enter into Higgins' explanation. The CIA's successful 1954 coup d'état in Guatemala provided a misleading

example. The confidence and, at times, arrogance of several CIA officials—including Latin American specialist J. C. King, as well as Richard Bissell and Tracy Barnes (two of the leading participants in planning the Guatemala operation)—is evident throughout the text. Bissell took charge of the plan to invade Cuba and soon established a direct working relationship with National Security Adviser McGeorge Bundy that bypassed customary administrative channels. The preparation of the force of Cuban exiles for the invasion moved ahead despite objections to the operation by General David Shoup, the commandant of the Marine Corps, and presidential adviser Arthur Schlesinger. Higgins' last chapter uses the findings of General Maxwell Taylor's Cuba Study Group, which assessed the flaws in the Bay of Pigs operation on orders of the embarrassed President Kennedy. Higgins concludes that the operation failed because it was too large to be kept secret (as Kennedy had hoped) and too small to establish a beachhead in Cuba.

Jenks, Leland. *Our Cuban Colony: A Study in Sugar*. 1928. Reprint. New York: Arno Press, 1970.
   The surge of United States political, military, and economic power in the Caribbean basin from the 1890's to the 1920's stimulated a vigorous debate on the issue of imperialism. Jenks's study originally appeared in 1928 as a part of this debate and contributed a forceful condemnation of the expansive economic power of the United States. As the subtitle indicates, Jenks focuses on sugar, but he also examines banking, tobacco, railroads, mining, and public utilities. Individual entrepreneurs such as William Van Horne (railroads) and Frank Steinhart (finance) amassed great personal wealth in the early 1900's. Furthermore, according to Jenks, by the 1920's, the individual entrepreneur gave way to large corporations, based on Wall Street, in the control of the island's economy. Corporations such as National City Bank, Electric Bond and Share, Bethlehem Steel, and United Fruit had extensive holdings in Cuba. Although recent studies have expanded on Jenks's findings (see the books by Louis Pérez, Jr., and Robert Freeman Smith discussed in this section), this book retains much value because of its place in the public debate on U.S. imperialism in the 1920's.

Matthews, Herbert L. *The Cuban Story*. New York: George Braziller, 1961.
   Matthews, a reporter for *The New York Times*, interviewed rebel leader Fidel Castro in the Sierra Maestra in eastern Cuba in early 1957. His story (which, as he admits, overestimated the size of rebel force) drew

attention to Castro in the United States and contributed to Castro's credibility as a guerrilla commander. This book appeared four years after the interview and two years after Castro took power. Matthews' retrospective provides a sympathetic portrait of Castro. The veteran journalist emphasizes the shift from the idealism of the bearded rebels in the Sierra Maestra in 1957 to the brutal struggle for power in Havana from 1959 to 1961. Matthews believes that Castro abandoned his early leftist idealism because the revolution unleashed ambitious individuals who challenged his control of the movement. According to Matthews, Castro could have revolution or democracy, but a combination of the two simply would not work. Nearly half of this book is devoted to commentary on the impact of Castro's revolution throughout the Western Hemisphere. The last chapter is an evaluative essay on the coverage of the Cuban revolution by the U.S. press.

Mills, C. Wright. *Listen, Yankee: The Revolution in Cuba.* New York: Ballantine Books, 1960.

The rapidity of Castro's triumph caught many observers in the United States by surprise. Mills, a well-known radical sociologist at Columbia University, traveled to Cuba in August, 1960, to attempt to capture the essence of the revolution for his readers in the United States. He presents his interviews with Cubans in the form of eight letters addressed to the U.S. public. Each letter takes up a particular issue. For example, the first discusses Cuba as a symbol for the poor and frustrated people of other Third World countries. The third letter expresses Cuba's fears of a counterrevolution or an attempt to overthrow the new Castro government by supporters of former dictator Fulgencio Batista and, more important, agents of the United States government. Perhaps the best letters are the last two, which explore the sense of cultural dynamism and revolutionary euphoria that were so strong on the island at the time of Mills's visit. The reader should be cautioned, however, that the author wrote during a time of great excitement in which many leftists overestimated the potential for revolutionary success in Cuba.

Morley, Morris. *Imperial State and Revolution: The United States and Cuba, 1952-1986.* Cambridge, England: Cambridge University Press, 1987.

Modern imperialism often is viewed in a mechanistic sense as the result of the economic power of large corporations dominating material resources and political systems of less developed countries. Morley takes a different approach in his emphasis on the policies of the United States government in its relations with Cuba during the era of Fidel

Castro. Morley gives a detailed discussion of U.S. economic policies intended to isolate and weaken Cuba. He cites the cessation of traditional trading patterns and the use of a financial squeeze through pressure on international banks. Morley also points out that Cuba managed to adjust its economic policies to have some modest success in trading with other capitalist nations such as Great Britain, Spain, and Japan. In general, however, the U.S. government and large multinational corporations carried out their main goal of isolating Cuba from the international market. Morley's book does not take into account the collapse of the Soviet Union in 1989, which significantly weakened the Cuban economy.

Paterson, Thomas. *Contesting Castro: The United States and the Triumph of the Cuban Revolution.* New York: Oxford University Press, 1994.
Fidel Castro brought Communism to power in Cuba only ninety miles from the state of Florida at a time when the United States was the world's most powerful opponent of the Marxist-Leninist ideology and its practitioners from Moscow to Peking. How did Castro stage his revolution in the Caribbean—an area subject to frequent U.S. military interventions and political/military hegemony? Paterson answers this question through a thorough examination of the reactions of U.S. diplomats, intelligence officials, politicians, journalists, and academics to Castro's rise from an obscure malcontent in the early 1950's to his triumphant entry into Havana in 1959. The Federal Bureau of Investigation observed Castro on his fund-raising trip from Mexico through Texas and on to Philadelphia and New York in 1955. Paterson includes of a photograph of the nattily dressed, well-groomed Castro walking through New York City's Central Park while on this trip. Paterson shows that U.S. officials had ample knowledge of Castro's activities but seriously underestimated the speed of the collapse of the last regime of Fulgencio Batista (1952-1959) and Castro's sudden military/political victory in 1958. This excellent study discusses Castro's rise to power in the context of the mingling of Cuban and U.S. cultures through tourism, popular music, baseball, and journalism as well as the more traditional themes of diplomacy, politics, and corporate investment.

Pérez, Louis A., Jr. *Cuba Under the Platt Amendment, 1920-1934.* Pittsburgh, PA: University of Pittsburgh Press, 1986.
When the United States imposed the Platt Amendment on the Cuban Constitution of 1901, it created a device to justify military and political intervention in the internal affairs of the island and, in so doing,

distorted the political and cultural development of the new nation. In this continuation of his 1978 book (discussed below), Pérez demonstrates persuasively that the United States used intervention and the threat of intervention to buttress the island's landholding elite and to block movements toward social reform and radicalism. The sudden drop in sugar prices in 1920-1921 not only brought an end to Cuba's great export boom but also created a major government fiscal crisis that destroyed Cuban banks and threatened to undermine U.S. investments in railroads and sugar mills. The United States government used the Platt Amendment to intervene in order to stabilize Cuban government finances and thereby bludgeoned the limited self-respect of the young Cuban republic. By the early 1930's, however, U.S. officials understood that the Platt Amendment had become a hindrance to the achievement of their aims in Cuba because of its immense unpopularity among the island's inhabitants. The United States ended the Platt Amendment in 1934, but, as Pérez points out, much damage had been done not only to the Cuban polity but also to U.S.-Cuban relations.

_____. *Intervention, Revolution, and Politics in Cuba, 1913-1921*. Pittsburgh, PA: University of Pittsburgh Press, 1978.
In addition to its provision for military intervention, the Platt Amendment to the Cuban Constitution of 1901 created a supervisory role for the United States in Cuban politics. The author concentrates on the presidency of Mario Menocal (1913-1921), a Conservative Party leader who faced political and revolutionary challenges from the opposition Liberal Party. The United States government used diplomatic notes, the presence of gunboats off Cuba's shores, and the landing of small units of soldiers to support the Menocal regime. These actions made it clear that not only direct military intervention but also the threat of intervention, political pronouncements from Washington, and the words of U.S. diplomatic representatives in Havana became significant factors in Cuban politics. This arrangement, according to Pérez, deeply affected Cuban politics by distorting the decision making of the nation's leaders and the outcomes of national elections. The Cuban political system committed its energies to responding to the government in Washington rather than the people of the island.

Quirk, Robert. *Fidel Castro*. New York: Norton, 1993.
Castro's impact on Latin American history and Cuban-U.S. relations attracted the attention of Quirk, an able historian whose earlier publications dealt mainly with the Mexican Revolution. Quirk carefully examined the books and articles published on Castro, tapes of Castro's

lengthy televised and radio speeches to the Cuban public, and his numerous interviews on U.S. television and with print journalists to construct this detailed biography. Unlike Tad Szulc's emphasis on Castro's life before the revolution (see the discussion of his book in this section), Quirk devotes 630 of his 840-page text to Castro's years in power from 1959 to the early 1990's. Quirk argues that Castro was a revolutionary long before he became a Communist. The Bay of Pigs invasion of April, 1961, although it failed, convinced Castro that he needed support from the Soviet Union because of the threat posed by the United States. In the months after this invasion, Castro began to use Marxist-Leninist terminology more frequently in his speeches and opened closer ties with Moscow. Quirk is even-handed in discussing Castro's triumphs and failures and includes an impressive analysis of his regime's declining fortunes in the 1980's and early 1990's.

Robbins, Carla. *The Cuban Threat*. New York: McGraw-Hill, 1983.
Castro's worldwide reputation as the promoter of Third World revolutionary movements was deeply embedded in the thinking not only of the U.S. public but also of most policymakers in Washington from the early 1960's into the 1980's. Robbins, a journalist with solid academic credentials, combined observation of current events with the analysis of long-term trends to write this persuasive attack on many of these assumptions about Cuban power. She argues that Cuba's impact on insurgent movements in Latin America was rather limited and sometimes ineffective, as exemplified by Che Guevara's failure in Bolivia in 1967. She also points out that the presence of Cuban doctors and teachers in Third World nations may boost support for Castro but does not pose a serious military threat to the interests of the United States. Robbins acknowledges the decisive role of Cuban combat troops in the leftist rebel victory in Angola in the early 1970's but also points out that this victory carried with it a burdensome military commitment to the new government. The crisis in Central America in the early 1980's led many foreign policy specialists in the Reagan Administration to claim that Castro's forces were deeply involved, but Robbins argues that in Nicaragua and El Salvador, as with most Third World revolutionary movements, the causes of the uprisings were primarily local in nature.

Ruiz, Ramón Eduardo. Cuba: The Making of a Revolution. New York: Norton, 1968.
Intended for the college classroom, this brief text is a suitable introduction for the general reader as well. Ruiz uses clear, straightforward

prose to explain the causes of the Cuban revolution of 1959. His explanation points to two major historical trends: Cuba's tendency to change governments by revolts rather than votes and the strident anti-United States nationalism that has been a powerful force on the island through much of the twentieth century. Fidel Castro used his gifts as a charismatic orator and astute political leader to turn the revolt of 1959 into an unleashing of Cuban nationalism that he channeled into a version of Communism. Ruiz includes chapters on the sugar industry, the place of José Martí in Cuban history, and the presence of socialism in Cuban politics from the early years of the twentieth century to the 1950's.

Smith, Robert Freeman. The United States and Cuba: Business and Diplomacy, 1917-1960. New Haven, CT: College and University Press, 1960.
Smith's sharply focused study of business influences in U.S. policy toward Cuba appeared in 1960, the year after Fidel Castro came to power. Smith's main thesis—that Washington's policies often were determined by the interests of private corporations involved in the sugar and tobacco businesses—touches on a basic cause of the revolution. Smith's research points to the probusiness orientation of the administrations of Presidents Warren G. Harding (1921-1923) and Calvin Coolidge (1923-1929) as crucial in the formulation of this policy. President Franklin D. Roosevelt's (1933-1945) Good Neighbor Policy responded to the economic crisis of the 1930's with a structured rearrangement of the role of U.S. corporate interests that, according to Smith, was acceptable to the major U.S. firms operating in Cuba. Smith discusses the complexities of loan renegotiation and tariff policy in language that is clear and generally free of jargon. The last chapter is an interpretive essay on U.S.-Cuban relations from Fulgencio Batista's rise to power in the 1930's to Castro's revolution in 1959. Although studies such as the one by Morris Morley (discussed in this section) have revised some of Smith's findings, this book retains considerable value because of its original research, the clarity of its thesis, and the context in which it appeared.

Smith, Wayne S. The Closest of Enemies: A Personal and Diplomatic Account of U.S.-Cuban Relations Since 1957. New York: Norton, 1987.
Most of Smith's work as a U.S. foreign service officer from 1957 to 1982 involved dealing with Cuba and Castro. One of his first assignments for the State Department was to prepare an intelligence analysis

of Castro's insurgent movement in 1957. In 1977, Smith was chief of the first group of U.S. diplomats to return to Cuba after the break in relations between the two countries in the early 1960's. Throughout these two decades, Smith closely watched the Castro regime, combining professional duties with an abiding personal interest. His book includes a carefully considered judgment as to why Castro adopted Communism as the revolution's ideology. Smith claims that the ambitious Castro envisioned himself as the twentieth century liberator of Latin America (and eventually the Third World) from the imperial power of the United States and Western Europe. Castro believed that the adoption of Communism and an alliance with the Soviet Union afforded him the best opportunity to reach these goals. Smith also gives detailed commentary on Cuba's relations with Nicaragua and Grenada in the 1970's and the Mariel boat lift of 1980. He concludes that the United States and Cuba should resume normal diplomatic relations. Smith retired from the foreign service in 1982 because of a dispute with Ronald Reagan's administration (1981-1989) on this issue.

Suárez, Andrés. *Cuba: Castroism and Communism, 1959-1966.* Cambridge: Massachusetts Institute of Technology Press, 1967.

Among the many controversial aspects of Fidel Castro's career are the questions surrounding his relationships with the ideology of Communism and international Communist organizations. Many U.S. observers insist that he was a disciple of Communism well before he came to power in Cuba in 1959. Suárez, however, has a different point of view. In this forcefully argued book, he builds an impressive case for Castro as a clever opportunist who secured his position as head of state in Cuba by committing his nation to the Soviet Union more as a source of strategic and military support than as a model for a new socialist society. In its early phases, Castro's movement received little help from the Cuban masses and had little contact with Cuba's long-established connection with international Communism, the PSP or People's Socialist Party. Che Guevara's break with Castro in 1963, according to Suárez, resulted from the former's realization that genuine revolution as a means for remaking economic and social structures meant less to Castro than the erection and protection of a strong national government. Suárez gives considerable attention to Castro's relationships with Communist China as well as the Soviet Union. The signal importance of this book is its challenge to widely held assumptions about Castro among U.S. political and intellectual leaders, as explained in Richard Welch's book discussed in this section.

Szulc, Tad. *Fidel: A Critical Portrait.* New York: William Morrow, 1986.
The longevity and ambiguities of Fidel Castro's life pose challenges to any biographer. Szulc responds to these challenges with positive results. He chose to devote more than 450 pages of his 653-page text to Castro's personality, family background, and youth. Of special interest is Szulc's discussion of Castro's first steps in the political arena as a law student at the University of Havana in the late 1940's. The author gives detailed attention to Castro's struggle to overthrow the second Batista government (1952-1959), from the failed raid on the Moncada Barracks in 1953, to the exile and reorganization of his movement in Mexico in 1955-1956, to the inauspicious return to Cuba in 1956 and the difficult years in the Sierra Maestra of eastern Cuba. In his approximately 140 pages on the revolution's first five years in power (1959-1963), Szulc emphasizes Castro's use of television to build his rapport with the Cuban people, his deteriorating relations with the United States, and the National Institute for Agrarian Reform's bold attempts to remake Cuba's rural economy. The last chapter, titled "The Maturity," is a mixture of reminiscences by Castro and evaluations by Szulc (based on the author's extensive interviews with Castro in 1984).

Thomas, Hugh. *Cuba: The Pursuit of Freedom.* New York: Harper & Row, 1971.
The ascendancy of Fidel Castro and Communism represents only a fraction of Cuba's long and eventful history. Thomas' classic study contains a readable survey of more than two hundred years of Cuba history, from the mid-1700's and the emergence of the sugar plantations under Spanish colonial rule to the 1960's, with the Bay of Pigs invasion of 1961, the Cuban Missile Crisis of 1962, and the social and economic experiments under Castro's version of a Communist state. On the two centuries in between, Thomas provides informative discussions of the sugar plantation system and slavery, the abolitionist movement, and the crisis and ultimate defeat of the Spanish Empire, concluding with the intrusion of the United States in 1898. Although the book focuses on Cuban history, it also contains much material on the United States as a major actor in this history. After 1898, the United States engaged in several interventions, cultivated a close working relationship with Fulgencio Batista during World War II and the 1950's, and persevered in its multidimensional conflicts with Castro after 1959. The text, nearly 1,500 pages, is supported by extensive footnotes, several useful appendices, and a lengthy bibliography.

Welch, Richard. *Response to Revolution: The United States and the Cuban Revolution, 1959-1961.* Chapel Hill: University of North Carolina Press, 1985.

The Cuban revolution had a large impact on the United States not only in foreign policy but also in intellectual circles and the amorphous area of public opinion. Welch examines these various responses in this important study. The first chapter provides a survey of events in Cuba. Chapters 2 through 4 cover the perceptions of diplomats and government officials, with emphasis on the role of Vice President Richard Nixon (of the Eisenhower Administration, 1953-1961) in the identification of Communism in Cuba as a major problem for the United States. The next four chapters look at the responses on the ideological right, including those of Senator Barry Goldwater; the responses from the ideological left, led by sociologist C. Wright Mills (see the annotation of his book in this section); and the responses on college campuses, in coffeehouses, and in the press in general. Welch's analysis is fair-minded on a subject that often succumbs to polemics. He concludes that most commentators on both the left and the right tended to elevate Castro's Communism to a higher, more threatening status as a result of the peculiar concerns and fears within U.S. politics and culture during the Cold War era.

Wyden, Peter. *The Bay of Pigs: The Untold Story.* New York: Simon and Schuster, 1979.

The defeat of the U.S.-sponsored Bay of Pigs invasion on the southern coast of Cuba was a profound embarrassment for President John F. Kennedy (1961-1963) and the Central Intelligence Agency, and a great triumph for Fidel Castro, who had a worldwide audience when he claimed that he had defeated Yankee imperialism. Wyden uses interviews with anti-Castro Cuban veterans of the invasion, the CIA strategists who planned the invasion, and the Cubans who responded to it, including Castro. Approximately half of the text deals with the origins of the plan in the CIA during the last years of the Eisenhower Administration (1953-1961) and its continuation under Kennedy. Wyden emphasizes the roles of CIA strategist Richard Bissell, CIA Director Allen Dulles, and President Kennedy. The last half of the book covers the invasion, with detailed information on what went wrong with the CIA plan, including the perspectives of both sides on Cuba's unexpected strength in combat aircraft.

The Dominican Republic

Atkins, G. Pope, and Larman Wilson. *The United States and the Trujillo Regime*. New Brunswick, NJ: Rutgers University Press, 1972.

Rafael Leonidas Trujillo ruled the Dominican Republic under a harsh and often cruel dictatorship from 1930 to 1961. Atkins and Wilson evaluate this dictatorship in the light of the frequently mentioned U.S. policy goal of promotion of representative democracy in Latin America. Clearly, Trujillo was a dictator who spurned democracy. To what extent was the United States responsible for this dictatorship? Atkins and Wilson document the supportive policies of the United States for Trujillo from World War II into the Cold War, but they argue that the administrations in Washington during these years had little opportunity to push for democracy within this island nation. Trujillo exploited the U.S. fixation with Western Hemisphere security from the 1930's to the 1950's to build the material and personnel foundations for his dictatorship. Only in the late 1950's did the United States pull away from Trujillo as his grip on the Dominican Republic began to weaken. The main thrust of the authors' analysis is that the United States had only a limited capacity to influence domestic politics in the Dominican Republic.

Calder, Bruce J. *The Impact of Intervention: The Dominican Republic During the U.S. Occupation of 1916-1924*. Austin: University of Texas Press, 1984.

The Dominican Republic faced political unrest and financial crisis in 1916. The United States dispatched an occupation force to restore stability and thereby eliminate a justification for intervention by European powers—especially Germany—which could have posed a threat to U.S. control of its new strategic asset, the Panama Canal. Caulder's analysis of the conduct and consequences of this military intervention is not only a study in U.S. diplomatic and military history but also a probing examination of the results of this episode on the historical development of the Dominican Republic. Military and civilian officials attempted to remake this Caribbean nation's society through several intrusive programs, including the expansion and reform of the public school system. The occupation authorities also modernized the road systems and initiated sanitation and public health programs. Calder emphasizes the training of a national constabulary (police force) that, in later years, would serve as the power base for Rafael Trujillo's dictatorship (1930-1961). Calder also explores Dominican resistance to the occupation, especially the outbreak of a guerrilla movement from 1917 to 1922. This thoroughly researched study places the Dominican experience in the larger context of U.S. interventions in the Caribbean in the early decades of the twentieth century.

Crassweller, Robert D. *Trujillo: The Life and Times of a Caribbean Dictator*. New York: Macmillan, 1966.
Rafael Leonidas Trujillo dominated not only the political system of the Dominican Republic from 1930 to 1961 but also the economic and cultural life of his nation. As a young man, he rose through the ranks of the constabulary (or police) force established by the United States during its military occupation of 1916-1924. Trujillo understood the power of U.S. diplomats, politicians, and business leaders and went to great lengths to cultivate their favor. Crassweller's biography is rich in its descriptions of the dictator's personal style and his idiosyncrasies, and it also explains the larger context in which Trujillo became the quintessential right-wing dictator who opposed liberal reformers, leftist ideologues, peasant and labor movements, and Communism, not only in the Dominican Republic but also throughout the Caribbean. Crassweller gives much attention to Trujillo's relations with the government in Washington and his efforts to create a favorable public image in the United States. In 1961, Trujillo's regime ended with his assassination by a group of dissident officials in his government aided by Dominican business leaders.

Kryzanek, Michael J., and Howard J. Wiarda. *The Politics of External Influence in the Dominican Republic*. New York: Praeger, 1988.
The Dominican Republic has long experienced a divided political culture. The traditional political system evolved from the Hispanic colonial period with its strong sense of personalistic, authoritarian government. In the twentieth century, strong outside influences—especially that of the United States—have pushed this nation toward an institutional, democratic framework. These conflicting tendencies have been further entangled by U.S. interventions (1916-1924 and 1965) and the extended U.S. support for the dictatorship of Rafael Trujillo (1930-1961). Kryzanek and Wiarda give the reader an exceptionally clear discussion of these often contradictory tendencies. The authors go beyond the customary limits of diplomatic history and foreign policy studies to probe a vital question: To what extent have the domestic politics and government of this nation been dominated by outside factors? In short, this approach traces the impact of foreign influences beyond discussions of treaties and tariff policies to encom-

pass the external pressures on the operation of the Dominican Republic's economic and cultural as well as political institutions.

Lowenthal, Abraham F. *The Dominican Intervention*. Cambridge, MA:
    Harvard University Press, 1972.
    Lowenthal was living in the Dominican Republic at the time of the
    U.S. military intervention in April of 1965, but his analysis not only
    involves events in that nation but also penetrates the information-gath-
    ering and decision-making processes within the government in Wash-
    ington. Lowenthal explains the instability of Dominican politics in the
    early 1960's, including an assessment of the weak and ineffective
    Communist presence in the agitation to return liberal reformer Juan
    Bosch to the presidency after his ouster in a 1963 military coup.
    According to the author, U.S. officials greatly overestimated the
    strength of the Communists in the pro-Bosch movement. Guided by
    their fixation on Castro's revolution as a prototype for similar move-
    ments in countries such as the Dominican Republic, the Central Intel-
    ligence Agency and the State Department concentrated their attention
    on Bosch and reported relatively little on military and civilian support-
    ers of Bosch. When U.S. officials finally grasped the full extent of
    popular unrest, the preponderance of their information on the small
    Communist group obscured the full range of political participants in
    the uprising. Lowenthal uses his interviews with more than 150 people
    involved in these events as a major part of his source material in this
    study.

Palmer, Bruce. *Intervention in the Caribbean: The Dominican Crisis of
    1965*. Lexington: University Press of Kentucky, 1989.
    The United States military intervention in the Dominican Republic
    took place ostensibly to prevent the seizure of that nation's government
    by Communists—in short, to avert another Castro-type revolution.
    Palmer, a military officer who was the U.S. Army's deputy chief of
    staff for operations at the time, writes from the point of view of one
    who was directly involved in the intervention. In general, Palmer
    considers the operation a success. U.S. forces occupied crucial posi-
    tions in Santo Domingo (the capital) and the countryside. The fighting
    resulted in approximately 5,000 Dominican casualties (rebels and
    civilians) and 350 U.S. casualties. Palmer is especially positive in his
    assessment of the work of the 82d Airborne Division (paratroopers).
    He also states his case for a genuine Communist threat in the Domini-
    can Republic in the months before the intervention and is critical of

U.S. press coverage of he occupation. (For contrary views, see the book by Abraham Lowenthal discussed in this section.)

Welles, Sumner. *Naboth's Vineyard: The Dominican Republic, 1844-1924.* 2 vols. 1928. Reprint. Mamaroneck, NY: P. P. Appel, 1966.
This lengthy study covers more than eight decades in Dominican history, and the second volume (440 pages of text) covers a quarter century of great importance in U.S. relations with that nation and for the author. Welles served as a diplomat involved in the arrangements for the ending of the U.S. intervention of 1916-1924. Later, he was a central figure in the development of the Good Neighbor Policy during the administration of President Franklin D. Roosevelt (1933-1945). His evaluation of the intervention in the Dominican Republic points to harmful results for both nations. For the Dominican people, the intervention brought foreign troops and the imposition of external policies in their homeland. For the United States, it brought entanglements in Dominican internal affairs and widespread criticism throughout the Western Hemisphere. Welles does not condemn the stated objectives of U.S. leaders including President Woodrow Wilson (1913-1921) and Secretary of State Charles Evans Hughes (1921-1925); instead, he concentrates his analysis on the unfortunate and often unintended impact of the intervention on Dominican people and institutions at the local level. Although somewhat dated because of more recent studies, this book has enduring value for its detailed account of the U.S. intervention and also because it contains insights into the ideas of Welles, who became one of the architects of the Good Neighbor Policy and one of the chief diplomats in charge of its implementation.

Haiti

Abbott, Elizabeth. *Haiti: The Duvaliers and Their Legacy.* New York: McGraw-Hill, 1988.
François Duvalier (known as "Papa Doc") and his son and political successor, Jean-Claude Duvalier, ruled Haiti with a mixture of authoritarian intimidation, tropical intrigue, and brutal repression from 1957 to 1986. Although Abbott's study of their regimes is concerned primarily with Haiti's internal affairs, it also makes clear that both men and their governments were affected by the dominating presence of the United States. The elder Duvalier's medical training in the United States in 1943 provided him with expertise that he used to build a large following among the nation's peasantry. Once in power, he and his son

drew criticism from U.S. observers because of their use of brutal tactics against their opponents. The U.S. government gave limited support to the flawed 1963 coup attempt against Papa Doc and the successful ouster of Jean-Claude Duvalier in 1986. Much of Abbott's information comes from interviews with Haitian leaders, some of whom were connected with the Duvaliers.

Dupuy, Alan. *Haiti in the World Economy: Class, Race, and Underdevelopment Since 1700*. Boulder, CO: Westview Press, 1989.
The economic history of Haiti is a long record of struggle, poverty, and external exploitation. Dupuy's clear, nontechnical prose covers this subject from the arrival of enslaved Africans during the heyday of sugar plantations under the eighteenth century French empire to the uphill quest for prosperity in the last half of the twentieth century. Chapters 5 and 6 concentrate on the internal problems of the divided middle class, the influence of the government in the economy, and the absence of local capital and modern technology. These chapters also cover the rivalries among the United States, France, Great Britain, and Germany for preeminence in the export and financial sectors of the Haitian economy in the late nineteenth and early twentieth centuries. The United States won this competition when its military and civilian officials occupied Haiti from 1915 to 1934. Chapter 6 covers the 1945-1986 period and the impact of U.S. investments and loans, the rise and fall of U.S. foreign aid programs, the rise of a sense of nationalism in Haiti, and the troublesome presence of the Duvalier dictatorship (father and son) that controlled the nation from 1957 to 1986. Dupuy traces the primary causes for Haiti's underdevelopment to the manner in which its economy is integrated into the international capitalist system. His analysis, following the pattern laid out by Immanuel Wallerstein, views Haiti as a peripheral agricultural economy outside the flow of profits and dependent on foreign (mainly U.S.) investment.

Healy, David. *Gunboat Diplomacy in the Wilson Era: The U.S. Navy in Haiti, 1915-1916*. Madison: University of Wisconsin Press, 1976.
Haiti's record of political and financial instability became a vital concern for the United States after the opening of the Panama Canal in 1914. Haiti's international debt tempted European powers to intervene in order to set up a collection agency which, in turn, could lead to a naval/military occupation and thereby pose a threat to the canal. The Haitian government's financial crisis of 1914-1915 and its conflict with the Banque National (controlled by the National City Bank of

New York) contributed to further tensions. A flotilla of U.S. Navy warships commanded by Admiral William S. Caperton arrived off Haiti in early 1915, carrying several hundred U.S. Marines. Healy discusses the relations between Caperton, a polite Tennessean who nevertheless shared his country's racist assumptions about Haiti, and Vilbrun Guillaume Sam, the president of Haiti. Sam became embroiled in a riot in which an angry mob killed him and dismembered his body. U.S. officials ordered the Marines and Navy to occupy key cities and restore order. Healy makes it clear that, although sincerely concerned about the Haitians, Caperton and his men were guided by racist assumptions in their operations. This study covers the Marines' campaign against the Cacos, rugged Haitian peasant rebels who opposed the U.S. intervention. In general, Healy provides a thorough examination of the formative phase of the U.S. occupation that continued until 1934.

Millspaugh, Arthur. *Haiti Under American Control, 1915-1930.* 1931. Reprint. Westport, CT: Greenwood Press, 1970.
By 1930, the military-civilian intervention in Haiti was a highly controversial subject in the United States. Millspaugh served as the chief financial officer with the U.S. occupation (both military and civilian) headed by Marine General John Russell from 1927 to 1928. He wrote this account of the first fifteen years of the occupation using documentary sources from U.S. congressional hearings and State Department publications together with his personal observations. Although Millspaugh gives attention to his specialty—management of Haitian finances—he also covers a wide range of topics from local politics to the occupation group's work to upgrade public health, transportation, and education. Millspaugh discusses the criticism directed at the intervention by anti-imperialists in the United States, but his overall conclusion emphasizes the more positive results. This book includes more than fifty pages of documents, and its detailed footnotes pinpoint relevant periodical articles and government publications that appeared at the height of the public debate in the United States.

Plummer, Brenda Gayle. *Haiti and the United States: The Psychological Moment.* Athens: University of Georgia Press, 1992.
Cultural differences and racial tensions have been important in United States-Haitian relations since their inception in the tumultuous 1790's. Plummer carefully places diplomacy within this larger historical context. The expression "psychological moment" comes from a statement by U.S. Secretary of State Elihu Root (1905-1909) that indicated his

growing awareness of Haitian sensitivity to the implications and complications of racial attitudes in the relations between the two countries. Plummer traces Haiti's isolation from the normal patterns of trade and diplomacy through the nineteenth century to the arrival of the Marines and U.S. tutelage in the early decades of the twentieth century. She views the United States as by far the dominant external influence in Haitian history thereafter. The author consistently maintains a balance between her coverage of diplomacy, politics, and economics and that of social and attitudinal factors. U.S. policymakers in the Cold War years generally seemed to tolerate Haitian elite control of the island nation—even many of the excesses of the dictatorships of the Duvaliers from the 1950's to the 1980's—as preferable to the inclusion of the unpredictable masses in the political system. Plummer's research in U.S. State Department archives coupled with her use of a wide range of published sources provides considerable depth to this study of an important and often neglected subject.

Schmidt, Hans. *The United States Occupation of Haiti, 1915-1934.* New Brunswick, NJ: Rutgers University Press, 1971.
The United States' armed intervention in Haiti left a legacy of racial tension, unfulfilled expectations, and arrogant imperialism in the relations between the two countries. Schmidt's thoroughly researched analysis of the results of two decades of Marine operations in Haiti underscores the depths of the misunderstandings that arose between whites from the United States and the predominantly black population of Haiti. He describes the attitudes of Marine officers such as Colonel Littleton Waller and Major Smedley Butler, who frequently disparaged the Haitian people in racist language. The author also describes the Marines' brutal suppression of the Cacos revolt of 1915, in which poorly armed peasants were no match for Marine rifles and bayonets. General John Russell was high commissioner for Haiti from 1922 to 1930, a job that placed him in charge of the U.S. occupation force. Free from the overt racism of many of his colleagues, Russell embarked on a vigorous program of social and economic uplift including provision of schools, public sanitation, roads, and bridges. In Schmidt's view, however, even these benevolent efforts brought limited long-term results. The Haitian occupation enhanced U.S. strategic security in the Caribbean, but it left few lasting benefits for the Haitian people and created new tensions between the two nations.

Puerto Rico

Carr, Raymond. *Puerto Rico: A Colonial Experiment*. New York: New York University Press, 1984.

According to Carr, the United States' "colonial experiment" with Puerto Rico, although not entirely a failure, has been far from success-ful. The veteran British historian, known for his studies of modern Europe, takes on the challenge of analyzing one of the twentieth century's most enduring colonial relationships. He concentrates on the period from 1948 to the early 1980's, during which the "common-wealth status" for Puerto Rico became established through the activism of Luís Muñoz Marín. Under this arrangement, Puerto Rico acquired the right to self-government at the local level within the framework of continued U.S. control. Commonwealth status, a compromise position that is neither full independence nor statehood on equal footing with the states of the United States, seemed to work in the 1950's and 1960's but became the object of criticism from a variety of perspectives thereafter. Carr has two thoughtful chapters on questions surrounding Puerto Rico's sense of identity versus the overwhelming influence of U.S. advertising and popular culture. He concludes that the Puerto Rican economy cannot survive complete independence but that the islanders will continue to debate their political and cultural status amid the frustrations and disappointments of the ambiguous relationship with the United States.

Clark, Truman R. *Puerto Rico and the United States, 1917-1933*. Pitts-burgh, PA: University of Pittsburgh Press, 1975.

Clark's book is a balanced political, economic, and social history of Puerto Rico based on research in manuscript collections on both the United States mainland and the island. The main body of the text begins with an explanation of the Jones Act of 1917, which established U.S. citizenship for Puerto Ricans. Clark contrasts the colonial administra-tion's imposition of prohibition on the island with the rise of a grass-roots reform movement that called for woman suffrage. Chapter 3 covers the fiasco of the ardent and awkward "pro-Americanization" governorship of E. M. Reily (1921-1923). Chapter 5 is a trenchant discussion of the weaknesses in the Puerto Rican economy from 1917 to 1933. Perhaps one of the brightest periods was the governorship of the energetic Theodore Roosevelt, Jr. (1929-1932), who seemed to be in the process of carrying out several promising policy initiatives when he decided to give up his post to become governor of the Philippines. A consistent theme in Clark's analysis of the impact of the colonial administration is the sense of estrangement between U.S. officials and the Puerto Rican people. Clark emphasizes the activities of several of the island's leaders, including working-class advocate Santiago Pantin and politician Antonio Barceló. The author includes extensive footnotes and a helpful bibliography.

Dietz, James L. *Economic History of Puerto Rico: Institutional Change and Capitalist Development.* Princeton, NJ: Princeton University Press, 1986.
This well-written survey of Puerto Rico's economic past provides solid coverage from the Spanish colonial period (1508-1898) through the economic surge under Operation Bootstrap of the 1940's and 1950's to the troubled conditions thereafter. Dietz stresses the long-term importance of the exportation of sugar in the island's history. Beginning with the establishment of U.S. colonial control, the author gives much attention to the role of investment capital in the development of the Puerto Rican economy. The text features low-keyed discussion and clearly stated statistical analyses. Dietz is generally critical of the extent to which the island's economy depends on special arrangements with Washington and investments from and sales to the United States. He insists that Puerto Rican development will be precarious as long as local government officials and business leaders are not able to create their own dynamism. In short, according to Dietz, Puerto Ricans sell to and buy from the huge U.S. economy but seldom buy and sell among themselves. The research value of this book in enhanced by its numerous footnotes and lengthy bibliography.

Diffie, Bailey W., and Justine Whitfield Diffie. *Porto Rico: A Broken Pledge.* New York: Vanguard Press, 1931.
This attack on U.S. policy toward Puerto Rico (Porto Rico is an antiquated spelling) eventually became a historical document in that it summarizes the case against imperialism on the island in terms of ideas in vogue in the early years of the Great Depression. The Diffies insist that the United States pledged to help Puerto Rico recover from the damages and civil strife connected with the Spanish-American War and further pledged to grant the island its independence. Instead, the Diffies argue, the United States continued to hold Puerto Rico as a colonial appendage in order to support the activities of private U.S. corporations in the island's sugar business as well as protecting investments in tobacco, fruit crops, and public utilities. These corporations prospered but kept the wages of Puerto Rican workers at very low levels. The Diffies' condemnation of these policies and practices concludes that

the United States played the role of an exploitative imperial power in both a political sense and an economic sense. The reader can consult the books by Truman Clark and Thomas Mathews (annotated in this section) for other perspectives on this period. The Diffies include a valuable annotated bibliography of documents and books available in the 1920's.

Jiménez de Wagenheim, Olga. *Puerto Rico: An Interpretative History from Pre-Colombian Times to 1900*. Princeton, NJ: Markus Weiner, 1996.

Even well-read students often fail to appreciate that Puerto Rico's history extends back for centuries to the years before the arrival of the Spanish Empire. Jiménez de Wagenheim covers this large topic with her survey of the island's social, political, and economic history over the course of six centuries. Her discussion of the island's economic history emphasizes the foundations for reliance on sugar and other export crops during the Spanish colonial era. The last portion of the text deals with crucial episodes in the history of modern Puerto Rico. The author explains the contradictions of the movement toward independence in the waning years of the Spanish Empire in the late 1800's with the abrupt intrusion of the United States during the Spanish-American War of 1898. This war did not bring independence but rather the shift of control over the island from Madrid to Washington, D.C.

Lewis, Gordon K. *Freedom and Power in the Caribbean*. New York: Harper & Row, 1963.

Puerto Rico experienced a surge of economic growth in the 1940's and 1950's under a program known as Operation Bootstrap, which offered incentives for U.S. corporations to build factories on the island. Lewis concentrates his study on this post-World War II period, when industrialization advanced rapidly but underlying problems continued to hold back Puerto Rican development. Lewis explains the origins of Operation Bootstrap and its positive image in the press and in the speeches of politicians. He also discusses the nagging difficulties of continued dependence on the United States for markets and investment capital, the widening gaps within the class structure, and the growing strength of "Americanization" in the island's traditionally Hispanic culture. Lewis devotes three chapters to government and politics within Puerto Rico and the struggle to find an acceptable political-administrative relationship with the United States. The last two chapters provide stimulating analyses of public education and public opinion during the 1940's and 1950's, with some valuable insights into Puerto Rican history.

Maldonado-Denis, Manuel. *Puerto Rico: A Socio-Historic Interpretation.* New York: Random House, 1972.

Maldonado-Denis was born in Santurce, Puerto Rico, in 1933 and was educated at the University of Puerto Rico and the University of Chicago, where he earned his Ph.D. in political science. He makes a case against the continuation of U.S. colonialism in Puerto Rico. Students can find in this study an example of radical anti-imperialism in which the United States is seen as a nation determined to dominate the commercial, financial, and industrial potential not only of Puerto Rico but also of the Western Hemisphere. The author is sharply critical of Puerto Rican politicians and business leaders who work with U.S. government and corporate officials. Maldonado-Denis brands these Puerto Ricans, including Luís Muñoz Marín, as collaborators with the imperialist interests. The author is also critical of U.S. efforts to supplant Puerto Rican native culture and nationalism with North American values.

Mathews, Thomas. *Puerto Rican Politics and the New Deal.* Gainesville: University of Florida Press, 1960.

The troubled relationship between the United States and Puerto Rico entered a particularly difficult phase in the 1930's. The Great Depression dealt the island's economy a severe blow, and a devastating hurricane in September of 1932 added another wave of material destruction. President Franklin D. Roosevelt's New Deal came into effect in March of the following year with a commitment to respond to the United States' economic collapse; Puerto Rico was included. Mathews conducted his research in U.S. government archives and the Roosevelt papers to document the successes and failures of the New Deal in Puerto Rico. The author examines the short, tumultuous administration of the overbearing Governor Robert Gore, who faced a rising tide of resentment carefully managed by the youthful Luís Muñoz Marín. Although Gore resigned amid controversy, the New Deal programs took hold on the island. Mathews gives particular attention to the work of Ernest Gruening as head of the Puerto Rico Reconstruction Administration and the conflicts involving Gruening with Secretary of the Interior Harold Ickes and Gore's successor as governor, Blanton Winship (1934-1938). Among the Puerto Rican leaders who figure prominently in this study are Muñoz Marín and his political rival, Antonio Barceló.

Perusse, Roland. *The United States and Puerto Rico*. Lanham, MD: University Press of America, 1987.

This brief, sharply focused book deals with the available options in the relationship between the United States and Puerto Rico. Although its status as a commonwealth (since 1952) allows for more local autonomy than its previous standing as a colony (1898-1952), Puerto Rico grew increasingly dissatisfied with this arrangement in the 1970's and 1980's. Perusse notes that the year 1998 marks the one hundredth anniversary of the U.S. invasion of the island. The United States and Puerto Rico have failed to find a formula for their relationship that satisfies all the constituencies involved. Perusse examines the case for the continuation of the commonwealth arrangement, outright statehood on equal footing with the other fifty states, and complete independence. His text contains several quotations from leading advocates of these positions. The foreword by Gerald Ford contains the former president's argument in favor of statehood. The text is supported by numerous footnotes that cite government reports, newspapers, and books in English.

Tugwell, Rexford Guy. *The Stricken Land: The Story of Puerto Rico*. 1946. Reprint. New York: Greenwood Press, 1968.

This lengthy volume is largely an account of Tugwell's term as governor of Puerto Rico from 1941 to 1946. Tugwell's 31-page introduction and 690-page text present the reader with an intimate—sometimes day-to-day—record of events in Puerto Rico from the governor's point of view. Important topics include the tensions associated with the early phases of World War II, when the defense of the British and French West Indian colonies was uncertain and the German submarine campaign placed Allied shipping in the Caribbean in a precarious position. Most of the text concerns Tugwell's efforts to grasp the nature of Puerto Rico's economic and political problems and his determination to engage in government-directed economic planning to solve these problems. Tugwell generally viewed his tenure as governor as an opportunity to revitalize the island on the basis of the ideals of the New Deal. He also discusses his work with Luís Muñoz Marín, who became the island's dominant political figure soon after Tugwell's departure. Another important figure in this book is Bolívar Pagan, a leftist who turned conservative and became an opponent of Tugwell and Muñoz Marín. Washington-based New Dealers Harold Ickes and Charles Taussig also played important roles in these years.

Smaller Caribbean Nations and Colonies

Adkin, Mark. *Urgent Fury: The Battle for Grenada*. Lexington, MA: Lexington Books, 1989.
Adkin, an officer involved in the operation code-named Urgent Fury, used interviews, published military documents, and his own experiences to write this detailed study of the military aspects of the 1983 invasion of Grenada. Adkin traces the origins of the Reagan Administration's decision to use military force to the execution of Grenada's Prime Minister Maurice Bishop by hard-line Marxist extremists who were determined to take control of this small island nation. Adkin supplies impressive detail on the actions of Rangers, paratroopers, and helicopter units as well as the rapid pace of events that created heavy pressures for the commanding officer, Vice Admiral Joseph Metcalfe. Adkin's evaluation of the U.S. invasion is generally favorable, but he also points out problems, including the absence of sufficient intelligence concerning the island, the failure of Navy SEALS to secure a path for the invasion force, and the crash of three Blackhawk helicopters in the assault on the capital city, St. George. Adkin concludes that the operation was a political and military success because it foiled the extension of Communism, but that the margin of victory was slender. The book includes relevant maps and photographs.

Heine, Jorge, ed. *A Revolution Aborted: The Lessons of Grenada*. Pittsburgh, PA: University of Pittsburgh Press, 1990.
The small Caribbean island of Grenada became the focus of debates about radical politics and military intervention in the 1980's. The rise of the New Jewel Movement in the 1970's, its linkage with Fidel Castro's Cuba, the internal divisions within the movement, and its overthrow by the U.S. intervention in 1983 created controversies that are discussed from various perspectives in this nicely edited volume of readings. Heine's introductory essay gives the political and social background for the 1979 revolution. Thereafter, the editor divides the essays into four sections. The first deals with the political, social, and economic trends in Grenada under the revolutionary government. The second covers international politics, including the policies of the Soviet Union and the United States. The third section examines the Grenadian political crisis resulting from Maurice Bishop's assassination, Bernard Coard's seizure of power, and the U.S. intervention. The final set of essays contains an assessment of the place of socialism in the smaller Caribbean nations.

Manley, Robert H. *Guyana Emergent: The Post-Independent Struggle for Nondependent Development*. Boston: G. K. Hall, 1979.

The former colony of British Guyana became the independent nation of Guyana in 1966. Manley's study deals with the new nation's first decade of independence, during which its leaders attempted to direct their energies toward a foreign policy of their own making and an economic system freed from dependence on Great Britain and the United States. The author also discusses the role of Cheddi Jagan, the charismatic leftist who pushed for Guyana's independence in the early 1960's using language similar to the revolutionary maxims of Fidel Castro. This radicalism attracted the attention of the United States, which closely followed events in Guyana. Although a more moderate politician, Forbes Burnham, became Guyana's prime minister (1966-1985), Jagan continued to exert much influence in his nation and throughout the Caribbean. Chapters 5 through 8 are concerned mainly with Guyana's efforts to assert itself as an independent nation (including nationalization of the foreign-owned bauxite mines), one that often was at odds with the U.S. goals of stability and security in the Caribbean region.

O'Shaughnessy, Hugh. *Grenada: An Eyewitness Account of the U.S. Invasion and the Caribbean History That Provoked It*. New York: Dodd, Mead & Company, 1984.

O'Shaughnessy not only witnessed the Grenada invasion but also studied the reasons why the world's most powerful nation decided to send fifteen thousand soldiers supported by air and naval power to this small Antillean island in October of 1983. The purpose was not simply to rescue the U.S. medical students enrolled in the island's St. George's Medical School. The author emphasizes the U.S. government's long-term concerns about Grenada's leftist prime minister, Maurice Bishop, the island's radical New Jewel Movement, and the apparently expanding presence of Communist Cuba. Nearly eight hundred Cubans were in Grenada working to complete their enlargement of an airport when the U.S. forces arrived by helicopter and parachute. Much of the actual fighting (which was limited) involved hostile fire exchanged by the Cubans and U.S. troops, although the author points out that only forty-three of the Cubans were soldiers. O'Shaughnessy probes deeper into Grenadian politics to discuss the split between the leftist Bishop and the violent extremists of the New Jewel Movement who were responsible for the prime minister's overthrow and assassination one week prior to the U.S. intervention. The tone of O'Shaughnessy's writing is calm and factual in spite of the controversies surrounding these events.

Palmer, Ransford. *Caribbean Dependence on the United States Economy.* New York: Praeger, 1979.

This important and in many ways unique study deals with the economic challenges faced by four of the leading English-speaking nations of the Caribbean: Jamaica, Trinidad and Tobago (one country), Guyana, and Barbados. These former colonies of Great Britain worked for and acquired their political independence during the 1950's and 1960's at the same time that the United States enjoyed an extended period of economic growth. In general, these small nations moved into the economic sphere of the United States. Palmer uses both statistical tables and analytical prose to explain the extent to which the economies of these four small countries came to depend on the United States for trade and investment. In particular, the author examines the bauxite industry, tourism, and human migration patterns in the 1960's and 1970's. Unlike many political and business commentators, Palmer is critical of the New World Order in which there are increases in the connections between small economies, such as those of the four Caribbean nations under study here, and the large U.S. economy. He warns that the process of international economic integration leaves the smaller nations more vulnerable to crises generated by external pressures from the large financial and industrial centers.

Stephens, Evelyne Huber, and John D. Stephens. *Democratic Socialism in Jamaica: The Political Movement and Social Transformation in Dependent Capitalism.* Princeton, NJ: Princeton University Press, 1986.

In spite of its small size, Jamaica came to international attention when the administration of President Michael Manley (1972-1980) attempted to enact an innovative reform program. The Stephenses' detailed examination of Manley's policy goals, his successes, and his failures not only sheds light on a critical period in Jamaican history but also provides a valuable perspective on the dominant influence of the United States on this Caribbean island. The authors argue that Manley—through a heavy tax on bauxite exports, the establishment of import controls, and the initiation of land reform—set Jamaica in the direction of a form of democratic socialism clearly more moderate than Castro's Communism but nevertheless a challenge to the international capitalist system. The authors give close attention to the role of the United States in Jamaican affairs as an importer of bauxite, as a source of investment, and as an opponent of leftist movements in the Caribbean. Their conclusions, though sympathetic to the Manley government, point out some of the regime's miscalculations, especially in its relations with the United States.

Weddell, D. A. G. *The West Indies and the Guianas.* Englewood Cliffs, NJ: Prentice Hall, 1967.
This survey text intended for the college classroom offers a convenient summary of the historical evolution of the smaller Caribbean nations, including the former British colonies of Jamaica, Barbados, Trinidad, Tobago, British Honduras (now Belize), and British Guiana (now Guyana); the French islands of Martinique and Guadeloupe; the Netherlands Antilles (Aruba, Bonaire, and Curaçao); and the U.S. possessions of Puerto Rico and the Virgin Islands. Weddell's first chapter is an overview of the social, political, and economic condition of the West Indies at the time of his writing in the late 1960's. The next two chapters cover the four centuries from European settlement in the 1500's to the end of slavery and the economic decline in the nineteenth century. Chapters 5 and 6 deal with the rise of the varieties of West Indian nationalism and the struggle to develop political and economic autonomy throughout the early and middle decades of the twentieth century. The penetrating presence of the United States is most evident in Chapters 1, 5, and 6, which cover the twentieth century.

Colombia

Bergquist, Charles. *Coffee and Conflict in Colombia, 1886-1910.* Durham, NC Duke University Press, 1978.
Popular culture in the United States often has associated Colombia with coffee. Bergquist's sophisticated, thoroughly researched volume explores the origins of the modern coffee-exporting sector of the Colombian economy. In general, this study deals with the impact of the export-oriented coffee industry on the internal economic and political structures of Colombia. Much of the discussion covers the connections between coffee production and the Liberal Party, which in general favored increased trade with the United States and other foreign markets. Bergquist also examines the clash between the Liberals and their Conservative opponents that eventually resulted in the bloody and destructive Thousand Days War of 1899-1902. The Liberals lost this civil war, but eventually many of their ideas found acceptance in the bipartisan administration of President Rafael Reyes (1905-

1909). Bergquist concludes this study with two excellent chapters on the Reyes presidency and the emergence of a "new order" in Colombia with heavy emphasis on the promotion of foreign trade, railroad construction, and the continued expansion of the coffee industry.

Bushnell, David. *Eduardo Santos and the Good Neighbor Policy, 1938-1942*. Gainesville: Center for Latin American Studies, University of Florida, 1967.
The Good Neighbor Policy faced some of its greatest challenges in the 1938 to 1942 period, when Axis influence in Latin America seemed to reach its peak at the same time that the German military overran Poland and France. Bushnell examines in great detail the relations between the United States and Colombia in this crucial period that coincided with the presidency of moderate Eduardo Santos. The general status of relations between his government and the administration of Franklin D. Roosevelt (1933-1945) was friendly, especially in the fields of military, naval, and aviation defense preparations, but Bushnell presents careful analyses of some points of controversy, including U.S. pressure to nationalize SCADTA (the German-Colombian airline); U.S. concerns about Axis propaganda and espionage in Colombia; the pro-Axis, anti-United States sympathies of leading Colombian conservatives; and the continued tensions regarding the operations of the United Fruit Company and Standard Oil. Bushnell is a master of clear, succinct prose and managed to compress an impressive amount of information into this 120-page text.

Fluharty, Vernon Lee. *Dance of the Millions: Military Rule and the Social Revolution in Colombia, 1930-1956*. Pittsburgh, PA: University of Pittsburgh Press, 1957.
The 1948 assassination of popular leftist leader Jorge Eliécer Gaitán unleashed a torrent of social unrest and violence that spread through much of Colombia. Fluharty, a student of politics and political history, completed this book only nine years after that traumatic event. From the point of view of a U.S. scholar, he expresses the frustrations of many Colombians who saw their movement toward democratic government in the previous decades wiped out by waves of disorder and bloodshed. Although Fluharty concentrates on the internal causes of Colombia's distress, the student who wants to understand the larger aspects of U.S.-Colombian relations will find much of value in this book. One of the author's main points is that the influx of U.S. investments and loans in the 1920's (the "Dance of the Millions" in the title) set off a period of unbalanced growth in which exports such as

coffee and bananas generated wealth for a few powerful families at the top of Colombia's social structure but left workers and peasants with little except a low standard of living. In short, the boom of the 1920's—viewed at the time as a welcome, progressive trend tied to the U.S. economy—contained the seeds of deeper social divisions and revolutionary ferment.

Lael, Richard. *Arrogant Diplomacy: U.S. Policy Toward Colombia, 1903-1922*. Wilmington, DE: Scholarly Resources, 1987.
The Panamanian revolt for independence in 1903, the subsequent U.S. recognition of its new government, and the rapid signing of the Panama Canal Treaty were pivotal events in the troubled relationship between Colombia and the United States. Other pivotal aspects of this difficult relationship—often neglected by students of the Panama Canal episode—are the protracted and problematic negotiations between the United States and Colombia concerning the aftermath of Panama's secession. Historian Lael traces these negotiations through the administrations of Theodore Roosevelt (1901-1909), William Howard Taft (1909-1913), and Woodrow Wilson (1913-1921). He finds variations in their policies but, in general, concludes that the United States consistently asserted its power to pressure Colombia for a settlement and also to limit that nation's efforts to regulate foreign-owned business enterprises within its boundaries. The final settlement of the Panama dispute, the Thomas-Urrutia Treaty of 1922, contained a $25 million indemnity paid by the United States to Colombia for the loss of Panama. In the ten years required to negotiate the treaty, however, the United States greatly expanded its economic base of operations in that South American nation.

McGreevey, William Paul. *An Economic History of Colombia, 1845-1930*. Cambridge, England: Cambridge University Press, 1971.
This widely respected survey of Colombian economic history has the strengths of sensible organization and a clear prose style. The last third of the book covers the expansion of the Colombian economy from the late 1800's to 1930, with particular emphasis on the export of coffee, bananas, petroleum, and minerals to foreign countries—largely the United States. Chapter 8 focuses on the energetic people of the province of Antioquia, where coffee production and textile manufacturing enjoyed rapid rates of expansion. Chapter 9 contains an explanation of why coffee cultivation for export was so successful in Antioquia during this period. Chapter 10 offers a useful analysis of the development of Colombia's transportation system and its importance for the export

sector of the Colombian economy. The conclusions in Chapter 11 offer insights into why the Antioquia coffee region was so successful in beginning the process of economic modernization.

Parks, E. Taylor. *Colombia and the United States, 1765-1934*. Durham, NC: Duke University Press, 1935.

In spite of the fact that Parks wrote this book in the mid-1930's, when much of the archival documentation on crucial episodes in Colombian-U.S. relations was unavailable, this book retains value in its narrative of the long history of diplomatic relations between the two countries and its evaluation of the controversial diplomacy of President Theodore Roosevelt (1901-1909). Relying on limited primary sources and published documents from both Colombia and the United States, Parks emphasizes the nineteenth century and the growing interest in both nations in the construction of a canal to link the Pacific with the Caribbean. The last eighty-five pages cover Theodore Roosevelt's policy toward the Panamanian revolt and the response of the Colombian government to the loss of the isthmus. Although moderate in his use of language, Parks is highly critical of Roosevelt's actions. He provides a stimulating commentary on Roosevelt's later justifications for these actions. The numerous footnotes in this section of the book will be helpful to many researchers because they point out published documents and newspaper accounts from the early twentieth century, many of which may be available in university and larger public libraries.

Randall, Stephen J. *Colombia and the United States: Hegemony and Interdependence*. Athens: University of Georgia Press, 1992.

The loss of Panama by Colombia and the economic potential of the Panama Canal are central in this survey, but Randall uses a multidimensional approach in which the loss of Panama and diplomacy in general are placed alongside cultural and commercial relations between the United States and Colombia in the nineteenth and twentieth centuries. The author contends that although the United States was concerned primarily with access to Colombia's resources (such as petroleum and platinum) and its strategic importance, the government in Bogotá was caught between often contradictory goals: The need to export raw materials to its powerful neighbor to the north often conflicted with the second goal, the need to maintain some degree of political, economic, and cultural autonomy. Randall emphasizes that in order to strengthen its sense of autonomy, Colombia turned to Germany as a source of economic and diplomatic leverage in crucial periods in the first decades of the twentieth century—especially the 1930's. He also discusses President Alfonso López Pumarejo's assertion of economic nationalism during the 1930's. In the Cold War era, the United States and Colombia shared an aversion to Fidel Castro and the revolutionary left (which was active in Colombia), but the emergence of the cocaine trade in the 1980's was a source of tension between the two countries.

_____. *The Diplomacy of Modernization: Colombian-American Relations, 1920-1940.* Toronto: University of Toronto Press, 1977.
On the surface, relations between the United States and Colombia seemed routine and uneventful during the period covered by this book, but, as Randall indicates, issues appeared that revealed fundamental differences between the two countries. The author stresses the economic aspects of the relationship. The United States was successful in its push for the 1935 treaty by which the two countries agreed to mutual tariff reductions. On the other hand, the repayment of U.S. loans made to Colombia during the prosperous 1920's proved to be too heavy a burden in the depression-ridden 1930's. The government in Bogotá defaulted on (announced that it would not repay) these loans. Another controversial event was the U.S. encouragement of the Colombian government's bloody suppression of the 1928 banana workers' strike against the United Fruit Company (headquartered in Boston). Randall has interesting chapters on the influence of the United States in the Bogotá government's decision to eliminate SCADTA, the Colombian airline with close connections to Germany, as an example of the growing concerns about Nazi influence in South America in the years just prior to World War II. In general, Randall contends that in spite of Washington's pullback from direct armed interventions under the Good Neighbor Policy, the Colombian experience made clear the expansion of U.S. hegemony in the economic development, politics, and diplomacy of that South American nation.

Rippy, J. Fred. *The Capitalists and Colombia.* New York: Vanguard Press, 1931.
The United States pushed aside Great Britain and other European powers to become the primary foreign investor in Colombia in the half century before this book appeared. Historian Rippy discusses this process in impressive depth considering the limited documentary sources available at the time. He provides an account of the activities of U.S. companies in urban streetcar lines, intercity railroads, mining, and banking. By the 1890's, the U.S. government used diplomatic

pressure and the presence of its modern navy to protect U.S. business interests in Colombia. Rippy builds a circumstantial case for U.S. instigation of the 1903 Panamanian revolt for independence that gave Washington easy access to the construction site of the transisthmian canal. The author discusses the flood of U.S. loans into Colombia in the 1920's known as the "Dance of the Millions." He also covers the frustrations of the oil companies in dealing with the confused state of Colombian land titles and the more profitable operations of the United Fruit Company in exporting bananas. Rippy is sharply critical of the working conditions for laborers in the United Fruit Company operations. The footnotes contain many references to published documents and journalistic accounts from the 1920's that were major sources for Rippy in this volume. Students may also wish to consult more recent studies by Stephen Randall and Richard Lael (annotated in this section), which have more depth in their research.

Venezuela

Ewell, Judith. *The Indictment of a Dictator: The Extradition and Trial of Marcos Pérez Jiménez.* College Station: Texas A&M Press, 1981.
This unusual book offers a remarkable perspective on the misdeeds of a dictator. Ewell makes full use of the legal records of the Pérez Jiménez case, in which Venezuela's former dictator (1952-1959), who fled to the United States, faced an extradition procedure from 1961 to 1963. The new Venezuelan government under President Rómulo Betancourt initiated the extradition process in order to have the authorities in the United States arrest Pérez Jiménez and return him to Venezuela to face charges on his abuses of power when he was head of state. Because of legal technicalities, the Venezuelan government was forced to concentrate on financial corruption rather than charges of murder and other more serious crimes. In 1968, after a lengthy trial, the Venezuelan Supreme Court found him guilty of the minor crime of profiting from public office. Because he already had spent more time in jail awaiting completion of the trial than the four-year sentence imposed by the court, the former dictator left Venezuela free but in disgrace. Ewell's book provides a rare insight into the internal finances of a corrupt dictatorship and the struggle of a nation to find the appropriate legal punishment for such wrongdoing.

_____. *Venezuela: A Century of Change.* Stanford, CA: Stanford University Press, 1984.

The international petroleum industry had a major impact on Venezuela's history throughout the twentieth century. Students who want to examine the petroleum industry, including the early ventures of the Rockefellers' Standard Oil Company and the working conditions and living standards of Venezuelan laborers, will find Ewell's exceptionally well-written survey text to be of much value. Moving in chronological sequence from the dictatorship of Juan Vicente Gómez (1908-1935) to the emergence of democratic tendencies in the 1940's to the return of dictatorship under Marcos Pérez Jiménez (1952-1958), Ewell identifies a general pattern in which most administrations catered to the needs of the foreign oil companies and did relatively little to respond to the situation of the oil workers (with the exception of the first presidency of Rómulo Betancourt from 1945 to 1948). The rise of national political parties coincided with the appearance of more assertive national policies toward the oil companies, especially in the later presidency of Betancourt (1959-1964), who was strongly anti-Communist. Ewell includes a thorough discussion of the nationalization of the foreign oil companies in the mid-1970's.

Herwig, Holger. *Germany's Vision of Empire in Venezuela, 1871-1914.* Princeton, NJ: Princeton University Press, 1986.
The excitable Theodore Roosevelt led prominent politicians and foreign policy experts in the United States in expressions of concern about German expansion in the Western Hemisphere in the late nineteenth and early twentieth centuries. Historian Herwig combed numerous archives in Germany to determine the extent to which U.S. fears of German expansion were justified. The results of his research confirm that many German government, business, and cultural leaders advocated a vigorous expansion into South America. In a sense, Germany "discovered" South America in the 1890's as a land of great potential wealth encumbered by weak and ineffective governments. Herwig concentrates on Venezuela as an important case study in this process. His research documents the construction of the Caracas to Valencia railroad as an example of German economic development in this South American nation. He also notes the arrival of thirty-eight German merchant companies in Venezuela and their energetic business practices. Soon German investments flowed into Venezuelan coffee plantations. These endeavors enjoyed the attention of the Pan-German League, which built public support in the fatherland for such overseas expansion through books, pamphlets, and speeches. Herwig's main point, however, is that in spite of these positive initial steps, Germany was unable to achieve its main goals in Venezuela. The railroad and

coffee plantations did not prosper as expected, and the demands of the German navy for major repair and supply bases in the Caribbean were never met. Instead, German naval and military strategists were impressed and intimidated by the U.S. completion of the Panama Canal, and politicians and diplomats met frustration in President Theodore Roosevelt's assertions of the Monroe Doctrine. German military advisers, business leaders, diplomats, and naval expeditions (including the joint blockade with Great Britain in 1903) played important roles in Venezuelan history, but Berlin did not realize its imperial ambitions in this South American nation.

Hood, Miriam. *Gunboat Diplomacy, 1895-1905: Great Power Pressure in Venezuela*. New York: A. S. Barnes, 1977.
Hood's brief book examines an often neglected episode in the emergence of the United States as a world power. Venezuela was not of primary interest to U.S. investors, but its strategic importance on the northern rim of South American and the southern margin of the Caribbean was obvious. Hood describes the political instability and financial woes of Venezuela throughout the nineteenth century. These problems were of little concern to the United States until Venezuela's two major creditors, Great Britain and Germany, decided to establish a naval blockade in order to force the Caracas government to pay its debts. Hood relies on the reports of London's diplomat in Caracas, W. H. D. Haggard, who wrote in detail about Venezuela's distress. The British-German intervention was directed against the government of Cipriano Castro (1899-1908), a strong-willed dictator who imposed his authority on Venezuela from his power base in the rugged Andes mountains. In his confrontation with the European powers, Castro revealed his impulsive, aggressive nature but lost out in the settlement handed down by the International Court in The Hague. Venezuela had to pay its debts, with priority given to Great Britain and Germany. According to Hood, this 1903 settlement with its rewards for naval intervention contributed to Theodore Roosevelt's announcement of his Corollary to the Monroe Doctrine in the following year, by which the United States asserted itself as the collector of foreign debts and the enforcer of political stability in the Western Hemisphere.

Lieuwen, Edwin. *Petroleum in Venezuela: A History*. Berkeley: University of California Press, 1954.
This pioneering study is a brief, thoughtful, historical account of the first half century of the oil industry in Venezuela. Lieuwen discusses the fundamentals of the petroleum business: government concessions,

geological explorations, exploratory drilling, transportation systems, refineries, and the ups and downs of the price of oil on the international market. His main interest, however, is the policy of the Venezuelan government. Writing in the early 1950's, Lieuwen is especially critical of the Juan Vicente Gómez dictatorship (1908-1935) and subsequent administrations for their failure to use the large tax revenues available from petroleum production to stimulate economic growth and provide for the social well-being of the Venezuelan people. Students can consult Judith Ewell's *Venezuela: A Century of Change* and the books by Sheldon Liss, Stephen Rabe, and Franklin Tugwell (all discussed in this section) for overviews of the changes in policies since the 1950's.

Liss, Sheldon. *Diplomacy & Dependency: Venezuela, the United States, and the Americas*. Salisbury, NC: Documentary Publications, 1978.
This study examines the diplomatic and economic relations between Venezuela and the United States within the larger framework of Western Hemisphere relations during the twentieth century. Liss organizes his book chronologically, beginning with the dictatorships of Cipriano Castro (1899-1908) and Juan Vicente Gómez (1908-1935) and moves through the experiments with democracy in the 1940's, the reversion to dictatorship under Marcos Pérez Jiménez (1952-1958), and the elected presidencies of Rómulo Betancourt (1959-1964) and Raúl Leoni (1964-1969). Liss examines Venezuela's difficulties in its foreign relations, with particular emphasis on the Dominican Republic and Cuba as well as the United States. One of his main theses is that Venezuela's attempts to reduce its dependence on the multinational oil corporations from the 1940's to the 1970's was one of the main tendencies that led to the formation of OPEC (Organization of Petroleum Exporting Countries).

Rabe, Stephen. *The Road to OPEC: United States Relations with Venezuela, 1919-1976*. Austin: University of Texas Press, 1982.
The discovery and exploitation of Venezuela's vast petroleum reserves brought drastic changes in the relations between that nation and the United States. In the years before World War I, the U.S. State Department gave marginal attention to its Venezuelan diplomacy except for worries about the presence of British and German influences there. As Rabe makes clear, however, in the 1920's the United States became concerned about British oil corporations' ownership of Venezuela's rich petroleum lands. In that decade, U.S. oil companies led by Standard Oil moved around the British to acquire control of the Venezuelan oil fields. The U.S. government maintained supportive policies toward

Juan Vicente Gómez, Venezuela's corrupt and cruel dictator. During the era of World War II, the U.S. government encouraged Standard Oil and other petroleum companies to accept higher taxes imposed by the Venezuelan government in order to secure a stable oil supply. After World War II, Venezuela began to experience periodic declines in its oil revenues because of unstable prices. Rabe discusses the perceptive and influential Venezuelan Juan Pablo Pérez Alfonso, who in 1960 formed OPEC (Organization of Petroleum Exporting Countries) with Saudi Arabia and other Middle Eastern countries in order to regulate the world's supply of petroleum and thereby stabilize prices. More concerned with the threats posed by Fidel Castro and the implementation of the Alliance for Progress, the United States underestimated the importance of OPEC until the oil crisis of the 1970's. Rabe's well-written text contains an extensive bibliography of scholarly and journalistic studies, with many of its citations published in English.

Tugwell, Franklin. *The Politics of Oil in Venezuela.* Stanford, CA: Stanford University Press, 1975.
Completed on the eve of the Venezuelan government's nationalization of foreign-owned oil properties, Tugwell's study examines the evolution of this country's policies toward the multinational petroleum companies—primarily Standard Oil but also Gulf, Texaco, and Royal Dutch Shell. Tugwell begins with the permissive practices that allowed oil companies much freedom of operation from the 1920's to the 1940's, but he concentrates his coverage on the "assertive experimentalism" of President Rómulo Betancourt (1959-1964) and subsequent administrations. A central figure in this study is Juan Pablo Pérez Alfonso, head of the Venezuelan ministry of mines, who was the primary architect of the oil policy of the 1960's and 1970's. Trained as a lawyer, Pérez Alfonso sought to establish conservation practices to protect the environment and to stabilize income from oil exports. In pursuit of this second goal, Pérez Alfonso and Saudi Arabia's representative, Abdullah Tariki, initiated a series of meetings in 1960 that resulted in the formation of OPEC (Organization of Petroleum Exporting Countries), an intergovernmental arrangement that enabled the world's major petroleum-exporting nations to regulate the amount of oil produced for the world market. Tugwell examines this process and Venezuela's oil policies in general up to the mid-1970's, with close attention to the perspective of the Caracas government.

Brazil

Burns, E. Bradford. *The Unwritten Alliance: Rio-Branco and Brazilian-American Relations.* New York: Columbia University Press, 1966.
Academic studies of relations between two countries generally concentrate on periods of tension, discord, and open warfare. Burns's pioneering examination of Brazilian-U.S. relations while Baron Rio-Branco was foreign minister (1902-1912) follows a different path. Burns makes good use of his extensive survey of primary documents in the foreign relations archives in Brazil, the United States, Argentina, Chile, Mexico, and Panama as well as private archives in Brazil. The result is a balanced combination of biography and history in which Rio-Branco emerges as a talented, intelligent diplomat who was at the center of the development of friendly relations between Brazil and the United States at a time when both nations were beginning to play more active roles in international affairs. For example, Rio-Branco dealt with boundary controversies and secured settlements favorable to Brazil. In many of his diplomatic efforts, Rio-Branco enjoyed a close working relationship with U.S. Secretary of State Elihu Root (1905-1909). Burns identifies a major transition during Rio-Branco's tenure as head of his nation's foreign relations ministry: the shift from Brazil's traditionally close ties with Great Britain to the "unwritten alliance" with the United States under which no formal treaty existed but the two nations generally cooperated.

Cobbs, Elizabeth Anne. *The Rich Neighbor Policy: Rockefeller and Kaiser in Brazil.* New Haven, CT: Yale University Press, 1992.
The most common perception of U.S. business operations in Latin America calls to mind selfish, profit-seeking corporations extracting oil and mineral resources and leaving little behind to benefit the local people. Cobbs documents the efforts of two individual industrialists, Nelson Rockefeller and Henry J. Kaiser, who were exceptions to this generalization in their activities in Brazil during the 1940's and 1950's. Both men worked as private citizens and not as official representatives of the U.S. government. Rockefeller used his political and business contacts to bring Brazilian and U.S. leaders together to smooth the way for economic growth in this South American nation. For example, he helped to organize an experiment in selling Brazilian stock on the U.S. stock market. Kaiser acted more directly through his formation of Willys-Overland do Brasil, a corporation that manufactured jeeps and automobiles in Brazil. Using Brazilian workers and managers, this company sold vehicles in Brazil and other South American countries.

Cobbs concludes that while the U.S. government turned away from the Good Neighbor Policy in the 1940's and 1950's, U.S. entrepreneurs opened new channels for the expansion of positive U.S. influences in Brazil.

Haines, Gerald K. *The Americanization of Brazil: A Study of U.S. Cold War Diplomacy in the Third World, 1945-1954.* Wilmington, DE: Scholarly Resources, 1989.

The early phase of the Cold War created special challenges and opportunities for the United States in its relations with Brazil. Historian Gerald Haines identifies two major preoccupations in U.S. policy toward Brazil: continued access to its raw materials and domestic market, and the promotion of a militant anticommunism. His thorough research combines an extensive study of U.S. government archives with a broad examination of published material and the mass media. From this research base, Haines presents an analysis of banking, technical and military assistance, industrialization, and propaganda. Although he concludes that the United States had considerable success in dealing with the administration of Brazilian Presidents Eurico Gaspar Dutra (1945-1951) and Getúlio Vargas (1951-1954), Haines also presents evidence of cultural arrogance, paternalism, and hypersensitivity to any movement that resembled Communism. The author takes issue with the notion that U.S. diplomacy in the Cold War neglected Latin America. He argues that the administrations of Presidents Harry Truman (1945-1953) and Dwight Eisenhower (1953-1961) gave much time and effort to Brazilian relations. This book's footnotes offer especially valuable citations for further study in contemporary publications.

Hilton, Stanley. *Brazil and the Great Powers, 1930-1939: The Politics of Trade Rivalry.* Austin: University of Texas Press, 1975.

This study gives a detailed examination of U.S.-German trade rivalry in Brazil in the tense years before the outbreak of World War II, but it also goes much further to discuss the larger diplomatic, political, and strategic issues involved in the multisided relationships that connected South America to Europe and the United States. Hilton provides a clear explanation of the Nazis' employment of special trading practices with Brazil. Germany paid for coffee, cotton, and other Brazilian exports in Aski marks, a special currency that could be exchanged only for German products. While U.S. Secretary of State Cordell Hull (1933-1944) pushed for free trade in the Western Hemisphere, Germany claimed larger portions of Brazilian trade by the opposite approach that tied Rio de Janeiro closer to Berlin. U.S. officials observed this successful trade campaign (including Brazil's purchases of Krupp artillery and other armaments) as well as the right-wing direction of the Brazilian government's domestic policies in the late 1930's and concluded that Germany was making serious inroads in South America. The early phase of World War II ended this trend, however, because the British blockade of German shipping severely cut the economic ties between the Third Reich and Brazil.

_____. *Brazil and the Soviet Challenge, 1917-1947.* Austin: University of Texas Press, 1991.
The influence of the Soviet Union and the possibility of a Communist revolution were important influences in Brazil in this period. Communist leader Luis Carlos Prestes initiated a disruptive if unsuccessful revolution in 1935 that seemed to confirm the worst fears of Brazil's conservative-to-moderate national leaders: that such a radical movement was a genuine threat to the nation. Brazilian head of state Getúlio Vargas (1930-1945, 1951-1954) initiated his Estado Novo in 1937 in large part as a security measure to prevent another such revolution. Hilton's research and analysis points out an unexpected twist in Brazilian politics and diplomacy that caused considerable consternation in the United States. Brazilian officials cooperated with Nazi Germany to establish a bastion in South America against the spread of Communism at a time when the United States was highly sensitive to the spread of Fascist influence as well as Communism in the Western Hemisphere. Hilton's use of private archives, especially the personal papers of Filinto Muller (the chief of security for the Federal District), offers important insights into the enforcement of the antileftist measures and establishes the historical background for the security-conscious military governments of the 1960's and 1970's.

_____. *Hitler's Secret War in South America, 1939-1945: Germany's Military Espionage and Allied Counterespionage in Brazil.* Baton Rouge: Louisiana State University Press, 1981.
World War II had a large impact on Brazil, and, as Hilton demonstrates in this heavily documented study, the German espionage effort in that country was of considerable international importance. Hilton argues that Germany's most extensive spy network was located in Brazil, not Argentina. He examines the work of William Canaris (head of German military intelligence) and discusses the activities of several of the Third Reich's agents, such as Albrecht Gustav Engels. Soon after leaving Germany in 1923, Engels became a successful businessman in the

electronics field, and in 1939 he began to work under the code name "Alfredo" to set up secret short-wave radios to transmit messages to Germany. The U.S. State Department and Federal Bureau of Investigation joined with Brazilian police to locate and apprehend German agents. In late 1942, a large portion of the German espionage effort in Brazil collapsed, but some individual agents continued their work until 1945. The first version of this book appeared in Portuguese in 1977 and created much debate in the Brazilian press. Hilton comments on this discussion in the introduction to this edition.

Leacock, Ruth. *Requiem for Revolution: The United States and Brazil, 1961-1969*. Kent, OH: Kent State University Press, 1990.
The Brazilian military overthrew the government of President João Goulart on April 1, 1964, and thereby brought to an end a period of growing tension in Brazil and in U.S.-Brazilian relations. One of the main sources of these tensions was the leftist administration of President Goulart (1961-1964), who, in the estimate of high-ranking Brazilian military officers, U.S. Ambassador Lincoln Gordon and other State Department officials, and the Central Intelligence Agency, was dangerously close to Communists and espoused anticapitalist policies. Leacock's extensive research in U.S. government archives reveals the extent to which the administrations of Presidents John F. Kennedy (1961-1963) and Lyndon Johnson (1963-1969) used diplomacy, intelligence, and propaganda to stimulate intense anticommunist attitudes among Brazilian military and civilian leaders. The U.S. government also encouraged the military coup against Goulart and positioned U.S. naval and military forces to provide support, but such support was not needed. Leacock criticizes the U.S. role in this coup. She points out that it brought to power repressive military governments that ruled Brazil in a twisted application of the U.S. policy of nation-building until the 1980's, when the country returned to civilian leadership.

Page, Joseph. *The Revolution That Never Was: Northeast Brazil, 1955-1964*. New York: Grossman, 1972.
Page combines first-person experiences with a broad perspective on U.S.-Brazilian relations in this study of peasant unrest and revolutionary frustration. His narrative centers on the activities of Francisco Julião, who became the political leader of a peasant movement in this historically poor region. Born into a wealthy family and trained as a lawyer, Julião dedicated his energies to land reform (the breakup of the region's large estates and the distribution of the land to impoverished sharecroppers). In the early 1960's, Julião visited Castro's Cuba and

became an internationally known leftist leader. The Brazilian military's coup of 1964 (see the book by Ruth Leacock annotated in this section), however, soon resulted in his arrest and deportation. Page also discusses the role of the U.S. Agency for International Development as a rival to Julião's more radical approach to rural development. During his efforts to study Julião's movement, Page was arrested and briefly jailed by Brazilian authorities in 1964.

Schneider, Ronald M. *Brazil: Foreign Policy of a Future World Power.* Boulder, CO: Westview Press, 1976.
Brazil's size and resources contain the potential to make that nation a major world power. Schneider's optimistic assessment, written in the mid-1970's before the impacts of the worldwide oil crisis and Brazil's international debt problems assumed their full dimensions, is focused on the government ministries that deal with foreign policy. Schneider emphasizes that Itamaraty (the foreign ministry) took a secondary, mainly formal, role in policy-making as a result of the expansion of the authority of government agencies concerned with economics, such as the finance ministry and the ministry of mines and energy. Schneider also examines the growing importance of the military during the administration of General Ernesto Geisel (1974-1979). This book offers the reader a balanced evaluation of the sources of power in Brazil and the formulation of its foreign policy within a broad international context.

Smith, Joseph. *Unequal Giants: Diplomatic Relations Between the United States and Brazil, 1889-1930.* Pittsburgh, PA: University of Pittsburgh Press, 1991.
Smith's study covers the shifting relationship between these two nations in a time of significant changes for both countries. While the United States emerged as the dominant power in the Western Hemisphere and, during and after World War I, a major world power, Brazil overthrew Emperor Dom Pedro II (1840-1889) and began the process of building the institutions of representative government and economic modernization. Smith uses a straightforward chronological organization that includes U.S.-Brazilian relations on several levels. The most obvious level is formal diplomacy involving relations between the two governments, but Smith also deals with economic issues such as Brazil's efforts to maintain healthy prices for its coffee sold in the United States. Chapter 3 covers Brazil's participation in World War I and the Versailles Conference. Smith also emphasizes the importance of Brazil's rivalry with its neighbor, Argentina, as a factor in its

long-term relations with the United States. The author provides an informative seven-page bibliographical essay.

Wesson, Robert. *The United States and Brazil: The Limits of Influence.* New York: Praeger, 1981.

This book concentrates on the 1960's and 1970's—two decades in which, according to Wesson, the United States began to discover the limits of its influence in Brazil. He examines the causes and the consequences of the coup of 1964 in which the Brazilian military removed a leftist government and then, in a break with national political traditions, held on to power for nearly twenty years. In spite of U.S. approval of this military coup, the two nations soon drifted in different directions, to a large extent because Brazil began to steer a more independent course in its own industrialization and its trade with countries outside North America. Chapter 4 covers the controversies that appeared during the presidency of Jimmy Carter (1977-1981). The United States had little success in its efforts to limit Brazil's development of nuclear power plants, but its attempts to promote human rights policies had a much larger impact. Wesson's subtle analysis concludes that although the two nations did not have a major confrontation in the 1960's and 1970's, Brazil began to follow a more independent course than in earlier decades, often to the apprehension of the United States.

Argentina

Braden, Spruille. *Diplomats and Demagogues: The Memoirs of Spruille Braden.* New York: Arlington House, 1991.

In a brazen act of political meddling, U.S. diplomat Braden challenged Juan Perón's candidacy for the presidency of Argentina in 1946 with the publication of the *Blue Book*, which alleged that the army colonel was closely tied to Nazis. Perón used this publication to accuse Braden (and the United States) of interference in Argentina's domestic politics. This point strengthened Perón's campaign, and he won the presidency by a substantial margin. In his memoir, Braden presents his case for these actions as ambassador to Argentina for most of 1945 and as assistant secretary of state for Latin American affairs from September, 1945, to June, 1947. Braden was a mining engineer and an executive in a large international copper company with holdings in South America. His career in diplomacy included participation in the settlement of the Chaco War (1932-1935), but his antifascist campaign in Argentina proved to be highly controversial. The gist of his defense of his actions is on pages 316 to 370. For the point of view of one of his opponents in the State Department, see the biography of George Messersmith by Jesse Stiller annotated in this section.

Bruce, James. *Those Perplexing Argentines.* London: Eyre & Spottiswoode, 1953.

Bruce served as U.S. ambassador to Argentina from 1947 to 1949, a period in which Juan Perón reached the peak of his strength. The country soon began to slide into the economic troubles and political decline that eventually led to his overthrow in 1955. Bruce witnessed many dramatic events, but the main purpose of his book is to provide the reader with a low-keyed discussion of life in Argentina at mid-century, thereby avoiding the tendency toward overstatement typical of much U.S. commentary on the homeland of Perón in this period. Bruce examines farming and ranching on the Pampas, the impact of European immigration on the nation, the legacy of the gaucho (Argentine cowboy), the nation's religious practices, its reading habits and educational institutions, its quest for industrialization, and the uniqueness of the political system. Bruce could not ignore the controversies of national politics, however, and his book contains interesting observations on the labor movement, Juan and Eva Perón, the ominous presence of the military, the increasing activism of the Communists, and the origins of Argentina's independent foreign policy, which often perplexed the United States in the 1940's.

Crassweller, Robert D. *Perón and the Enigmas of Argentina.* New York: Norton, 1987.

Juan Perón was a powerful influence in U.S.-Argentine relations from the time that he appeared as a rising personality in the military in 1943 until the overthrow of his government in 1955 and, again, in his short-lived return to the presidency in 1973-1974. Crassweller's biography is an exceptional combination of detailed personal information on Perón interlaced with the broader historical and cultural factors that shaped his political career. Pages 97 to 283 present the rise and fall of Perón from 1943 to 1955, with emphasis on his ideas and values (much more Argentine and Hispanic than Germanic fascist), his conflicts with Spruille Braden, and his policies toward the United States. Crassweller also gives a balanced discussion of Perón's internal political and economic policies as well as the often exaggerated perceptions of the pro-Axis direction of these policies as viewed by U.S. diplomats and journalists.

Josephs, Ray. *Argentine Diary: The Inside Story of the Coming of Fascism*. New York: Random House, 1944.

At about the time that Germany and Italy began to taste defeat in Europe in 1943 and 1944, Argentina received attention in the U.S. press because of its apparent shift toward Fascism and military dictatorship. Josephs, a U.S. journalist who had lived in Argentina since 1940, discusses this tendency in the language of an alarmist. He incorporates commentary of the victory of Fascism in Spain in the late 1930's; the cultural influence of Spain, Italy, and Germany in Argentina; and the ambition of the South American nation's new military rulers to build a case for Buenos Aires as a center for Fascist intrigue and a refuge for the defeated Nazis. Josephs' book is organized as a diary, giving day-by-day coverage of politics, propaganda, subterfuge, and rumors in Argentina from January, 1943, to January, 1944. This book should be used primarily as an example of alarmist overstatement that presents a point of view considerably revised in more recent studies by Robert Crassweller, Ronald Newton, and Randall Bennett Woods (all annotated in this section).

McGann, Thomas F. *Argentina, the United States, and the Inter-American System, 1880-1914*. Cambridge, MA: Harvard University Press, 1957.

Argentina and the United States experienced a distant but sometimes tense relationship in the late 1800's. Many of the elements in this tension appeared in the period under study in McGann's exceptionally well-written book. He examines in detail the economic, political, and cultural factors that brought Argentina to the forefront of Latin American nations as a rival to the United States in the Western Hemisphere. He also explains the Argentine political/landowning elite's close ties with Great Britain (for finance and trade) and France (for culture), as well as the elite's ambivalent attitude toward the United States—a mixture of admiration and suspicion. Approximately two-thirds of the text concerns the development of the Inter-American system and in particular the Pan American conferences in Washington (1899-1890), Mexico City (1901-1902), Rio de Janeiro (1906), and Buenos Aires (1910), in which Argentina and the United States played out their often antagonistic and sometimes friendly rivalry. McGann gives special attention to Argentine diplomat Luis Drago, who devised his doctrine that opposed the use of force (military intervention) to collect debts owed to foreign powers. By the last years of the period under study, U.S.-Argentine relations improved as U.S. investors began to supplant British banking houses in the Argentine economy.

Newton, Ronald C. *The "Nazi Menace" in Argentina, 1931-1947.* Stanford, CA: Stanford University Press, 1992.

The general public in the United States, influenced by some journalists and high-ranking public officials, tended to believe that Nazi Germany was on the verge of establishing a Western Hemisphere foothold in Argentina in the 1930's and the early years of World War II. Newton's main thesis, based on research in German—as well as U.S., Argentine, and British—records, is that the Third Reich and its supporters made some highly visible propagandistic demonstrations of energy and arrogance in that South American nation but, in reality, lacked the organization and resources to have a significant impact in the Rio de la Plata region. Probably Germany's most solid achievement in Argentina was the impressive growth of trade between the two countries from 1937 to 1939. U.S. journalists and diplomats often took the high-profile presence of Nazi sympathizers in the Argentine military and business community as evidence of deeply rooted support for Hitler, but Newton points to calmer assessments by British and Argentine officials who, in most cases, did not agree with the loud, alarmist pronouncements from U.S. observers.

Peterson, Harold. *Argentina and the United States, 1810-1960.* New York: State University of New York, 1964.

This study provides a comprehensive survey of the diplomatic relations between the two countries. Peterson begins with the Argentine struggle for independence from Spain (completed in 1816) and the quest for formal diplomatic recognition from the United States (achieved in 1822-1823). He also devotes an entire chapter to a summary of the Falkland Islands (or Malvinas) dispute from the 1830's to 1960 and has three chapters on the role of the United States in the coming of the Paraguayan War and its aftermath from the 1850's to the 1870's. Approximately half of the 537-page text deals with the relations between the two nations in the twentieth century, with emphasis on Argentina's maintenance of independent diplomatic policies that often placed it outside the bounds of hemispheric unity and at odds with the United States. In particular, he examines Argentine neutrality in World War I and the early phases of World War II. The controversial presidency of Juan Perón (1946-1955) is covered in three chapters. Although Peterson was unable to gain access to Argentine diplomatic archives, his examination of U.S. primary and published sources in the 1940's and 1950's is impressive. His extensive footnotes provide the reader with a long list of published books and articles available in many college and some public libraries.

Rapoport, Mario. "Argentina and the Soviet Union: History of Political and Commercial Relations (1917-1955)." *Hispanic American Historical Review* 66 (May, 1986): 239-285.

Argentina's leanings toward Fascism have been examined closely by scholars, but the connections between that nation and the Soviet Union have had little attention from academics and journalists. This study concentrates on the period from 1945 to 1955, when Fascism and the Perón Administration were at the forefront of Argentine history. Rapoport's research reveals that Argentina and the Soviet Union enjoyed a fairly close relationship based largely on the establishment of trade agreements after World War II. Argentina exported mutton, other food products, and flax oil to the Soviet Union and its satellite states in exchange for railroad equipment and petroleum. The United States became increasingly concerned with this unexpected rapport between the Perón government and Moscow. During the Cold War, as in World War II, Argentina followed an independent course within the Western Hemisphere, very much to the dismay of the security-conscious anti-Communists in the United States. For a larger study on this theme, see Aldo Vacs's book (annotated in this section).

Rock, David. *Argentina, 1516-1982: From Spanish Colonization to the Falklands War*. Berkeley: University of California Press, 1985.

Argentina's long and unique history receives a thorough analysis in this book designed for the college classroom. Rock devotes nearly 300 of the text's 378 pages to the post-1810 period. His political narrative includes well-defined portraits of Bernadino Rivadavia, the modernizer of the 1820's; Juan Manuel de Rosas, the prototypical caudillo of the 1830's; the rise of the landowning elite of the late nineteenth century; the enigmatic populist Hipólito Irigoyen (1916-1922, 1928-1930); the rise and fall of Juan Perón; the legendary presence of Eva Perón; and the troubled decades of the 1960's and 1970's. Rock also examines the surge of the Argentine economy in the nineteenth century and its problems over the years since the 1920's. These political and economic trends are essential to understanding Argentina's relations with the United States. In particular, Rock stresses the period from 1930 to 1955, when political and economic tensions dominated the often hostile interactions of the two nations. Rock takes a broader perspective than most commentators on the economic problems that beset the Perón government—especially the loss of grain sales to Great Britain and continental Europe as a result of the United States' sale of its own grain reserves to Europe under the Marshall Plan of 1947.

Stiller, Jesse. *George S. Messersmith: Diplomat of Democracy*. Chapel
Hill: University of North Carolina Press, 1987.

This thoroughly researched, full-scale biography of Messersmith, who
was the U.S. ambassador to Argentina in the critical 1946-1947 period,
contains important details on the infighting within the State Department concerning Washington's policies toward the nascent Perón
regime. Messersmith was working for reconciliation with Perón. The
thirty-five pages of Chapter 7 concentrate on the conflict between
Ambassador Messersmith and Assistant Secretary of State for Latin
American Affairs Spruille Braden, a staunch opponent of Perón who
had served as U.S. ambassador in Buenos Aires in 1945. This book also
covers Messersmith's diplomatic assignments in Havana from 1940 to
1942 and Mexico City from 1942 to 1946. In Mexico, he became aware
of the State Department's growing concern about Argentina's tilt
toward the Axis Powers in the early part of World War II. For Spruille
Braden's view of these events, see his memoir annotated in this section.

Vacs, Aldo César. *Discreet Partners: Argentina and the USSR Since 1917*.
Pittsburgh, PA: University of Pittsburgh Press, 1984.

The governments of Argentina and the Soviet Union have experienced
troubled relations since the Bolshevik Revolution of 1917, but these
tensions were limited to superficial diplomatic and ideological differences. U.S. observers often were puzzled that although governments
in Buenos Aires were unfriendly and often openly hostile to the
Argentine Communist Party, these same governments arranged closer
economic ties with the Soviet Union. Vacs emphasizes the role of the
second regime of Juan Perón (1973-1974) in the expansion of Argentine trade with the Soviet Union. The main Argentine exports were
grain crops and meat; the Soviet Union supplied electrical equipment.
Argentina increased its exports to the Soviet Union in the early 1980's
as a result of U.S. President Jimmy Carter's trade embargo against
Moscow. Vacs also discusses the strategic, diplomatic, and ideological
factors in the Buenos Aires-Moscow relationship but concludes that
trade was the main consideration. Vacs's findings parallel those of
Mario Rapoport in his article (discussed in this section) that deals
primarily with Argentine-Soviet relations during the first Perón era
(1946-1955).

Whitaker, Arthur P. *The United States and Argentina*. Cambridge, MA:
Harvard University Press, 1954.

Whitaker was a close observer of the rise of Juan Perón to power in the
1940's and the troubled relations between his government and the

United States. This book is an exceptionally well-written contemporary account of the tumultuous 1940's and early 1950's by a highly respected historian. Although the main purpose of this volume is to explain U.S.-Argentine relations, Whitaker also provides an extended discussion of the cultural, economic, and political elements of Argentina's history and how Juan and Eva Perón emerged from this milieu. Whitaker traces Perón's consolidation of the dictatorship by intimidation of the press, the nation's courts, and the universities. He also has a chapter on Perón's foreign policy—"The Third Position"—in which Argentina sought a middle course between the United States and the Soviet Union during the early years of the Cold War. Whitaker sees more opportunistic maneuvering than ideological innovation in this policy. This book appeared in 1954, the year before Perón's regime fell to a military coup. The bibliography has a convenient listing of the major contemporary publications on Argentina during the Perón years.

_____. *The United States and the Southern Cone: Argentina, Chile, and Uruguay*. Cambridge, MA: Harvard University Press, 1976. Whitaker brings a lifetime of experience in Latin American history to full use in this survey of the histories of the three southernmost nations of the Western Hemisphere. The first 350 pages are composed of surveys of the domestic histories of these three nations from the independence era of the early 1800's to the early 1970's. The last sixty-seven pages contain Whitaker's analysis of the place of Argentina, Chile, and Uruguay in U.S. foreign policy. His discussion covers the economic and diplomatic influence of Great Britain in the late nineteenth century, the U.S. application of the Good Neighbor Policy in the Southern Cone in the 1930's, the problems of Axis influence—especially in Argentina—during World War II, and the impact of the Cold War, with special emphasis on the Alliance for Progress. Whitaker's seventeen-page annotated bibliography has useful commentary on additional published works.

Woods, Randall Bennett. *The Roosevelt Foreign Policy Establishment and the "Good Neighbor": The United States and Argentina, 1941-1945*. Lawrence: Regents Press of Kansas, 1979.
Argentina's goal of establishing a foreign policy independent of the influence of the United States was never more evident than during World War II. As Woods explains in this important and insightful study, successive Argentine governments from the late 1930's to 1943 seemed to be receptive to Axis overtures and adamantly refused to give up their policy of neutrality regarding the belligerents in World War II. Woods

concentrates on the rival agencies within the U.S. government—including the Treasury Department, the Federal Bureau of Investigation, and the War Department as well as the State Department—to explain why and how Washington insisted that Nazi influence was strong enough in Argentina to pose a threat to the security of the Western Hemisphere. Woods's examination of government archives explains the origins and conclusions of several reports that emphasized the extent and potential of Fascist influence in Argentina. The administration of President Franklin D. Roosevelt (1933-1945) used a variety tactics (including propaganda, nonrecognition of new governments, and the freezing of Argentine assets in U.S. banks) to try to discredit the regimes in Buenos Aires in order to pressure that South American nation to abandon neutrality and join in the fight against the Axis. Argentina eventually declared war against the Axis in March of 1945.

Chile

Bowers, Claude. *Chile Through Embassy Windows: 1939-1953.* New York: Simon and Schuster, 1958.

After serving as ambassador to Spain (1933-1939) during that nation's civil war, in which fascists fought against republicans, Bowers hoped to enjoy a quiet tenure as the chief U.S. diplomat in Chile. Instead, as Bowers explains in this well-written memoir, he encountered another version of the struggle of Fascism against democracy. Chile was the target of significant Axis propaganda and had its share of rumors concerning Fascist intrigue. For the United States, the most frustrating aspect of Chilean politics was the nation's apparent reluctance to break relations with the Axis Powers. As the U.S. ambassador, Bowers obviously had much at stake on this issue, but in his text he consistently defends Chile. Bowers explains that the administration of President Juan Antonio Ríos chose to abide by democratic procedures and respect public opinion in its dealings with the Axis Powers. In a situation that Bowers compares to the U.S. support of the British without a declaration of war (from the fall of 1939 to December, 1941), the Chilean government leaned toward the United States while allowing time for public opinion to coalesce and the proper constitutional obligations to be met. Chile broke relations with the Axis in January of 1943. Bowers also recounts the activities of Communists in Chile during the early Cold War. Among the many strengths of this book are the author's sympathetic portrayal of the land and the people of Chile and his carefully etched portraits of that nation's political leaders, such as Arturo Alessandri and Carlos Ibáñez.

Burr, Robert N. *By Reason of Force: Chile and the Balancing of Power in South America, 1830-1905.* Berkeley: University of California Press, 1967.
This groundbreaking study examines the relations among the nations of South America through the concept of balance-of-power politics. Earlier works on foreign relations in South America after 1810 concentrated on the influence of Great Britain, Spain, other European nations, or the United States, but Burr clearly demonstrates that there was an evolving mix of negotiations, treaties, and policies among the governments of South America that constituted an international system. His focus is on Chile in its striving to assert its national self-interest, first in its regional setting on the western coast of South America and, by the last half of the nineteenth century, on a continental level. Chile's integration into the international economic system through its exports of guano and nitrates made the area where its northern territories came together with Bolivia and Peru valuable and subject to competing land claims. Chile's self-image improved as its people became aware of the nation's political and economic stability, in contrast to the disorder typical of its neighbors. Chile emerged as a continental power with its victory over Peru and Bolivia in the War of the Pacific (1879-1883) and through continued maneuvering for strategic advantage in its relations with Argentina. Burr also makes it clear that the United States played a role in this international arena but that its role generally was peripheral in the time frame of this study. For students who assume that the United States was the dominant power in the Western Hemisphere in these years, this study will provide a convincing alternate perspective.

Davis, Nathaniel. *The Last Two Years of Salvador Allende.* Ithaca, NY: Cornell University Press, 1985.
Davis was the U.S. ambassador to Chile from 1971 to 1973, a period that coincided with the last two years of Allende's controversial socialist government. Davis presents his analysis of the political conflicts and economic problems that undermined Allende's ambitious plans to remake Chilean society according to a flexible Marxist model for far-reaching but peaceful change. He also discusses the role of the United States in bringing the Allende Administration to an end in October, 1973. The four-hundred-page text often provides detailed and, in some cases, day-by-day accounts of the decline and fall of

Allende. These events remain the subject of much controversy even among the most fair-minded historians. Davis discusses the opposition to Allende from the administration of President Richard Nixon (1969-1974), including National Security Adviser Henry Kissinger, but his main conclusion is that the Allende Administration fell largely as a result of internal or domestic factors in Chile's struggling economy and weakened, polemicized political system. Davis tends to minimize the role of the Central Intelligence Agency in undermining Allende's experiment in finding a peaceful road to socialism. Readers who disagree with Davis' conclusion may nevertheless find value in this detailed examination of the events and personalities in this important historical episode. Those seeking balance to the former ambassador's interpretation can consult the works by Brian Loveman, James Petras and Morris Morley, and Paul Sigmund annotated in this section.

Falcoff, Mark. *Modern Chile, 1970-1989: A Critical History*. New Brunswick, NJ: Transaction Publishers, 1989.
Salvador Allende's victory in the presidential election of 1970 was a blow to the United States' hopes of rolling back the influence of Marxism in the Western Hemisphere. Falcoff finds no indication that Allende's presidency was the culmination of an inevitable shift to the radical left in Chile. Instead, he argues that this election was the result of the three-sided rivalry among Christian Democrats (moderate left), Nationalists (right), and Allende's Popular Unity that divided the electorate into roughly equal thirds. Under these circumstances, Allende won a narrow victory. The author's analysis of the Allende Administration's (1970-1973) efforts to remake the nation's economic structure also emphasizes the weaknesses of the left. Agrarian reform (the breakup and distribution of large farms among peasants) caused a severe decline in food production. The most ambitious project in terms of international business was the nationalization of the copper mines owned by the Kennecott and Anaconda companies. Falcoff's overview of the push for nationalization from the 1920's to the 1970's concludes that there was broad public support for this decision but that the results of government control included serious declines in productivity. The United States actively opposed Allende's election, but, according to the author, the overthrow of his government was not the doing of the Central Intelligence Agency. The Allende Administration fell as a result of its own mistaken economic policies, which led conservative military officers to intervene in order to prevent what they believed would become a national disaster. Falcoff's assessment of the regime of Augusto Pinochet (1973-1989) points out the tensions between this

dictatorship and the U.S. government. Falcoff's views contrast with those of Brian Loveman, James Petras and Morris Morley, and Paul Sigmund, whose books are annotated in this section.

Francis, Michael J. *The Limits of Hegemony: United States Relations with Argentina and Chile During World War II*. Notre Dame, IN: University of Notre Dame Press, 1977.

The two nations in South America most distant from the United States, Chile and Argentina, had contrasting experiences with the United States during the era of World War II. These two nations, however, did share political inclinations toward Fascism in the late 1930's and early 1940's, which aroused the consternation of U.S. policymakers who were fearful of Axis inroads in the Western Hemisphere. The central purpose of Francis' book is to explain why U.S. relations with these two countries followed considerably different patterns, with different results. Francis observes that Chile moved in the direction signaled by Washington (although slowly at times) largely because of the importance of Chile's copper exports to the United States and because most of Chile's political parties (even on the far right) saw the United States in a favorable light. U.S. Ambassador Claude Bowers played a prominent role in smoothing the way for U.S. influence in Chile (see his book annotated in this section). In Argentina, the situation was different. The United States had less economic influence because of Buenos Aires' long-established ties with Great Britain. In the Argentine political arena, the appeal of Francisco Franco's Spanish corporate state was stronger than the appeal of U.S. model. The rise of Juan Perón gave Argentina a stridently nationalistic impetus to resist U.S. influence. Francis concludes that U.S. pressures on Argentina to break off relations with the Axis Powers were "ineffectual and possibly dysfunctional." In summary, the author analyzes the limits of U.S. power in the Western Hemisphere in a time of serious international crisis in this interesting contrast of U.S. relations with Chile and with Argentina.

Goldberg, Joyce S. *The "Baltimore" Affair*. Lincoln: University of Nebraska Press, 1986.

Two U.S. sailors from the cruiser *Baltimore* died in a riot outside the True Blue Saloon in Valparaiso, Chile, in October, 1891. Relations between the two countries already were strained because of U.S. policy in Chile's recently concluded civil war, and this event brought the two countries close to a major international conflict. Goldberg's archival research gives the reader the perspectives of both U.S. and Chilean observers on the riots, a discussion of the consequent judicial and diplomatic proceedings, and an analysis of the possibilities of war. The United States, represented by its minister to Chile, Patrick Egan, and led by its president, Benjamin Harrison, demanded an apology and an indemnity. The Chilean judicial system rendered its verdict on the deaths of the U.S. sailors, and the government in Santiago, under the leadership of the strong-willed foreign minister, Manuel Matta, refused to comply with these demands from Washington. (Later, however, the Chilean government paid indemnities to the families of the sailors.) Goldberg's account of the contemporary assessment of the war readiness of the two nations reveals that a potentially strong Chilean navy, temporarily handicapped by heavy duty in that nation's civil war of 1891, posed a serious challenge to the U.S. Navy, which was in the midst of an expansion that continued with renewed vigor after diplomats of the two nations reached a compromise settlement. The aggressiveness of the Harrison Administration in this affair left a lasting legacy of anti-U.S. feelings in Chile.

Kinsbruner, Jay. *Chile: A Historical Interpretation*. New York: Harper & Row, 1973.
This volume is a brief, well-organized, and clearly written summary of four centuries of Chilean history from the beginnings of the Spanish colonial period in the 1530's to the administration of Salvador Allende. (This book appeared shortly before Allende's overthrow.) Nearly three-fourths of the text's 161 pages deal with the nineteenth and twentieth centuries, during which the independent nation of Chile established itself as a relatively stable and prosperous country. Kinsbruner uses a form of neo-Marxist analysis to examine the strengths and weaknesses of Chile's role in the international free market economy. He emphasizes the growing impact of the United States in Chile's economic difficulties from the 1940's to the 1970's, including issues such as inflation, foreign (especially U.S.) control of copper mining, and the problems of securing foreign investment to stimulate economic development. Kinsbruner views the rise of the left in Chile's politics, culminating with Allende's victory in 1970, as the logical outcome of these economic difficulties. For a contrasting perspective, students can consult the books by Nathaniel Davis and Mark Falcoff annotated in this section.

Loveman, Brian. *Chile: The Legacy of Hispanic Capitalism*. 2d ed. New York: Oxford University Press, 1988.
The crises in Chile of the 1960's and 1970's that drew the United States deeply into that nation's history grew out of long-term trends that

originated in the Hispanic colonial era. Loveman's provocative study ties the crisis period to these long-term trends, in which Hispanic capitalism was a major component. Loveman defines Hispanic capitalism as a mixture of private enterprise, government policies, and the process that linked these two (including high-level corruption). Salvador Allende's administration (1970-1973) attempted to break with the tradition of Hispanic capitalism only to encounter the opposition of the United States and the Chilean military. Loveman is critical of Allende for his use of radical rhetoric in an institutional setting that made radical change difficult. The author also is critical of the military government that seized power in 1973 for its excessively repressive methods used against a broad range of leftists. In summary, this text covers the essential trends in Chile's domestic history to give the reader a solid understanding of the twentieth century environment in which U.S. economic and political influences became significant factors in that nation's history.

Monaghan, James. *Chile, Peru, and the California Gold Rush of 1849.* Berkeley: University of California Press, 1973.
A little-known aspect of the California gold rush of 1849 and the early 1850's is the participation of Chileans in that legendary scramble for quick riches. Monaghan's popular history is intended for general readers, but it also includes research in academic monographs published in the United States and Chile. According to Monaghan, approximately fifty thousand South Americans arrived in California between 1848 and 1852. Most of them were Chileans, although a considerable number were from Peru. Monaghan relies on the writings of Chilean Vicente Pérez Rosales, whose experiences in the rough-and-tumble gold fields were set down in a series of articles and books written after his return to Chile in late 1851. Chileans made contributions in the technology of mining based on their experiences in South America. Monaghan makes the point that most Chileans felt the brunt of virulent prejudice in their relations with the predominantly Anglo-Saxon North Americans. The anti-Chilean riot of July, 1849, and other manifestations of prejudice sent many Chileans back to their homeland with little gold but a large amount of resentment against the United States.

Muñoz, Heraldo, and Carlos Portales. *Elusive Friendship: A Survey of U.S.-Chilean Relations.* Boulder, CO: Lynne Rienner, 1991.
This brief text is mainly a study of U.S.-Chilean relations during the dictatorship of Augusto Pinochet, who was in power from 1973 to

1989. In their survey of the historical background, the authors develop the thesis that over the previous century and a half, relations between the two countries were more contentious and tense than harmonious and calm. They also identify cycles of discord and harmony in U.S. policy toward the Pinochet government. Washington lent considerable support to the dictatorship until, during the presidency of Jimmy Carter (1977-1981), relations cooled because of U.S. criticisms of human rights violations. The administration of Ronald Reagan (1981-1989) used more supportive policies toward Pinochet but eventually became critical because the Chilean dictator was slow to move toward representative government. The authors conclude with the 1989 election of Patricio Aylwin to the presidency and the return to democracy. A special strength of this book is its presentation of the perspectives of two respected Chilean scholars on recent events in their nation's history in a highly readable translation by Orlando García Valverde.

Petras, James, and Morris Morley. *The United States and Chile: Imperialism and the Overthrow of the Allende Government.* New York: Monthly Review Press, 1975.

Salvador Allende's narrow victory in the election of 1970 brought him to the presidency of Chile. The fact that he was the first Marxist to win such a high post in an open election in the Western Hemisphere caused great concern in the administration of President Richard Nixon. Three years later, the Chilean military overthrew this leftist government by force in a coup that resulted in Allende's death. Petras and Morley, writing in the aftermath of this bloody episode, built a case for U.S. involvement in the destruction of the Allende government. The authors employ a neo-Marxist analysis to present the United States as an imperial power that used a variety of devices to weaken Chile. For example, they pinpoint the National Security Council, led by Henry Kissinger, for taking the initiative within the Nixon Administration to undermine Allende. Kissinger and other U.S. officials greatly curtailed Chile's opportunity to borrow money from international banks and other lending institutions. At the same time, the International Telegraph and Telephone Company, a U.S.-based multinational corporation, used its influence to discredit Allende. In addition, the United States government strengthened its ties with the Chilean military, which eventually overthrew Allende. The authors argue that the United States pushed Chile toward this coup following the example of the Brazilian military revolt that overthrew a leftist government in that nation in 1964. Students who want to find balance for this neo-Marxist interpretation can consult the books by Nathaniel Davis, Mark Falcoff, and Paul Sigmund discussed in this section.

Pike, Fredrick. *Chile and the United States, 1880-1962: The Emergence of Chile's Social Crisis and the Challenge to United States Diplomacy.* Notre Dame, IN: University of Notre Dame Press, 1963.
Written several years before the election of Marxist Salvador Allende to the Chilean presidency in 1970, this book now has a prescient quality that most historical studies lack. Although Pike did not predict Allende's victory and the turmoil and dictatorship that followed, he did establish a connection between the hierarchical, paternalistic nature of Chile's social structure and its relationship with the United States. He traces the evolution of Chilean-U.S. diplomacy from the early nineteenth century to the middle of the twentieth century, with emphasis on the impact of social tensions within Chile on this relationship. Approximately two-thirds of the text covers the period from the 1890's to the 1950's, when the nation's dominant leftist and rightist political movements disagreed on the issue of how to deal with the large gap between the poor and the more prosperous sectors of society. The last chapter is titled "The United States and the Two Chiles" and contains a critique of the U.S. tendency to align itself with the traditional elite in Chile. Pike's extensive footnotes mention several valuable published sources, including many in English.

Sigmund, Paul E. *The United States and Democracy in Chile.* Baltimore: Johns Hopkins University Press, 1993.
Chile and the United States share traditional commitments to government by representative democracy. Sigmund's absorbing analysis reveals, however, that in the troubled years from the 1960's to the early 1990's, U.S. policy toward this South American nation was deeply ambivalent about and sometimes opposed to the practice of democracy. The Alliance for Progress initiated land reform and other elements of liberal democracy in the 1960's, but the United States Central Intelligence Agency also began covert intrusions into Chilean politics in a futile effort to stop the voters' shift to leftist parties. The victory of Marxist Salvador Allende in the 1970 presidential election was followed by an intensive U.S. effort to buttress the Chilean military and to undermine the nation's economy in order to destabilize the Allende government. The military coup that ousted Allende in 1973 brought to power Augusto Pinochet, who ruled Chile under a dictatorship from 1973 until 1989. Sigmund views U.S. support for Pinochet and the military as counterproductive for democracy, although he also points

out that the administration of Ronald Reagan (1981-1989) began to turn against the military dictatorship in the mid-1980's. This external pressure, along with tremendous internal demands from Chile's general population for a return to civilian government, led to the revival of representative government in 1989-1990.

Spooner, Mary Helen. *Soldiers in a Narrow Land: The Pinochet Regime in Chile*. Berkeley: University of California Press, 1994.
Spooner lived and worked in Chile for most of the 1980's as a journalist covering the military dictatorship of Augusto Pinochet (1973-1989). She interviewed many Chileans, from government officials to ordinary citizens, during these years and combines these interviews with extensive reading in published sources to provide a sharply etched portrait of a nation in the agony of a harsh dictatorship. Much of her text is relevant to Chilean-U.S. relations in this period. She takes issue with U.S. Ambassador Nathaniel Davis' account (see his book annotated in this section) of his efforts to help U.S. citizens taken by the Chilean military during the bloody overthrow of the government of Salvador Allende (1970-1973). She also discusses the Chilean military government's public relations campaign to obtain a favorable image in the United States and the influence in Chile of the "Chicago boys," the economists trained at the University of Chicago in the free enterprise policies of Milton Friedman. The operations of Chile's rabidly anti-Communist DINA (National Intelligence Office) included the assassination of former Allende government official Orlando Letelier in Washington, D.C. Such brutal treatment of dissidents, political prisoners, and exiled leftists became an issue in U.S.-Chilean relations and form a prominent part of Spooner's text. Her footnotes include several articles from U.S. newspapers and newsmagazines.

The Andean Nations as a Region

Pike, Fredrick. *The United States and the Andean Republics: Peru, Bolivia, and Ecuador*. Cambridge, MA: Harvard University Press, 1977.
The relationships between the United States and these three countries have been distant—especially when compared with U.S. involvements in Mexico, Cuba, and Central America—but they have had important consequences when viewed in a broad perspective. Pike offers just such a perspective in this exceptional study. He explains the cultural and political bases for the history of Andean America in a manner that

the typical U.S. reader can understand, even if unfamiliar with this part of the world. Pike stresses the lingering and pervasive influence of corporatism (not to be confused with the large organizational structures of U.S. business), under which the general population from rich to poor is set up in various groups that are tied to the central government through bureaucracy and patronage. Using this unifying theme, Pike presents the histories of Peru, Bolivia, and Ecuador in a clearly written survey from the colonial period into the 1970's. His analysis of U.S. influence in the Andean nations begins with the arrival of North American capital in the early decades of the twentieth century, then continues with the growth of U.S. diplomatic influence beginning with the 1920's and extends further in the Good Neighbor Policy in the next two decades, the arrival of the Cold War in the 1950's and the Alliance for Progress in the 1960's, and the uncertainties of economic develop-ment and social change in the 1970's. A unique strength of this book is its weaving together of the internal histories of these three countries with the expansive economic, cultural, and diplomatic influences of the United States.

Individual Andean Nations

Bolivia

Andrade, Victor. *My Mission for Revolutionary Bolivia, 1946-1952*. Pitts-burgh, PA: University of Pittsburgh Press, 1976.
   The precarious nature of Bolivia's tin-dominated economy and the wide gap between the rich and the poor drove that nation toward social revolution in the 1940's. In 1952, miners and other workers began a social revolution that resulted in the nationalization of foreign-owned tin mines and stimulated a sharp debate in Washington concerning the allegation that this movement was Communist-inspired. The challenge of representing Bolivia in Washington in the crucial years of 1946 and 1952 faced Victor Andrade, an educator and military officer who turned to a diplomatic career as representative of Bolivia's revolutionary government. Andrade's informative first-person account of his work as a diplomat includes his meetings with several prominent figures in U.S. diplomacy and politics. He records his productive meetings with Secretary of State Edward Stettinius, Assistant Secretary of State for Latin American Affairs Nelson Rockefeller, and Presidents Harry Truman and Dwight Eisenhower. He also records his conflicts with diplomat Spruille Braden and Senator Millard Tydings, along with his

difficulties with powerful Senator Bourke Hickenlooper. According to Andrade's account, he represented the interests of the revolutionary government in Bolivia against the international tin mining companies and their advocates within the U.S. government. The introductory essay by Cole Blasier adds important depth to Andrade's story.

Klein, Herbert S. *Bolivia: The Evolution of a Multi-Ethnic Society.* 2d ed. New York: Oxford University Press, 1992.
For students who want to delve into the history of Bolivia, this text is an excellent starting point. Klein covers the pre-Columbian era of native American societies and the Spanish colonial period in the first third of the book. He then discusses the revolution for independence and the struggles to build a nation-state in the nineteenth century, along with presenting an outstanding chapter on the development of the export economy based on silver and tin in the period from 1880 to 1930. Klein offers a coherent summary of the revolution of 1952 and traces the growing concerns of the United States in the internal affairs of Bolivia from this point onward. The last portion of the text is concerned with the politics and policies of the post-revolutionary military governments, with astute commentary on their efforts to promote economic development not only in the export economy but also in local agriculture. Klein includes a discussion of land reform (the breakup of large properties among peasant farmers), a controversial topic with international ramifications. The fifteen-page annotated bibliography is a valuable source for additional readings on all phases of Bolivian history.

Marsh, Margaret. *The Bankers in Bolivia.* New York: Vanguard Press, 1928.
United States economic expansion encompassed key South American primary resources in the 1920's. In the case of Bolivia, tin attracted investments from New York, accompanied by similar financial commitments to railroad construction and speculation in potential petroleum properties. Marsh brings together considerable amounts of financial and legal information to document the extent of U.S. involvement in Bolivian mining, transportation, and finance, and the consequent burdensome debt carried by that nation's fragile government with its limited tax revenues. Marsh emphasizes that tin mining produced impressive profits but that most of these profits left Bolivia for corporate headquarters in the United States and Europe. She argues that although U.S. military intervention had not occurred in Bolivia, the potential for such intervention existed. This study, written in the late

1920's, was one of a series of attacks on U.S. business activities in Latin America and constitutes a polemical but nevertheless important expression of opinion regarding the harmful effects of expansive capitalism. Marsh's book includes the contract for the Bolivian loan of 1922 from the Equitable Trust Company of New York. The footnotes and bibliography are built on an extensive survey of the existing published material on Bolivia in the early decades of the twentieth century.

Wilkie, James. *The Bolivian Revolution and U.S. Aid Since 1952: Financial Background and Context of Political Decisions.* Los Angeles: Latin American Center of the University of California, Los Angeles, 1969.
The Bolivian revolution of 1952 resulted in increased pressure on that nation's government to create programs to stimulate social change and economic growth. James Wilkie, an expert in the study of budget and finance, examines the budget allocation process in Bolivia in the 1950's and early 1960's with special attention to the role of the United States Agency for International Development, or USAID. This agency took on the challenge of assisting the Bolivian government in its social programs in education and housing and its economic programs in agriculture and public works. Although Wilkie's findings in this brief text are not conclusive, they do represent a valuable "snapshot" of the operations of USAID and the Bolivian government in their efforts to use fiscal resources to carry through with the nation's revolutionary aims. Much of the text and a twenty-eight-page appendix include useful statistics.

Ecuador

Conaghan, Catherine M. *Restructuring Domination: Industrialists and the State in Ecuador.* Pittsburgh, PA: University of Pittsburgh Press, 1988.
The United States and Ecuador have experienced few diplomatic disagreements, and there have been no major U.S. military interventions in that country. One area of significant interaction between these two nations involves the process of industrialization. Like most of the smaller Latin American states, Ecuador entered the process of industrialization relatively late, after World War II. Conaghan focuses this sophisticated analysis on those members of the Ecuadoran middle class engaged in industrial and agricultural enterprises. A central theme in

her study is the arrival of large multinational corporations (usually involved in the export of bananas and cacao to the United States) and the efforts of Ecuadoran entrepreneurs to deal with the consequences of this foreign-dominated economic expansion. Ecuadoran business leaders want the government to be a supporter of their enterprises. These same business leaders see little need for reformist projects such as welfare or labor legislation. It is this government-business alignment that most often establishes the points of contact between the multinational corporations and the nation of Ecuador.

Fitch, John Samuel. *The Military Coup d'État as a Political Process: Ecuador, 1948-1956.* Baltimore: Johns Hopkins University Press, 1977.
Ecuador experienced four occasions in which the military overthrew a civilian government in the years from 1948 to 1966. Fitch examines the causes and consequences of these coups d'état in Ecuador's political process and concludes that such interventions by the armed forces have come to be regarded by military officers, civilian politicians, and the public in general as an integral part of the nation's political system. The role of the United States in these coups was evident but not the decisive factor. The U.S. Central Intelligence Agency promoted anti-Communist policies in Ecuador, and U.S. military advisers tended to reinforce that position. Fitch's main purpose is to explore the Ecuadoran political, social, and economic bases of military coups, but those readers interested in U.S. opposition to Communism in the Western Hemisphere in the early Cold War can find much evidence of the Ecuadoran armed forces acting in accord with Washington's overall goals even though direct links among the diplomatic, military, and intelligence agencies of the two countries was minimal.

Martz, John D. *Ecuador: Conflicting Political Culture and the Quest for Progress.* Boston: Allyn and Bacon, 1972.
This convenient, brief summary of the basic characteristics of Ecuador's political system also includes the social, cultural, and economic conditions in this Andean republic in the 1950's and 1960's. Martz's talent for writing clear prose and providing logical organization is very much in evidence. The discussion of Ecuadoran politics in Chapter 2 includes an examination of Marxist and other radical criticisms of U.S. influence. Of particular relevance to U.S.-Ecuadoran relations are Chapter 5, which deals with the "clash of tradition and modernization" and provides commentary on the impact of U.S. investments on economic development, and Chapter 6, which discusses "dependency and

nationalism" as manifested in the growth of concern among Ecuadorans about the enlargement of the economic impact of the United States. Martz also mentions provisional president Otto Arosemena Gomez's confrontation with the U.S. delegation at the meeting of hemispheric presidents and diplomats at Punta del Este, Uruguay, in 1967.

Peru

Dobyns, Henry, and Paul Doughty. *Peru: A Cultural History*. New York: Oxford University Press, 1976.

United States-Peruvian relations have large historical significance only in the most recent decades of Peru's long and eventful history. Dobyns and Doughty begin this survey text with an account of native American groups in the centuries before the rise of the Inca state and culture in the 1400's. They continue this story through the Spanish conquest and the erection of Spanish monuments on the ruins of the Inca empire in the 1500's, then devote an entire chapter to the struggle for Peru's independence from 1808 to 1826. Approximately half of the text concerns Peru's quest for political and cultural unity and economic prosperity in the nineteenth and twentieth centuries. The authors place U.S.-Peruvian relations in a large historical context that includes succinct discussions of the impact of foreign corporations in mining, agricultural, communications, trade, and investment activities, as well as the local and national reactions to these intrusions from the outside. The authors furnish a helpful chronological chart and an annotated bibliography.

Goodsell, Charles T. *American Corporations and Peruvian Politics*. Cambridge, MA: Harvard University Press, 1974.

The relationship between multinational corporations and the governments of developing nations such as Peru is the subject of much debate. Critics of these powerful business organizations claim that they practice a form of imperialism by applying pressure to the host country's political leaders for favorable treatment. Social scientist Charles Goodsell studies this issue through a close examination of the political activities of large U.S.-based companies in Peru, mainly in the 1950's and 1960's. Included in his examination are the International Petroleum Company (Standard Oil), W. R. Grace, International Telephone and Telegraph, and Cerro de Pasco (mining). Goodsell's conclusions do not support the notion that these corporations impose their wills on

the Peruvian political system through an imperialistic grasp of power. Instead, Goodsell finds that although such corporations frequently acquire special tax advantages and resource concessions, they do not dominate politics and the press. The expropriation of foreign-owned mining and agricultural holdings by the military government of Juan Velasco Alvarado (1968-1975) was a clear indication of the limits of multinational corporations' power in Peru.

Gootenberg, Paul. *Between Silver and Guano: Commercial Policy and the State in Postindependence Peru*. Princeton, NJ: Princeton University Press, 1989.

Peru entered the world of international trade in the middle part of the nineteenth century after three hundred years within the confines of the Spanish Empire and a relatively brief three decades (1820's-1850's) of high tariffs to bring revenue into the impoverished treasury of the new government. This tariff on imports greatly limited commerce with other nations. After the establishment of liberal trade policies (reduction or elimination of tariffs), Peru opened its economy to the international system and became more closely tied to the United States and Great Britain through the booming guano (bird droppings used as fertilizer) trade in the later decades of the nineteenth century. Although Gootenberg does not provide much detail on Peru's trade with the United States in these years, his analysis of the origins and impact of free trade on the nation offers a valuable explanation of the importance of the intermeshing of Peru's economy with the world economy. This experience is crucial to an understanding of Peru's economic strengths and weaknesses in later years, when the U.S. economic presence became even larger. Gootenberg's work complements Larry Clayton's study of W. R. Grace and Company (discussed in the section on economic development in Chapter 4). The author includes an intelligent critique of the use of dependency theory in explaining the Peruvian economy and a thorough discussion of the role of nationalism in this period of Peru's history.

Sharp, Daniel A., ed. *U.S. Foreign Policy and Peru*. Austin: University of Texas Press, 1972.

Juan Velasco Alvarado came to power in Peru in a 1968 military coup d'état that defied the conventional understanding of Latin American barracks revolts as conservative or reactionary grabs for power. By contrast, Velasco attempted a fundamental restructuring of the nation's economy with the apparent purpose of benefiting the workers and peasants while challenging the Peruvian elites and the large multinational corporations. The unique value of this collection of essays is that it focuses on U.S.-Peruvian relations at a time when the potential of the Velasco Administration seemed to be at its peak. Topics covered in these studies include an overview of U.S. policy toward Peru, U.S. relations with the Peruvian military, U.S. responses to Velasco's land reform proposals, and the operations of U.S. private banks and corporations. (The early promise of the Velasco regime did not materialize, however, and this government fell victim to a coup in 1975.)

Thorp, Rosemary, and Geoffrey Bertram. *Peru, 1890-1977: Growth and Policy in an Open Economy*. New York: Columbia University Press, 1978.
Much of the relationship between the United States and Peru has been based on trade and investment, not diplomacy and intervention. Thorp and Bertram provide an excellent historical overview of the economic cycles of Peruvian history through the operations of foreign (mainly U.S.) corporations. The authors divide their coverage into three phases. The first runs from 1890 to 1930 and features intensification of the activities of several corporations, such as W. R. Grace and Cerro de Pasco, engaged in agricultural and mining operations for export to overseas markets. The second phase runs from the Depression era through World War II (1930-1948); during that era, economic dislocations caused by worldwide events gave Peru the opportunity to attempt to develop its own locally based enterprises. The last period extends from 1948 to 1977. The meager results in local industrialization obtained in the Depression and war years gave way to a return to export-oriented growth through large multinational corporations. The expansion of this process prompted the military regime of Juan Velasco Alvarado (1968-1975) to challenge these arrangements and take control of the properties of several foreign-owned corporations. Among the themes in this book is the authors' conclusion that the presence of multinational corporations distorted Peru's economic history by stifling local initiative in business entrepreneurship. This text includes informative footnotes and an extensive bibliography.

Werlich, David. *Admiral of the Amazon: John Randolph Tucker, His Confederate Colleagues, and Peru*. Charlottesville: University of Virginia Press, 1990.
Eastern Peru contains a large section of the headwaters of the Amazon River, but, because of the rugged Andes Mountains, this region is isolated from Lima and the other major urban centers of the country on the Pacific side of the highlands. Confederate Navy veteran John

Randolph Tucker went to Peru after the Union victory in the Civil War
to work as an explorer, cartographer, and geographer in this isolated
region. His expeditions in the late 1860's and 1870's, based in the small
frontier settlement of Iquitos, mapped the tributaries of the Amazon
and contributed to the opening of this section of Peru to oceangoing
ships by way of the Amazon. Werlich's archival research in the United
States and Peru provides rare insights on the contributions of Tucker
and his former Confederate colleagues to the scientific and economic
development of Amazonian Peru in the late nineteenth and twentieth
centuries.

Paraguay

Garner, William R. *The Chaco Dispute: A Study of Prestige Diplomacy.*
Washington, DC: Public Affairs, 1966.
The Chaco War was a devastating conflict between Paraguay and
Bolivia over possession of a previously neglected, oil-rich tropical
lowland area in heart of South America. The fighting from 1932 to
1935 prompted diplomatic negotiations that involved several nations—most prominently Argentina and the United States. Garner's
succinct account concentrates on this diplomacy and stresses that the
Chaco War became a struggle for prestige between Buenos Aires and
Washington as much as the fighting itself was a struggle for territory
between Paraguay and Bolivia. The Argentine officials, led by the
resourceful Carlos Saavedra Lamas, outmaneuvered U.S. Good Neighbor Policy diplomats, particularly with the inclusion of the League of
Nations as a device to focus the last stages of the negotiations on
Buenos Aires. Saavedra Lamas won a Nobel Prize for his labors for
peace, and, according to Garner, Argentina won a significant victory
in "prestige diplomacy" with its strong showing in the world press in
contrast to the less impressive performance of the United States.
Paraguay won the war and claimed the disputed territory in a military
triumph that matched the Argentine diplomatic victory. For a contrasting view of the motives behind this war, see the book by Leslie Rout
annotated in this section.

Grow, Michael. *The Good Neighbor Policy and Authoritarianism in
Paraguay: United States Economic Expansion and Great Power Rivalry in Latin America During World War II.* Lawrence: Regents Press
of Kansas, 1981.

Paraguay, a nation of only marginal concern for the United States for most of the twentieth century, became an important element in hemispheric defense against potential Nazi incursions into southern South America. Grow's study includes relevant information on the 1930's as well as the war years from 1941 to 1945. His archival research reveals that the United States was genuinely concerned about German influence in Paraguay and that President Franklin D. Roosevelt's administration employed a combination of economic and military aid to lure the Asunción government into the Allied camp. In the process, the United States displaced both its enemy (Germany) and an ally (Great Britain) in securing a central place in the Paraguayan economy and polity. Grow examines U.S. dealings with the government of Higino Moringo (1940-1948), which used twists and turns from authoritarian practices to democratic rhetoric and ended in a destructive civil war. Grow concludes that Paraguay's experiences with the United States in the World War II era taught Moringo's successors a valuable lesson: that alliance with the United States brought loans and other important sources of external support.

Lewis, Paul H. *Paraguay Under Stroessner*. Chapel Hill: University of North Carolina Press, 1980.
Paraguay's longtime dictator, Alfredo Stroessner, ruled his country with an iron and often brutal hand from 1954 to 1989. Lewis carefully explains the origins of the Stroessner dictatorship. In many ways comparable to the Somoza dynasty in Nicaragua (1935-1979) in its rigid opposition to Communism and the left in general, the Stroessner regime tended to operate in concert with the military establishments and conservative governments of the regional powers Argentina and Brazil in addition to observing the Cold War policies of the United States. One of Lewis' main themes, however, is Paraguay's efforts to balance the influences of more powerful nations. A landlocked country dependent on its trade outlets through the Rio de la Plata system, Paraguay traditionally accepted a degree of domination by Argentina. Stroessner also entered into dam construction projects with Brazil and turned to Argentina and Brazil as well as the United States for foreign loans. According to Lewis, Paraguay often avoided submission to U.S. pressures. For example, Lewis discusses Stroessner's response to U.S. calls for democratization as a few empty gestures and little more. The dictator, however, often sent his young military officers for training in antiguerrilla tactics at the U.S.-run School of the Americas at Fort Gulick in the Panama Canal Zone. In general, Lewis concludes that Stroessner managed to move away from the type of interlocking

arrangements with the United States that were typical of the World War II era (as discussed in the book by Michael Grow annotated in this section).

Rout, Leslie. *Politics of the Chaco Peace Conference, 1935-1939.* Austin: University of Texas Press, 1970.

The Paraguayan victories on the battlefields of the Chaco War brought territorial gains in the diplomatic negotiations to end the conflict. Rout's detailed examination of the diplomacy surrounding the Chaco War emphasizes the strains and stresses in these negotiations, in which personalities and politics often carried large importance. Rout also makes it clear that economic factors were of prime consideration in the origins of the war and the struggle for a peace settlement. The Chaco had value for cattle grazing and its Quebracho trees (which produce tannin) in addition to the presence of significant petroleum reserves. Rout consulted archives in Paraguay, Bolivia, Argentina, Uruguay, and the United States to provide impressive depth in this diplomatic study. He gives more credit to Paraguayan General José Felíx Estigarribia's mature decisions for the final settlement than Argentina's high-profile diplomat Carlos Saavedra Lamas. Rout also discusses the work of U.S. diplomat Spruille Braden. This book also contains relevant maps and several important documents from the negotiations.

Zook, David H. *The Conduct of the Chaco War.* New Haven, CT: Book-man, 1960.

The four years (1932-1935) of violent conflict between Paraguay and Bolivia, two landlocked South American countries, greatly distressed the United States and other leading nations of the Western Hemisphere and Europe. Zook examines the diplomatic background of the dispute over the Chaco territory, a tropical lowland area along the border between Paraguay and Bolivia that ranges from moist fertile land to arid, desertlike conditions. He attributes scant importance to the petroleum potential of the region as a cause for the war and instead emphasizes the buildup of frustrations in both nations as a result of decades of prolonged and fruitless negotiations. The strong point of this book is its examination of the war itself. Familiar with developments in military strategy and tactics in the years between World War I and World War II, Zook explains the victory of the outnumbered Paraguayan forces as the result of the resourceful Colonel José Felíx Estigarribia, who grasped the value of motorized transportation as a means of outmaneuvering his Bolivian enemy. The environment of the Chaco made the foot soldiers the main combatants, and Estigarribia's

quick movement of his troops on trucks left the Bolivians (who tried
to rely on scarce and poorly located railroads) at a great disadvantage
in key battles. Although Zook gives only slight attention to U.S. policy
toward the belligerents in this book, his depiction of the nature of the
fighting helps to clarify why so many people in the United States,
Argentina, and other nations worked vigorously to bring the conflict
to an end.

Uruguay

Alisky, Marvin. *Uruguay: A Contemporary Survey.* New York: Praeger,
1969.
A small nation located between Argentina and Brazil on the southeastern coast of South America, Uruguay has played a secondary role in
hemispheric affairs. As Alisky points out in this overview of Uruguayan history, for the first half of the twentieth century, this small,
predominantly agricultural country produced not only wool and meat
but also stable, progressive democracy. Alisky wrote this book during
the decade when signs of trouble became evident in Uruguay's economy and political system. International prices for wool and meat did
not keep pace with the costs of Uruguay's advanced welfare system,
which was in many ways comparable with the U.S. system. Inflation
also hit the Uruguayan economy hard in the 1960's. The United States
began to play an increasingly important role in the Uruguayan economy with the decline of British overseas trade and investment in the
1940's and 1950's, and with the establishment of the Alliance for
Progress in the following decade. (Latin American and U.S. delegates
signed its charter at Punta del Este, Uruguay, in 1961.) Alisky explains
the growth of the U.S. economic presence in Uruguay in Chapter 5 and
the cooperation of these two nations in their foreign policies in Chapter
9.

Finch, M. H. J. *A Political Economy of Uruguay Since 1870.* New York:
St. Martin's Press, 1981.
This sophisticated economic analysis covers the rise and decline of the
Uruguayan economy during the century in which it first emerged as an
exporter of wool, mutton, wheat, and meat only to encounter severe
economic difficulties in the 1950's and 1960's. Chapter 5 discusses the
problems of the meat exporting business, in which the Uruguayan
government's maintenance of artificially high export prices drove
foreign corporations (including Armour and Swift, both based in the

United States) to find less expensive suppliers. Chapter 7 covers the economic crisis of the 1955-1970 period, in which the decline of meat and other export products and government budget deficits led Uruguay to appeal to the International Monetary Fund and the Alliance for Progress for help. The responses of these agencies did not bring the necessary results, and the downward economic spiral accelerated with the withdrawal of nearly $250 million in U.S. private investments in the 1960's. Finch does not present the U.S. government or private corporations as villains in Uruguay's economic crisis, but his analysis does make it clear that the United States replaced Great Britain as the main source of credit and trade in the 1950's and after.

Wilson, Carlos. *The Tupamaros: The Unmentionables*. Boston: Branden, 1974.

The Uruguayan economic crisis of the 1950's and 1960's severely damaged the standard of living of the general population and was accompanied by serious challenges to the nation's long history of democratic government. One outcome of this turmoil was the appearance in the 1960's of the Tupamaros, a radical leftist urban guerrilla group. Wilson's brief account is clearly sympathetic to this group. The author explains its origins, its philosophy, and many of its actions as justified within the context of recent Uruguayan history. A significant portion of this book discusses the hostility of the Tupamaros toward the United States, as exemplified by their capture and execution of the Central Intelligence Agency's antiguerrilla expert Dan Mitrione in 1970. This book's pro-Tupamaro content should be balanced by a reading of M. H. J. Finch's study and other publications on this period in Uruguayan history.

Chapter 6
VIDEO DOCUMENTARIES

Americas. Color. Approx. 10 hours. Boston: WGBH, 1993.
This ten-part documentary covers the large field of Latin American history, with emphasis on social and economic issues. The part titled "Migrants" deals with the large movement of people within Mexico from the countryside to the cities—especially Mexico City—in search of jobs and a better life. Central characters are Marcela and Atenacio Aguayo, who left the village of Malpaso in the state of Zacatecas for Mexico City in 1972. Although they prospered for a while in the 1970's, the economic crisis of 1982 and its consequences ended their prosperity and destroyed their hopes. Poignant scenes reveal Marcela's sense of frustration and personal loss. There is also coverage of the difficult working conditions in the maquiladoras (factories) in northern Mexico, located along the border, where U.S. corporations employ Mexican workers. This documentary connects persistent poverty and internal migration to the plans and policies of the administration of President Carlos Salinas de Gortari (1988-1994) for economic reform and, in particular, the establishment of the North American Free Trade Agreement (NAFTA). The protests of peasant farmers from Zacatecas and other states and the experiences of Marcela Aguayo call into question the basic assumptions behind NAFTA and the Mexican government's large-scale economic projects, which have done much damage to the lives of peasants in the countryside and workers in the cities. By implication, this documentary provides background information on why many Mexicans decide to migrate to the United States in search of better job opportunities.

Can Tropical Rainforests Be Saved? Color. 116 minutes. New York: Richter Productions, 1994.
This three-part documentary provides a global perspective on the value of rain forests and the threats to their existence from extensive cutting by international corporations. The broad coverage includes Latin America, Africa, and Asia. Part 1 focuses on the Amazon basin and the intrusion of logging, cattle ranching, paved highways, and gold mining, and also on the less-publicized deforestation of Panama. Part 3 covers the development of the park system in Costa Rica that protects a substantial portion of that nation's rain forests and the efforts of the members of the native American Kuna tribe of Panama in their work

to preserve the rain forests in which they live. The issue of deforestation is examined from several perspectives, including those of the local peoples in the path of expansive development, the settlers and squatters who move into the cleared areas, and government and corporate interests involved in this process.

Castro's Cuba: Two Views. Color and black and white. 136 minutes. Minneapolis, MN: Twin Cities Public Television, 1990.

Fidel Castro has been one of the most controversial figures in the Western Hemisphere through the last half of the twentieth century. This documentary's exceptional value is in its presentation of two opposing perspectives on Castro's first three decades as head of state in Cuba. The first half of the documentary—titled "Nobody Listened"—is the work of journalist Jorge Ulloa, who concentrates on the plight of political prisoners in Cuba from the early 1960's to the late 1980's. Revolutionary leaders such as Huber Matos and Jorge Vells had supported Castro in the struggle against the dictatorship of Fulgencio Batista and in the formative period of the revolutionary government, but they lost favor with the new regime and served long terms in Cuban prisons. Much of the information is presented through interviews with Matos, Vells, and other former political prisoners who, after their releases in the 1980's, went to the United States or Europe and began to tell of the conditions that they had experienced while incarcerated. This part of the documentary also includes remarkable footage of the large prison on the Isle of Pines and similar institutions. In general, "Nobody Listened" provides a bleak portrait of the status of individual rights and the prevalence of political persecution in Castro's Cuba. The second half of this documentary is titled "The Uncompromising Revolution" and is the work of journalist Saul Landau. It presents a much more positive view of recent Cuban history, with emphasis on the expansion of public education and medical care, as well as on the development of a sense of national pride among the Cuban people. The impact of these trends is expressed by several Cubans in their own words (translated in easy-to-read captions). This portion of the documentary also focuses on Cuba's biogenetics laboratories and Cuban work on the cutting edge of medical innovations in the 1980's. Landau interviews the inmates of a Cuban women's prison, where conditions were much better than those described in "Nobody Listened." In Landau's presentation, Fidel Castro is the center of attention. The journalist pieced together recent interviews with Castro and archival footage of earlier interviews and speeches to provide a sympathetic but also penetrating look at the evolution of Castro's policies over three decades.

Crisis in Central America. Color and black and white. Approx. 4 hours. Boston: WGBH, 1986.

This four-part series appeared when U.S. policy in Central America confronted opposition at home and abroad. Part 1 is titled "Yankee Years" and gives a historical overview of U.S. policy in the Caribbean from the 1840's to the 1950's, with emphasis on the strategic impact of the Panama Canal, Augusto César Sandino's guerrilla war against U.S. intervention in Nicaragua (1927-1933), Fulgencio Batista's rise to power in Cuba in the 1930's, the Guatemalan revolution of 1944, its subsequent leftist governments, and the CIA's overthrow of Guatemalan President Jacobo Arbenz Guzmán in 1954. Strengths of this segment include vintage newsreels and interviews with U.S. diplomat Dana Munro. The second part, "Castro's Challenge," covers the Cuban revolution from its struggles in eastern Cuba through the collapse of Batista's government and Castro's ascension to power in Havana in 1959. This segment includes footage of some of Castro's early speeches, Castro's defeat of the CIA-sponsored Bay of Pigs invasion, and the struggles for efficiency and productivity in the Cuban economy in the 1960's and 1970's. Part 3 is called "Revolutionary Nicaragua" and deals with the fall of Anastasio Somoza's dictatorship in 1979, with particular attention to the assassination of respected Nicaraguan journalist Pedro Joaquín Chamorro and the depiction of the Nicaraguan crisis on U.S. television, including videotape of the killing of correspondent Bill Stewart. This portion of the documentary also traces the rise of Daniel Ortega to power and the withdrawal of Violeta Chamorro (the widow of Pedro Joaquín Chamorro) from politics in the early 1980's. This presentation is supported by interviews with many Nicaraguan leaders and U.S. officials directly involved in these events. Part 4 is called "The Battle for El Salvador" and examines the civil strife in that nation. The administration of President Ronald Reagan (1981-1989) alleged that Communists including agents of Nicaraguan President Daniel Ortega were the primary sources of opposition to the Salvadoran government and sent military aid and advisers to that strife-torn nation. This segment also includes videotape of material from U.S. television news coverage of these events.

Emerging Powers. Color. Approx. 4 hours. New York: Wall Street Journal Television, 1996.

The surge of internationalization in the world's economy sparked interest in the problems and promise of developing nations in this process. This four-part documentary covers four major developing nations: China, India, and two Latin American countries: Brazil and Mexico. The segment on Brazil ranges from the industrial center of São Paulo to the Amazon basin in its portrait of a wide cross section of the nation's economic activity. The program begins with Brazilian popular music, which reaches a large international audience. Much of Brazil's economy is connected to the world market. Individual segments deal with an Avon cosmetics salesperson in Amazonia, the state of television advertising, the production and export of Brazilian telenovelas or television soap operas (in translation), the emergence of an agribusiness operation that includes oranges and coffee for export, and the privatization of the Brazilian steel industry. Interviews include Brazilian President Fernando Henrique Cardoso. The last part deals with Mexico and concentrates on the period immediately following the onset of the economic crisis of 1995. Interviews with a middle-class family in Mexico City reveal the hardships imposed by higher interest rates and the general uncertainty of the economy. The documentary also includes optimistic notes, including a profile of the Monterrey Institute of Technology and the hopes of one of its graduates as he enters a family-owned business. Another optimistic note is found in grassroots capital formation through a small savings and investment organization made up of a group of industrious women in a low-income neighborhood in Mexico City. Interviews and dramatic scenery highlight the efforts of an entrepreneur who guided the completion of a modernized railroad connection from Texas to the agriculturally productive state of Sinaloa.

Eva Perón. Black and white. 27 minutes. New York: Wolper Productions, 1963.
This portrait of the controversial Argentine actress-turned-political activist has many revealing visual images but does little to resolve the questions regarding her life. It also abounds with examples of the presumptions and prejudices in the U.S. media toward her, her husband Juan Perón (Argentine president from 1946 to 1955 and again from 1973 to 1974), and the mass sociopolitical movement that they led. The narrative script, read by Mike Wallace, emphasizes the seamy side of Eva's early life, including allegations that she "made her way from colonel to colonel" as a tactic for personal advancement. Juan Perón is described as a fascist who used techniques learned from Hitler and Mussolini to gain power. The narrative exaggerates Eva's role in Juan

Perón's political campaigns of 1945 and 1946 by claiming that she harangued the Argentine masses and thereby saved her husband from imprisonment. Newsreel footage shows Perón's "Nazi-style" army and police. Perón's electoral victory is characterized as a farce dominated by fascist gangsterism. By contrast with this political commentary, the coverage on Eva's 1947 tour of Europe is even-handed. In general, however, the narrative information in most of this documentary is similar to the anti-Perón judgments of Spruille Braden. Although its visual images of mass demonstrations and the central characters are quite insightful, this documentary should be used in conjunction with other sources including the books by Robert Crassweller, Ronald Newton, David Rock, Jesse Stiller, Arthur Whitaker, and Randall Woods as well as Braden, all of which are annotated in Chapter 5 in the section on Argentina.

The Godfather of Cocaine. Color. 82 minutes. Boston: WGBH, 1995.
Pablo Escobar's meteoric rise from petty criminal in the 1970's to head of a multibillion dollar drug smuggling empire is the subject of this fast-moving biography. This program includes information on Escobar's family background (based largely on interviews with his mother and brother), his earliest criminal activity, and his beginnings in the drug trade. Interviews with former U.S. ambassador to Colombia Lewis Tambs, former drug smuggler Max Mermelstein, and several U.S. Drug Enforcement Agency investigators provide important details on how Escobar ran his international drug smuggling organization, which included huge processing plants and a fleet of airplanes. There is also an account of the violent war between Escobar's organized crime empire and the Colombian government, from the 1984 raid on the huge processing plant at Tranquilandia to Escobar's revenge attacks on the Colombian law enforcement system, including the assassination of Minister of Justice Rodrigo Lara Bonilla. The role of pilot-smuggler-DEA informant Barry Seal is examined, as is his murder (on Escobar's orders) after the administration of President Ronald Reagan publicized photographs Seal had taken of drug shipments passing through Nicaragua. (The Reagan administration intended to discredit the leftist Sandinista government.) The final portion of this documentary deals with the hunt for the elusive Escobar in 1992 and 1993 and his death in a gun battle with members of the Colombian military special unit assigned to track him down.

Grenada. Color. 55 minutes. Boston: WGBH, 1985.

The 1983 United States military intervention on the small island of Grenada seemed, on the surface, to be an impressive display of Cold War policing of the Caribbean against Communist expansion. The main purpose of this documentary is to explore the problems and the failures that escaped public attention in the news media at the time. Grenada was a major concern for the administration of President Ronald Reagan for several months because of the leftist inclinations of its government under Maurice Bishop and because of the construction by Cuban workers of a 10,000-foot runway that could accommodate large, presumably Soviet, jet aircraft. The assassination of Bishop by an even more radical Grenadian faction on October 19, 1983, led the Reagan Administration to intervene, ostensibly to protect the six hundred U.S. medical students attending St. George's University on the island, but also to bring an end to the pro-Cuban, pro-Soviet policies of the island's leaders. This documentary uses interviews with State Department officials and military officers (including a highly demonstrative General Norman Schwarzkopf, who participated in the invasion) to explain the numerous mistakes made by U.S. forces in the operation. Schwarzkopf and others blamed failures in intelligence that left the U.S. troops with inadequate maps and a poor understanding of their mission. In an operation that the Defense Department expected to encounter virtually no opposition and to require only a few hours for completion, the U.S. military suffered nineteen deaths and more than one hundred wounded, and it needed several days to reach all the U.S. medical students on the island.

The Hunt for Pancho Villa. Black and white with color. 55 minutes. Boston: WGBH, 1993.

Mexico and the United States came perilously close to war in 1916, largely because of Pancho Villa's raid across the border into Columbus, New Mexico. This documentary examines Villa's background as a popular bandit leader who emerged as a major force in the early years of the Mexican Revolution. On-screen interviews with historians and elderly survivors of these episodes underscore the ambiguities in Villa's reputation: He was a heroic revolutionary of unquestioned courage and also a man of dark and violent moods. Villa also had a friendly—even protective—attitude toward U.S. businesses operating in northern Mexico. This attitude changed abruptly, however, after President Woodrow Wilson turned his support from Villa to his rival, Venustiano Carranza. Soon after that switch, Villa launched his attack on Columbus. Approximately half of this program deals with U.S. General John Pershing and his punitive expedition into Mexico to defeat and capture (or possibly kill) Villa as punishment for the raid on Columbus. Pershing's forces were unsuccessful in pursuit of this goal and also engaged in embarrassing and bloody conflicts with Mexicans that nearly brought the two countries into a much larger conflict.

Mexico. Color and black and white. Approx. 4 hours. Boston: WGBH, 1988.

Mexico's twentieth century history includes one of the world's major social revolutions followed by an unusually long period of single-party rule. This three-part documentary spans the years from the early 1900's, when Porfirio Díaz enjoyed the last decade of his thirty-four-year dictatorship (1876-1910), to 1988, when the PRI (Party of the Institutional Revolution) showed signs of losing its grasp on power after sixty years of near political monopoly. The United States was a generally powerful, often intrusive influence in Mexico during these years. Part 1 covers the collapse of the Díaz dictatorship, the rise and brief presidency of Francisco Madero (1911-1913), the revolutionary careers of Pancho Villa and Emiliano Zapata, U.S. diplomatic interference and military interventions, and the ascension to the presidency of Venustiano Carranza (1917-1920) and Alvaro Obregón (1920-1924). Obregón's assassination in 1929 broke the line of presidential succession and prompted Plutarco Elías Calles to bring together various political factions to form the party that was to direct Mexico's national life into the 1980's. Part 1 also covers the presidency of Lázaro Cárdenas (1934-1940), who responded to the demands of peasants and workers with such measures as the 1938 nationalization of foreign-owned oil companies, which caused a crisis in U.S.-Mexican relations. This historical section includes interviews with surviving veterans of the revolution along with commentary from leading academics. Part 2 contains the story of the national party (called the PRI after a reorganization in 1946) through the economic prosperity of the 1960's and the period of harmonious relations with the United States to the troubled presidency of Gustavo Díaz Ordaz (1964-1970), when Mexico's plans for boosting its international image by hosting the 1968 Olympics brought on a major political crisis and a violent confrontation between students and the government (dramatic footage of these events is included). The oil boom of the 1970's stimulated a temporary spurt in national prosperity and excessive borrowing from foreign—mainly U.S.—banks. This borrowing, in turn, brought on the economic crisis at the end of the José López Portillo Administration (1976-1982). Part 3 is concerned largely with the government of Miguel de la Madrid (1982-1988) and its efforts to restore a balanced economy and political stability. Although de la Madrid had some success and enjoyed good relations with Washington, the PRI's presidential candidate in 1988, Carlos Salinas de Gortari, had to campaign vigorously (as the visual images of this documentary reveal). Salinas won the election, but the PRI showed that its power clearly had eroded. The coverage of the period since 1960 includes excerpts from key presidential addresses (in translation) and interviews with important government decision makers including treasury officials Hugo Margain and Jesús Silva Herzog.

Mr. Ludwig's Tropical Dreamland. Color. 57 minutes. Boston: WGBH, 1980.

The Amazon has become the scene of ambitious enterprises that eventually surrender to the complexity and unpredictability of the tropical rain forest. Multibillionaire Daniel Ludwig poured a substantial part of his personal fortune into the Jari region about three hundred miles west of the south of the Amazon. He purchased more than three million acres of rain forest in 1967 and immediately began to implement his plans to grow and harvest the quick-maturing gmelina tree as a source of pulp for paper. He also shipped, by oceangoing tugboat, a ready-made pulp mill from Japan to Jari in 1977-1978. This documentary uses interviews with Ludwig's employees, including agronomists, botanists, and engineers, to give details on the internal workings of this giant project. Excellent photography provides graphic illustrations of the removal of the rain forest, the planting of the gmelina trees, and the operation of the pulp mill. The viewer also sees the living conditions of the workers, with particular insights on the problems of recruiting and retaining the approximately thirty thousand workers needed on the project. The documentary concludes with a balanced discussion of an important question: Should Ludwig's methods in Jari be used elsewhere in the Amazon basin and in other tropical rain forests? For more information on Ludwig's Jari project, consult Jerry Shields, *The Invisible Billionaire: Daniel Ludwig* (Boston: Houghton Mifflin, 1986).

Murder on the Rio San Juan. Color. 54 minutes. Boston: WGBH, 1988.

A group of international journalists, disgruntled Sandinistas, and a single, secretive assassin gathered in a riverfront building on May 30, 1984, on the southern border of Nicaragua for a press conference to be held by the legendary rebel Edén Pastora, also known as Comandante Zero for his audacious leadership in the overthrow of the Somoza dictatorship in the late 1970's. Pastora had become disillusioned with the Sandinista government in the early 1980's and was attempting to form his own revolutionary army to oppose the Managua regime. This press conference proved to be a trap in which the lone assassin attempted to kill Pastora by detonating a powerful explosive. Pastora was wounded but survived. The casualties included the death of U.S. reporter Linda Frazier. The documentary contains a biographical sketch of Pastora, but the main focus concerns who was responsible for the bombing. Videotapes made by several journalists contain clear pictures of the assassin. Through interviews with journalists, Nicaraguan and Costa Rican officials, and Pastora himself, this documentary provides an interesting portrait of intrigue and revolutionary violence that was typical of Central America in the 1980's. U.S. officials—especially ambassador to Costa Rica Curtin Winsor—give the point of view of Reagan Administration officials. The information in this documentary narrows the field of possible sponsors of the bombing to two: the CIA or the Sandinista government. For more details on the bombing and the assassin (identified as Per Anker Hansen), students should consult Martha Honey's book *Hostile Acts*, annotated in the section on Costa Rica in Chapter 5.

The Noriega Connection. Color. 57 minutes. Boston: WGBH, 1990.
Manuel Noriega used ruthlessness and ambition to become one of the most powerful men in the Western Hemisphere in the 1980's. He exploited his positions of authority in the Panamanian military and government to make deals with Colombian cocaine smugglers at the same time that he was a highly paid informant for the U.S. Central Intelligence Agency. This documentary traces Noriega's life from his humble beginnings in a poverty-stricken, broken family in the 1930's though his career in the Panamanian military in the 1950's to the height of his power as a strong-arm dictator in the 1980's. He became an informant for the CIA after the 1964 riots in the Panama Canal Zone. Panama's popular leader Omar Torrijos found Noriega's talent for espionage and his penchant for violence to be useful in the formation of his government (1968-1981). After Torrijos' death in 1981, Noriega used his talents to build his own dictatorship (1983-1989). This documentary uses interviews, newsreel footage, and video news coverage to link Noriega with the CIA under Presidents Richard Nixon, Jimmy Carter, and Ronald Reagan. It also reveals that the Panamanian dictator made deals with Fidel Castro and the leftist Sandinistas in Nicaragua as well as the Colombian drug smugglers.

The Ragged Revolution. Color and black and white. 35 minutes. London: Yorkshire Films, 1972.

This documentary uses the colorful artistry of several of Diego Rivera's murals to introduce the viewer to the turmoil and violence of the first years of the Mexican Revolution, from 1909 to 1915. Black and white images from film and photograph archives highlight the 1909 meeting of dictator Porfirio Díaz (1876-1910) with U.S. President William Howard Taft (1909-1913) on the U.S.-Mexican border, the 1910 celebration of the centennial of Mexico's independence from Spain, and the beginning of the revolution in that same year. Students can observe the physical characteristics and mannerisms of the leading figures of the revolution who are prominently featured in this documentary: Francisco Madero, Pascual Orozco, Pancho Villa, Emiliano Zapata, and Venustiano Carranza. Other central characters are the duo who collaborated in the demise of Madero: the intrusive U.S. Ambassador Henry Lane Wilson and the dictatorial, violence-prone General Victoriano Huerta, who took control of the government after the overthrow and murder of the ill-fated first leader of the revolution.

School of Assassins. Color. 18 minutes. New York: Richter Productions, 1994.

This brief, provocative documentary focuses on the U.S. Army's School of the Americas. Established in 1946 as a training institution for officers in the Latin American armed forces during the Cold War era, the School of the Americas faces a wide range of charges in this scathing attack. U.S. Representative Joseph Kennedy of Massachusetts is among those who argue that the institution has trained officers who returned to their homelands (Argentina, Bolivia, El Salvador, and Panama) to join right-wing governments that engaged in repressive policies and violations of civil liberties. This documentary is an important condemnation of this link between the U.S. government and many dictatorial regimes in Latin America, but it can be placed in a broader perspective by reading other sources annotated in the section on the United States and the Latin American armed forces.

AUTHOR INDEX

SUBJECT INDEX

Adams, John Quincy 21-23, 25-26
Adams-Onís Treaty 25
Allende, Salvador 11, 19, 56, 67,
    82, 232-233, 235-239
Alliance for Progress 14, 79-82,
    218, 230, 238, 240, 250-251
Alvarado, Juan Velasco. *See* Velasco
    Alvarado, Juan
Alvarez, Alejandro 95
Alvarez, Carlos Jader. *See* Jader
    Alvarez, Carlos
Amazon, basin and river 116-117,
    123-124, 126-129, 246, 255, 259
Anslinger, Harry J. 134, 140
Anti-imperialism 21, 57, 99, 162,
    204. *See also* imperialism
Antillean Islands. *See* Netherlands
    Antilles
Arbenz Guzmán, Jacobo 58, 91,
    118, 168-170, 254
Arévalo, Juan José 118, 169
Argentina 5, 7, 11, 14, 18, 22, 26,
    47-48, 50-52, 58, 62, 64, 70, 72,
    77-80, 82, 86, 92, 95, 99, 109-110,
    114, 119-120, 125, 144, 223-231,
    234, 247-248, 255, 261
Arias Sánchez, Oscar 166
Armed forces 7, 83, 85-88, 171,
    261. *See also* militarism, United
    States military, *and* warfare
Axis 11, 18, 47, 50-51, 84, 92, 96,
    110, 210, 225, 229-231, 234. *See
    also* Nazi Party

Babassu 124
Bahamas 9, 134
Banks and banking 67-68, 72, 76,
    78, 94, 144, 149, 159, 185, 188,
    199, 213, 220, 237, 241, 246, 258.
    See also business, capital,
    capitalism, economic

development, foreign investment,
    investment, *and* private enterprise
Barbados 208-209
Barco, Virgilio 130
Baseball 110-111, 113, 187
Batista, Fulgencio 16, 47, 183-184,
    186-187, 190, 192, 253-254
Bay of Pigs 3, 10, 57, 63, 87, 89,
    183-184, 189, 192-193, 254
Beals, Carleton 113
Belize 134, 209
Betancourt, Rómulo 214-215,
    217-218
Bishop, Maurice 206-207, 257
Bogotá, Colombia 48
Bolívar, Simón 14
Bolivia 9, 11, 13, 50, 54, 56, 60-61,
    63, 65-66, 68, 85, 89, 92, 119,
    127, 131, 133-134, 136, 138, 189,
    232, 239-242, 247, 249, 261
Borodin, Michael 59
Bowers, Claude 234
Bracero program 103
Braden, Spruille 173, 224-225, 229,
    240, 249
Brazil 6-8, 11, 14, 18, 47, 50-51,
    54, 69-70, 72, 77-79, 82, 92, 99,
    109-110, 116, 120, 123-129, 144,
    219-224, 248, 255
British and British Empire 22-23,
    42-43, 98. *See also* Great Britain
British Guiana. *See* Guyana
British Honduras. *See* Belize
Buenos Aires, Argentina 22, 48, 62
Bunau-Varilla, Philippe 43, 45,
    178-179
Bush, George 177
Business 18, 73-74, 141, 143, 145-
    147, 151, 155-156, 163, 190, 202,
    204, 211, 214, 216, 219, 233,
    242-246, 257. *See also* banks and
    banking, capital, capitalism,

91, 93, 95, 102, 106, 109-110, 112, 131, 134, 179-180, 182-193, 206, 217, 229, 253-254
Cuban immigrant community in Miami, Florida   105-106
Cuban Missile Crisis   3, 10, 57, 84, 192
Cultural life and history   14, 28
Culture   18, 113-115, 123, 141, 148, 152-153, 187, 203, 240. *See also* popular culture
Curtis, William Eleroy   26

Daniels, Josephus   53, 148
DEA. *See* Drug Enforcement Agency
Debray, Regis   61, 65
Debt   19, 68, 72, 78, 155-156, 198, 213, 216, 223, 226, 241, 248, 258
Debt crisis   67, 72-73, 78, 143, 145
Deforestation   123-124, 127, 253
Democracy   7, 15, 76-82, 95, 164, 180, 194, 231, 237-238, 250
Dependency theory   75
Depression. *See* Great Depression
Dewey, George   42
Díaz, Porfirio   100, 145, 147, 151, 153, 155, 158, 258, 261
Diplomatic history   3-5
Dominican Republic   6, 8, 10, 12, 14, 19, 42, 44, 46, 71, 80-81, 91, 93, 110, 113, 180-181, 194-197, 217
Drago Doctrine. *See* Drago, Luis
Drago, Luis   26, 226
Drug Enforcement Agency   132-133, 137-138, 256
Drug trade   17, 19, 134, 140, 256. *See also* cocaine, international drug trade, *and* marijuana
Duarte, José Napoleón   158, 167
Dulles, John Foster   92
Duvalier, François   105, 197-198, 200
Duvalier, Jean-Claude   105, 197-198, 200

Ecology   124-125, 127-129
Economic crisis   142-143, 145, 156, 251, 255, 258
Economic development   7, 67-77, 79, 82, 93, 117, 126-128, 130, 137, 143, 153, 155, 158-159, 168, 171, 202-203, 207, 212, 215, 219, 240-241, 243, 246. *See also* banks and banking, business, capital, capitalism, foreign investment, investment, *and* private enterprise
Economic history   67, 143, 159, 201-203, 211
Economics   73, 75, 138, 141, 145, 232, 239, 252
Economy   69, 102, 146, 156, 198, 201, 204, 207-209, 213, 228, 233, 235, 241, 245-246, 250, 255, 258
Ecuador   11, 68, 92, 119, 127, 239, 242-244
Editorial cartoons   109
Eisenhower, Dwight   3, 10, 58, 170, 193, 220, 240
El Salvador   15, 61, 83, 87, 89-90, 120, 158-160, 162, 164, 166-167, 171, 184, 254, 261
Environment   8, 123-129, 140, 142
Escobar, Pablo   130, 132, 135, 256
Estefan, Gloria   3
Estigarribia, José Félix   249
Estrada Palma, Tomás   38-39

Fabela, Isidro   22
Falkland Islands   86, 98, 227-228
Fascism   24, 50-51, 109, 221, 226, 228, 231, 234
Federal Bureau of Narcotics   134-135
Figueres, José   165
Flores Magón, Ricardo   155
Florida   20, 105, 131, 135
Ford, Gerald   181
Foreign investment   68, 73, 76, 143, 151, 153, 156-157, 198, 202-203, 210, 213, 226. *See also* investment

ABOUT THE AUTHOR

John A. Britton grew up in Jackson, North Carolina, and attended the University of North Carolina at Chapel Hill for his undergraduate education. He earned his Ph.D. in history from Tulane University in 1971. His publications include *Educación y radicalism en Mexico, 1931-1940* (1976), *Carleton Beals: A Radical Journalist in Latin America* (1987), and *Revolution and Ideology: The Image of the Mexican Revolution in the United States* (1995), which won the A. B. Thomas Award of the South Eastern Council on Latin American Studies. He edited *Molding the Hearts and Minds: Education, Communications, and Social Change in Latin America* (1994) and has written several essays in encyclopedic works. He also is a contributing editor for the *Handbook of Latin American Studies*. He began teaching history at Francis Marion University in 1972 and currently holds the Suzanne Lucas and Benjamin Pratt Gasque Chair in History there. He and his wife, Kathy, have three children: Jeannie, Dan, and Maria. They reside in Florence, South Carolina.